Y0-DLV-928

Bossard, James Herbe/The large family sy
HQ728 .B715 1975 C.1 STACKS 1975

```
HQ      Bossard, James Her-
728       bert Siward, 1888-
B715      1960.
1975
            The large family
        system
```

```
HQ      Bossard, James Her-
728       bert Siward, 1888-
B715      1960.
1975
            The large family
        system
```

DATE	ISSUED TO
APR 1 0 1997	
	APR 1 4 1998
APR 0 9 2004	

COLLEGE FOR HUMAN SERVICES
LIBRARY
345 HUDSON STREET
NEW YORK, N.Y. 10014

The Large Family System

The Large Family System

AN ORIGINAL STUDY IN THE SOCIOLOGY OF FAMILY BEHAVIOR

James H. S. Bossard
Professor of Sociology, William T. Carter Professor of Child Development, and Professor of Sociology in Psychiatry, The School of Medicine, University of Pennsylvania

With the aid and partial collaboration of

Eleanor Stoker Boll
Research Associate, The William T. Carter Foundation, and Assistant Professor of Sociology University of Pennsylvania

GREENWOOD PRESS, PUBLISHERS
WESTPORT, CONNECTICUT

Library of Congress Cataloging in Publication Data
Bossard, James Herbert Siward, 1888-1960.
  The large family system.

  Reprint of the ed. published by University of Pennsylvania Press, Philadelphia.
  Includes indexes.
  1. Family. 2. Child study. I. Boll, Eleanor Stoker. II. Title.
HQ728.B715 1975   301.42   74-25536
ISBN 0-8371-7871-1

© 1956 University of Pennsylvania Press

Originally published in 1956 by the University of Pennsylvania Press, Philadelphia

Reprinted with the permission of University of Pennsylvania Press

Reprinted in 1975 by Greenwood Press
A division of Congressional Information Service, Inc.
88 Post Road West, Westport, Connecticut 06881

Library of Congress catalog card number 74-25536
ISBN 0-8371-7871-1

Printed in the United States of America

10 9 8 7 6 5 4 3 2

To

My Father and Mother
who were reared in large families

and

The Hundred Families
whose coöperation made this study possible

Foreword

Living for the first fifteen years of my life as an only child, I would look with longing at my schoolmates who were growing up in large families. Some of them did not have the material advantages which I did, but they seemed to me to have so many other things in their common family life that I would envy them many times. Once, when very young, I hurried home from school to ask my mother to provide a large family by the end of the week. Later I came to enjoy, with particular zest, visits to my grandparents where many children and grandchildren gathered periodically for gala family parties.

For a number of years, I have devoted myself to the study of the social processes involved in family life and child rearing. As far back as 1940, Dr. Eleanor S. Boll, my Research Associate, suggested that the significance of family size in child development deserved much more attention than it had thus far received. In 1947, another research associate, the oldest of ten children, crystallized this long-latent interest in large family living in the insistence that the large family had been unduly ignored in the study of child development. Since then, I have sought to fill this gap by gathering the material on which this book is based.

Without the material support of The William T. Carter Foundation and the present members of the Carter family, this study would not have been possible. For a number of years, their aid has made it possible for me to work under ideal conditions. Progress in this particular project has been facilitated by two grants from the Board of Graduate Education and Research of the University of Pennsylvania, upon recommendation of the Faculty Committee on the Advancement of Research. Mrs. Winogene Pratt Sanger, formerly of the staff of the Carter Foundation, made valuable suggestions which were incorporated in the earlier stages of the study. Dr. Eleanor Stoker Boll, long-time Research Associate, has been of invaluable help in the organization and interpretation of the material, is the author of most of Chapter 11, and co-author of various other sections of the volume. To Dr. Joan L. Gordon, of the Savannah State College, in Savannah, Georgia, I am indebted for seven histories of large families in the Deep South. For permission to reprint parts of this volume previously published, acknowledgment is due to the *American Sociological Review, Mental Hygiene, Child Development,* and *Marriage and Family Living.* Above all, I am indebted to the numerous members of many large families for their forbearance and patience in answering so many questions.

James H. S. Bossard

At Wynnebourn, in Wynnewood, Pa.
July 20, 1955

Contents

	Foreword	7
1	Purpose: What This Book Is About	13
2	Method: How the Study Was Made	24
3	Subject: Children in a Hundred Large Families	39
4	Attitudes and Motives: How Its Members Regard the Large Family	53
5	Interaction—Personal Relations Within the Large Family	76
6	The Vulnerability of the Large Family	106
7	Child Rearing in the Large Family	126
8	Interaction Among the Siblings	148
9	Interaction Among the Siblings (*continued*)	167
10	Personality Patterns Among the Siblings	201
11	Selected By-products of Large Family Living	222
12	Family Formation in the Next Generation	262
13	Marital Happiness of Persons Reared in Large Families	285
14	The Large Family System	305
	Subject Index	323
	Index of Authors	325

The Large Family System

· 1 ·

Purpose: What This Book Is About

THIS IS A BOOK about the large family as a way of family living and child rearing. It is an original study, based on case histories of one hundred large families, members of whom have contributed the facts of their family experiences. Persons reared in fifty additional large families were consulted on selected aspects of the study, but the hundred case histories constitute the hard core on which the succeeding pages are based.

The study originated from a conviction that, in their preoccupation with the prevailing small family system, present-day students have neglected the large family, in spite of its importance. Further incentive came from an interest in two basic questions: first, is there a large family system, with its own distinctive features; and second, if so, how does it affect the processes of child rearing and personality formation of the child members of such families?

This first chapter will develop these points and summarize the nature and scope of the study. More specifically, it will deal with (a) the importance of the large family in child development; (b) the existence of a large family system; (c) personality development in the large family; (d) the history of the present study; (e) a summary picture of the hundred families included; and (f) what this book is not.

THE IMPORTANCE OF THE LARGE FAMILY

Current thinking concerning child and personality development has become so family-minded that it even counts in terms of families rather than of children; this in spite of the obvious fact that a family with twelve children is twelve times as important statistically as a family with one child. Examination of United States Census data on types of families by size will illustrate the contrast that has just been made. Of all households (35,087,440) enumerated in 1940, only 2.2 per cent (765,560) had six or more related children under eighteen years of age. Reckoning in terms of household units, families of such size seem relatively unimportant. Counting in terms of children, however, a total of 5,134,159, or 13 per cent of all children under eighteen years of age, was found in these families. To put it another way, one out of every forty-six families had six or more children under eighteen, but almost one out of every seven children was reared in families of such size. If the same comparison is made for households with five or more related children under eighteen, the percentage of all households is 4.2 but the percentage of all children found in these households is 22.1. This might be compared with the fact that 19 per cent of all children under eighteen were enumerated in households with but one related child, and with 25.8 per cent of all children in households with two related children under eighteen years of age.[1]

Another index of value in this connection is the order of birth for children born during the calendar year. The National Office of Vital Statistics now issues annual reports on births by age of mother, race, and birth order. A compilation of these reports for the five years 1946 to 1950, inclusive, shows that of the total number of 17,637,358 births reported, 717,928, or 4.1 per cent, were sixth and seventh births, and 552,216, or 3.1 per cent, were of eighth order or over. Thus a total of 1,270,144, or 7.2 per cent, of all births during this five-year period were sixth and over in the order of birth.[2]

On the basis of the foregoing data, it seems reasonable to

[1] Bureau of the Census, Special Report of the 1940 Census, *Types of Families*, Table 5.
[2] National Office of Vital Statistics, *Births by Age of Mother, Race, and Birth Order,* Special Reports, 1946-1950.

conclude that the large family is of considerable importance, as a type of family situation, in the rearing of American childhood. It would seem, too, that inadequate attention has been given to this fact by students of child development.

IS LARGE FAMILY LIVING DISTINCTIVE IN KIND?

Earlier students of the family were prone to consider it primarily as a type of personal relationship, between husband and wife and parents and children. The problems of the family were those which arose from the interaction between persons of differing ages, sexes, temperaments, and traits. Admonition, discipline, forbearance, and restraint were the answers to these problems.

More recently, the family has come to be considered as constituting a segment of the life of a people. This viewpoint has resulted largely from the study of culture, which has come to emphasize the life of a people as a unified cultural system, and the family as an integral part of that system. This approach implies that there is a family culture, which takes the form of a pattern consisting of the ways of doing and thinking that cluster around the family and sex aspects of group life. This family culture pattern includes courtship and marriage procedures, sex mores, husband-wife relationships, status of men and women, parent-child relationships, family routines and rituals, sex obligations in marriage, child-rearing practices, attitudes toward education, responsibility toward aging parents, norms of personal conduct, forms of intimate behavior, divorce, sense of group responsibility, and many other aspects. In other words, there exists in every society a series of socially accepted attitudes, forms of behavior, and values, centering around the sex, procreative, homemaking, child-rearing, and affectional relationships and activities of the family group which constitute the family culture pattern of that society.

Once this concept is grasped, it becomes clear that, in addition to the generalized ideal family pattern, there exist, in the realities of everyday living, not one but many such patterns. Since they are patterns of living, they are the product of all the factors that affect and differentiate human behavior. From this it follows that each nation, region, social class, religious group, in fact, every cultural group, has its own distinctive family pattern. The family is, then, a way of group life. As such, it represents a group adjustment to the conditions which surround it and the problems that confront it.

Is size also a determinant of family life? Is there a pattern of family living which is peculiar to the large, as compared with the small, family? Does size *per se* tend to create certain forms of family relationships between the parents, between children and parents, and among the siblings? Is a large family prone to emphasize certain values and exert certain pressures distinct from those in smaller families? Does it foster certain ways of rearing children? Do children in large families have problems, and do they develop patterns of adjustment which tend to be peculiar to it? These are questions of one type which present themselves in any study of the large family and its relation to the processes of child development.

PERSONALITY DEVELOPMENT IN THE LARGE FAMILY

A second series of questions grow out of an accepted principle of personality development: namely, that the group experience, and particularly the family group experience, is of major importance in molding the personality of its members. Especially is this true of its child members who are continuously exposed to family group influences during the formative years. Within reasonable limitations, children tend to be what their families and other group contacts make them to be.

To the extent that this is true, it follows that significant differences in the family patterns of living will tend to produce different personality types. It is generally recognized that family life patterns in Germany, Bali, Somaliland, and New England differ from each other, and tend to produce different personality types. Similarly, Back Bay Boston produces a type that differs from that which is found characteristically among sharecroppers in Mississippi. It seems equally obvious, then, that if there is a large family system in distinction to a small family system, the two would tend to produce different personality types. What are the emphases in child rearing that are peculiar to large families and what personality types do they tend to produce? Does the large family produce any characteristic traits among its child members? Do children in large families have their own distinctive problems, not customarily found in small families, for example?

It would seem possible to find some answers to questions of this kind, and such answers might conceivably be of great importance. A host of questions of importance suggest themselves. Does the large family produce good matrimonial risks? Does growing up in a large family tend to create persons who will have large families in turn? Does it produce persons interested in, or surfeited with, children by the time they become adults? Do children from large families tend to be well or ill adjusted? Are they good occupational risks? Do they tend to work in large occupational groups when they are older? Do significant differences appear among them on the basis of order of birth?

HISTORY OF THE PRESENT STUDY

The convictions and questions that have been mentioned led to an exploratory study of twenty-five large families, having a total of 222 children. All but one of these families had six or more children; eight had ten or more. The material gathered seemed so significant that a portion of this study was presented to the family section of the American Sociological Society, and was subsequently published in the *American Sociological Review*.[3]

Although there was every scientific reason for extending the scope of the study, considerations of finance and time seemed to make this impossible. Support from large foundations was solicited, but without success. Just as the study was about to be discontinued, adequate aid came from three quarters. One came through the medium of Mrs. Dorothy Barclay, of the staff of *The New York Times*, who summarized the study on her page in the magazine section of the Sunday *New York Times*. In her write-up, Mrs. Barclay mentioned that reprints of the study were available. Within a month, more than eight hundred requests for reprints were received, from twenty states of the Union. In fulfilling these requests, many of which came from persons who had been reared in large families, their coöperation was solicited in extending the scope of the study. A second source of aid was the William T. Carter Foundation at the University of Pennsylvania. Members of the Carter family generously supplemented the regular income from the endowment in order to permit the extension of the research work of the Foundation, thus enabling the inclusion of the larger study. Finally, the Board of Graduate Education and Research of the University of Pennsylvania, upon recommendation of the Faculty Committee on the Advancement of Research, twice made grants to facilitate work on the project. The combination of these three factors made possible the present study, based on case histories of one hundred large families.

THE ONE HUNDRED LARGE FAMILIES

The hundred families of this study were wholly unselected, save for one stipulation: at least six children must have been

[3] James H. S. Bossard and Winogene Pratt Sanger, "The Large Family System—A Research Report," *American Sociological Review*, February, 1952, pp. 3-9.

born to the parents. Otherwise, they were accepted as they were located and indicated a willingness to coöperate in meeting the requirements of the study. In spite of this fact, they constitute in many ways a cross section of the American population, as the following summaries will show.

1. *By Nativity and Race.*   In sixty of the families, both parents were native-born whites of native-born parentage. Another seventeen reported both parents as native-born white but of foreign or mixed parentage. In ten families, both parents were foreign born; eight were Negro families; and in five cases, the father was foreign born and the mother was native born.

2. *By Religious Preference.*   When the study was begun, it was anticipated that most of the large families that would be found would be Roman Catholic. Actually, only twenty-six of the cases fall into this category, with both parents of this faith. In three additional cases, the father was Roman Catholic and the mother was Protestant. Eight of the families are Jewish. The remaining sixty-three are Protestant, with Baptists and Methodists predominating. Episcopalians, Lutherans, Presbyterians, Congregationalists, Mennonites, and Friends are found in lesser proportions.

3. *By Fathers' Occupations.*   A wide distribution of occupations are found in the hundred families. Twenty-two were skilled workers, including carpenters, painters, machinists, miners, upholsterers, tinsmiths, and the like. Next in numerical order was the professional group. Eighteen fathers were teachers, clergymen, lawyers, doctors, and other professional representatives. Seventeen fathers were farmers, including four who combined farming and public school teaching. There were fourteen proprietors, mostly of smaller businesses, such as retail merchants, contractors, and managers of personally owned business concerns. Next were eleven executives, including bank presidents, investment brokers, and executives

of larger business establishments. Five fathers were salesmen, five were unskilled workers, and one was a public official. Occupations of the remaining seven either were not reported at all or without sufficient clarity to permit classification.

A word should be said about the occupation of the mothers. In only two cases did the mothers have an occupation other than that of housewife. That does not necessarily mean that they did not participate in earning the family income. In the case of two farm families, the mothers maintained butter and egg businesses; in another case, the mother sold other farm products; in still another, she kept a rooming-house. In the overwhelming proportion of cases, however, she was housewife and home maker. Obviously, bearing and raising a houseful of children is a full-time occupation in itself.

4. *By Type of Community.*   Most of the families are small-town, village, or farm families. Thirty-six described the communities in which they grew up, wholly or in major part, as "village," "farm village," or small town. The last named often was designated as under 2,000 population. Nineteen more grew up on farms. These two account, then, for fifty-five of our families. Another twelve are small-city families, in all cases cities of less than 100,000 population. There are twenty-four big-city families, chiefly from Philadelphia, New York, and Brooklyn. Eight more grew up in the suburbs of large cities, chiefly Philadelphia and New York. Then there was one family who moved about so much and lived in so many different types of communities that it was not possible to classify it.

5. *By State of Residence.*   Exactly half of the one hundred families came from Pennsylvania and New York: the former contributing thirty-seven, the latter thirteen. Twenty-one additional states and the District of Columbia are represented in the following proportions: Georgia, Maryland, and Michigan, four each; Illinois and Massachusetts, three each; Indi-

ana, Mississippi, North Carolina, and Virginia, two each; Arkansas, Colorado, Connecticut, Florida, Louisiana, New Hampshire, New Jersey, Oregon, South Carolina, Tennessee, West Virginia, Wisconsin, and the District of Columbia, one each. In eleven cases, the families lived in several states during the period when the children were growing up. In eight of these cases, the several states were all located in the Middle West; in the remaining three, they were highly scattered.

6. *By Age of Parents.* Data on the age of the parents of the hundred families were obtained for ninety-seven of the fathers and for ninety-three of the mothers. Since the case histories were obtained over a period of several years, and since some of the parents were deceased, ages are indicated as they were, or would have been, if the parents were living, as of 1950. Table 1 indicates the age distribution of both parents.

TABLE 1

Age of Parents, by Five-Year Periods, as of 1950

Fathers' Ages	Number	Mothers' Ages	Number
		35–39	1
40–44	1	40–44	3
45–49	2	45–49	9
50–54	13	50–54	6
55–59	8	55–59	11
60–64	15	60–64	17
65–69	6	65–69	8
70–74	11	70–74	12
75–79	12	75–79	4
80–84	11	80–84	9
85–89	10	85–89	7
90 and over	8	90 and over	6
Total	97		93

7. *By Age Differentials Between Parents.* The ages of both parents were obtained in ninety-three of the one hundred

families. Table 2 presents the data on the age differences between the parents.

TABLE 2

Age Differentials of Parents of One Hundred Large Families

		Number
Both parents the same age		3
Mother older than father		6
By one year	4	
By two years	2	
Father older than mother		84
By one year	6	
By two years	21	
By three years	12	
By four years	8	
By five years	7	
By six years	3	
By seven years	6	
By eight years	4	
By nine years	4	
By ten years	7	
By eleven years	1	
By twelve years	3	
By fifteen years	1	
By twenty-eight years	1	

WHAT THIS BOOK IS NOT

This book is not a statistical study, except incidentally and to suggest leads for further analysis. To assume differently is to miss the purpose of the entire project. No claim is made that the hundred cases are representative of the American large family population. The number of cases in separate categories is, with few exceptions, too small to call for the application of advanced statistical techniques or to permit an attempted identification of the role or interrelationships of separate variables. This is a pioneer study. All conclusions are offered tentatively, to suggest insights and hypotheses for subsequent determination.

SUMMARY

1. This book is an original study of one hundred large families.

2. The study was undertaken because of a conviction that the large family was not given adequate attention by students of family relations and child development, and also because of interest in the ways in which size of family affects the processes in these two areas.

3. The one hundred families represent a variety of groups and cultural backgrounds. They are prevailingly native-born white, but with foreign-born and Negro representation; they are largely Protestant, although Roman Catholics and Jews are included; occupationally, the fathers are found in a wide range of occupations, and with some preponderance in farming and small-town occupations. More than half of the families grew up on farms or in small rural towns, the rest are city and suburban products. A total of twenty-three states and the District of Columbia are represented. The parents are mostly in middle and in past middle age, as parents of large families naturally would be. As is customary, fathers are generally older than mothers, mostly from two to seven years older.

4. This book is not a statistical study of the American large family population, but rather an analysis which seeks to suggest some features of large family living and its possible meaning for child development.

· 2 ·

Method: How the Study Was Made

WITH A HUNDRED FAMILIES, each with six or more children, scattered over twenty-three states and reared in a wide variety of situations, as the subject of this study, and with the object of gaining insight into the process of family living and child rearing in these families, questions of methodology naturally presented themselves. How should this study be made? What specific items of information should be obtained? How should it be gathered and from whom? The answers to these and related questions which emerged in the course of the study constitute the second chapter of this volume. The topics that are discussed include: (a) undesigned life history documents—the first step; (b) the outline of the study; (c) sources of information; and (d) a general comment on methodology.

UNDESIGNED LIFE HISTORY DOCUMENTS

Although many proven techniques of social research are now available, it remains true that each exploration of a new area of study necessitates a continuing adaptation of these techniques to the particular project involved. In a sense, then, each research project is an adventure in methodology just as it is a search for new insights. Paradoxical as it may seem, one never fully knows how a problem or an area should be studied until it has been studied. Our experience and judgment here coincide with those expressed in an excellent study of child behavior just published. Barker and Wright, in their analysis of *Midwest and Its Children*, after facing the choice of whether to concentrate on methods or on problems, elected to emphasize the latter and to deal with methodological issues only as necessary in the progress of the analysis. "We did this in the belief that the perfection of scientific methods more profitably follows than precedes their initial application to a problem." [1]

The first step in the present study was experimental and exploratory. It involved the use of *undesigned life history documents*. This term is used to indicate a case study which is not written to follow design. It is not written for publication, like an autobiography; nor to present a set of answers, as in response to a questionnaire; nor to follow a series of assigned topics, as is done in many literary compositions. An *undesigned life history document* is one written by a person about his experiences, recollections, and thoughts, and is planned only in the sense of being confined to a given area of life. Such a record is not "tailored" to the design of a researcher, nor is it a series of responses manipulated by his interests. It reveals the emphases of the writer, furnishing data and interpretation as selected by the contributor of the record.

In the present instance, fifteen persons, who had grown up in large families, were asked to write about their family life during the days of their childhood and youth, with special reference to their own development as maturing persons. No other stipulation of topic was made, nor questions asked. All of them were persons of intelligence, and nine of them had since lived, as adults, as members of small families, thus having had experience in living in families of contrasting sizes. The life records which they contributed were of unequal length and value. Several consisted of more than forty typed pages, single spaced, and spelled out in considerable detail their early family experiences. Others were less outgoing in

[1] Roger G. Barker and Herbert F. Wright, *Midwest and Its Children* (Evanston, Illinois: Row, Peterson and Co., 1955), p. 471.

their recollections, confining themselves to summary statements of selected facets of their family life.

To utilize these undesigned records seemed a natural and advantageous way to begin the study and to serve as bases for its further organization. Throughout the entire project, these undirected contributions were encouraged, along with other methods of securing information. No evaluation of "unsolicited information," in contrast to other types of data, however, is made nor implied at any time in this volume. Any and every kind of data and source of information have their own values and limitations.

THE OUTLINE FOR THE STUDY

The fifteen records thus obtained were then analyzed by two persons, one of whom was the oldest of ten children; the other, the older of two. The result was the formulation of a series of questions and topics, which were "tried" on twenty-five persons who had been reared in large families. The case records thus obtained were analyzed again, and an outline was then constructed that has been utilized throughout the study.

This outline consists of two parts. Part one called for the following base data:

1. Parents:
    (a) Age of father; if deceased, age and date of death
    (b) Age of mother; if deceased, age and date of death
    (c) Age of step-parents; if deceased, age and date of death
    (d) Occupations of father and/or mother

2. Children ever born to parents, indicating
    (a) Age; if deceased, age and date of death
    (b) Sex
    (c) Marital status
    (d) Number of children of each sibling married, including stepchildren, if any
    (e) Happiness in marriage: happy, medium, unhappy

Method: How the Study Was Made

3. Order of birth of informant

4. Type of community in which family lived: farm, village, small town, small city, large city, suburb, etc.

5. Nativity of parents:
   (a) Native-born white of native-born white parents, or
   (b) Native-born white of foreign or mixed parentage
   (c) Foreign-born white
   (d) Negro

6. Religion of parents and children

Part two consisted of topics to write about or to talk about in interviews. These follow.

1. Attitude toward the large family
   (a) Father's attitude
   (b) Mother's attitude
   (c) Informant's attitude
   (d) Attitude of other siblings, as known

2. General tone of family life: happy, unhappy, medium, etc.

3. Relations of children to each other: happy, unhappy, medium, etc. The extent to which cliques and combinations developed among the children. Who "ganged up" with whom?

4. Parent-child relationships
   (a) With father
   (b) With mother

5. What persons other than parents and children lived in the household, and over what periods of time? Include relatives, servants, and others. Rate relations with such persons.

6. To what extent did the children discipline each other? Which children did the disciplining? How?

7. Explain the parents' role in discipline
   (a) Father's role
   (b) Mother's role

8. Explain the parents' methods of discipline
   (a) Father's method
   (b) Mother's method

9. On the basis of your experience, what size family do you want?

10. On the basis of your experience, what do you wish your birth order had been? Why?

11. Do you think a large family makes for a sense of security among its members
    (a) Economic security
    (b) Emotional security

12. To what extent did the children in your family play together? Give details.

13. To what extent did you play with other children? Why?

14. To what extent have you and your brothers and sisters "clung together" since you have grown up? Give details.

15. At what age did you leave home? Why?

16. At what ages did your brothers and sisters leave home? Why?

17. This study is particularly interested in obtaining information on the specialized roles of children in large families. For example, was one child in your family the household drudge, another the social butterfly, another the responsible one, another the finance-minded one, etc.? Describe such specialized personality types among your brothers and sisters as fully as you can.

18. The study is particularly interested in the dietary habits which prevail in large families. How much were dietary whims and dislikes honored in your family, and to what extent were menus standardized, with little or no attention to likes or dislikes of an individual member? To what extent were special dishes prepared for such persons?

19. To what extent do you think living in a large family socializes a child?

20. Do you have a strong sense of possession? Do you think family size affects this?

21. Considering your brothers and sisters one by one, do you consider them
    (a) Well adjusted
    (b) Not well adjusted
    (c) Medium

22. Which of your brothers and/or sisters is closest to you? Is the attachment very pronounced?

23. How many such factions or pairings were there in your family?

24. What is your outstanding reaction to having been reared in a large family? That is to say, what have you been in the habit of saying about large families in general and yours in particular?

25. What other aspects of large family living do you think should be stressed?

METHODS OF SECURING INFORMATION

In gathering the information, every effort was made to secure the interest, coöperation, and confidence of the informants. Particular efforts were made to emphasize the confidential nature of the material contributed. At the very beginning, each family was given a number and all information, it was explained, was recorded with the use of a system of symbols which precluded the use of names and other items of identification. Assurance was given that only one analyst would have access to the records after their recording. Informants were encouraged thus to write and to talk themselves out frankly and completely.

Relatively complete records centering around the foregoing outline were secured from at least one child in each of the hundred families included in the study. Written records centering around this outline were obtained for seventy-two families. In fourteen of these seventy-two cases, more than one member made a written contribution; in three cases, more than two members did so.

In the case of the other twenty-eight families, oral interviews only were conducted, in the course of which the general outline was followed, but the informants were encouraged to talk freely and over as wide a range as they wished. Particular emphasis was given to the last point in the outline, in which they were asked to discuss topics and points not previously covered.

In fifty-four cases, it was possible to combine both the written and oral approach. In these cases, the informant first "wrote himself out" on the outline given to him. This was then read, after which at least one interview, and in some instances more than one interview, followed. In these cases the informants were led over their written accounts, and asked to clarify them and to supplement them.

Not all questions were answered by all of the informants, so that tabulations of answers presented subsequently will not always total to one hundred. In some cases, these omissions appear in the cases where only written contributions are available; in a few interviews, there was evidenced a reluctance to answer certain questions. Since the good will and coöperation of the informant were highly valued, nothing resembling pressure was exerted in any case.

SOURCES OF INFORMATION

A. The chief effort in this study has been to look at large families through the eyes of the children who grew up in them. As a result, the children have been the chief source of information. At least one child member in each of the hundred families has contributed a case record based on the outline that has been presented, and an analysis of these one hundred informants is presented herewith.

1. *By Age of Informants.* Table 3 presents the age of the informants at the time they made their contribution to the study, classified by ten-year periods. This table shows that these informants are mature persons. None of them was under

TABLE 3

Informants, by Classified Age Grouping

Age Grouping	Number of Informants
Under 20	4
20–29	32
30–39	26
40–49	22
50 and over	16

eighteen years of age; yet more than a third were under thirty. Approximately two out of every three were under forty.

2. *By Order of Birth.* Supplementary to the age distribution of the informants, and a partial explanation of it, is their distribution by order of birth. In eighteen cases, the informant was the youngest child; in eighteen cases, the oldest; and in sixty-four, an inbetween child. If birth order was considered only in respect to those siblings who survived infancy, thirty-eight of the informants were in the upper third, thirty-seven were in the lower third, and twenty-five were in the middle third of the children. In families with seven children, the first two were considered upper-third children and the last two as the lowest third; in the case of eight, the first three were upper, and the last three were the lowest third, respectively; and so on alternately in the case of all numbers not divisible by three.

3. *By Sex Distribution.* Seventy-two of the hundred informants were women and twenty-eight were men. The number of women, while disproportionate on a numerical basis, is

believed to have been of distinct advantage in a number of ways. Female children as a rule spend more time at and within the home, and hence have more opportunity to see the family in operation from within. Again, women tend to be more concerned with family life and home making. In all events, the case records obtained from women are invariably more complete than those obtained from the male informants. It can be argued, however, that large family living, as presented in this volume, is viewed heavily through female eyes, even though analyzed through male insight.

4. *By Marital Status.* A majority of the informants had left home and married at the time the study was made. A total of fifty-eight were married, forty were single, and two were divorced. Combining the data on sex distribution with those of marital status, of the fifty-eight married informants, twenty-two were men and thirty-six were women; of the forty single ones, six were men and thirty-four were women. Both of the divorced contributors were women. The fact that a majority of the informants were married was again considered an advantage, for it meant that a large part of the information came from persons who had been reared in large families but had also since formed their own families and could look in an objective yet understanding way at life in the families in which they were reared.

B. In addition to these one hundred main informants, case records were obtained from seventeen additional children in the hundred families. As previously noted, these gave information on the points of the outline used in the study, independently and without consultation with the other sibling who had given information. It would be highly desirable, in a study of this kind, if several siblings in each family might have made their contribution to the study, and it is hoped that at some future time a study of this kind may be financed to an extent which makes such procedure possible.

Method: How the Study Was Made

A comparison of the case material made by two or more child members of the same family, centering around the same points, is both interesting and instructive. The following points may be noted briefly. First, they differ at times in regard to certain specific facts, such as age of parents, age of siblings, father's occupation, and the like. In all cases, these differences are not great. Second, they differ at times in rating the marital happiness of their brothers and sisters. Usually the difference is that of one category: one sibling will rate another's marriage as happy while the other rates it as of medium happiness. Similarly with ratings of personal adjustment. These represent differences in judgments or in opportunities to form definite opinions. They tend to differ, too, in such matters as would be affected by order of birth. Older children, for example, lay more emphasis upon the financial problems of the large family than do the younger ones. On the other hand, comparisons of such case records show marked similarity in regard to certain basic facts, such as the happiness of the family life, the family policy regarding diets, the prevailing methods of discipline, and the like.

C. A third source of information was utilized on the subject of the motivation for large families. In addition to the hundred case records which recorded the attitudes of the parents and children toward large families, the subject was discussed with parents of eighteen large families. Of these, ten were from families included in the study, and eight were from families not so included. In all cases, these parents were in middle age and over. Since the author is of mature years, it may be recorded that these conversations were conducted with relative frankness.

D. Finally, the author has talked with a number of persons who were reared in large families but who were not included in the study. To them were presented in impersonal form various facts that appeared in the course of the study, for the purpose of obtaining further insight and suggestion. Such contacts, while casual and conducted in sporadic fashion, were helpful in a number of ways.

A FOOTNOTE ON METHODOLOGY

To make explorations over a six-year period into the life histories of a hundred families, including more than a thousand persons, is a unique and rewarding experience. Not only does one learn much about life, but also something about the methods of studying family life. This latter subject, too, is one that we need to know a great deal more about than we do now, so that as one studies family situations one must always be alert and open minded in regard to the ultimate goal, that of gaining new insight into family life. The value of research lies not so much in its adherence to current methodological orthodoxy as in the sights and suggestive leads which it reveals.

Although the main objective in this study has been upon the discovery of qualitative insights, the authors have made mathematical summaries of the data in the chapters that follow. These have been made purely for their suggestive value. The limited number of cases, as well as their doubtful representativeness, preclude any general statistical significance for these summaries. Critical readers will keep this clearly in mind.

If there is one outstanding impression which this study has made upon those who have participated in it, it is an appreciation of the vast amount of investigation that is needed in an unexplored field before pertinent and promising hypotheses can be formed. The large family as a way of life and child rearing has received little attention from sociologists thus far. This is, therefore, a pioneer study in which we have sought to break new ground and open new vistas. Our efforts have been focused on the unearthing of new leads which can subsequently be utilized for the formulation of hypotheses

Method: How the Study Was Made

which more comprehensive research studies may prove or disprove. Our methodology has been adjusted to this end, and it is on this basis that both our findings and methodology should be judged.

This must not be interpreted as implying a cavalier attitude toward methodological procedures currently in vogue. Once pertinent hypotheses have been formed, there remains the quantitative task of checking them. That the standardization and manipulation of large groups of social facts call for sound scientific craftsmanship, goes without saying. One is reminded here of the distinction made by W. I. Thomas, between the life-experience document, which is not designed to prove anything but whose unique value lies in the recounting of human experience in individual terms, and the role of statistics, which is the establishment of the relative weight of suggested variables and their interrelationship. But the human situation is truly very complex, and "it must be obvious that very important aspects of the environment are probably not touched by these measurements, and likewise important aspects of personality make-up are not included." [2]

Another comment concerns the use of the questionnaire type of approach. Major or even appreciable reliance upon formal questions seemed less desirable the longer any use was made of it in the present study, for it clearly tended to confine the investigation to prescribed items and forms of answer. The question-and-answer technique elicits information only on the points of inquiry. It is much like the lawyer and a witness in the courtroom. Skillful or inept counsel, by confining testimony to the answer to specific questions, often creates impressions which are contrary to the facts and the witness' knowledge of them. Second, since this method tends to force complex human relationships into simple and countable categories, the net result may be wholly misleading.

[2] W. I. and Dorothy S. Thomas, *The Child in America* (New York: Alfred A. Knopf, 1932), p. 567. *See also* Edmund H. Volkart, *Social Behavior and Personality* (New York: Social Science Research Council, 1951), pp. 18-28.

Moreover, when they can be thus reduced, the appropriate categorical pigeonholes may not be available. Accordingly, as the present study progressed, less and less use was made of the direct questionnaire in interviewing, save for the purpose of suggesting the areas of experience to be considered, allowing the informant to follow the course of his own recollections.

Finally, the present study has reaffirmed a conviction that research methods need to be adapted to the differing abilities and attitudes of the persons concerned.[3] Some people are "ear and tongue" minded. That is, they will talk, often quite freely and frankly, concerning even the most intimate aspects of family life. They will answer questions freely and supplement them with various kinds of additional information. Mention of one subject will call forth responses on other matters mentally associated with it. In marked contrast will be any written records that can be obtained. They will talk but they won't write. This may be due to an inability in the art of written expression or an uneasiness about committing anything to a written record. "Never put anything on paper." This is a social as well as a business principle with some people.

Experience with other informants is exactly the reverse. These people write easily, often they write well, and they are quite willing to do so. Ability in the art of written expression exceeds aptitude in framing the oral word. The informant in the present study who contributed the longest and certainly one of the most revealing and helpful records of large family living is a shy, retiring person whose laconic replies to questions were given with a hesitant diffidence that was in marked contrast to the easy flow of the written record.

Fortunately, in fifty-four of the cases, it was possible to combine both the written contributions of the informants

[3] For a more complete discussion of this and also of other methods of studying family life, the reader is referred to James H. S. Bossard and Eleanor S. Boll, *Ritual in Family Living* (Philadelphia: University of Pennsylvania Press, 1950), chap. X.

with a record of interviews. This combination seems, whenever feasible, to be most desirable in studies of this kind.

The present study has utilized whatever methodology was needed at the moment to further its objectives. These objectives have been twofold. One has been to find out all that is possible about large family living, utilizing the outline presented in the preceding pages as a kind of framework around which to group the material that could be secured. Once assembled, the second main effort has been to organize it into some kind of a collective unity. Here various refinements of methodology were employed, but much of the progress that resulted came in a way so aptly described by another student of a hundred families. "My understanding," writes Rebecca Reyher in her book on *The Fon and His Hundred Wives*, "seemingly comes by osmosis and irrelevancy. Like a jig-saw puzzle, all the pieces are in a heap, and then suddenly they begin to fall into place, have purpose and meaning." [4]

SUMMARY

1. This study began experimentally with fifteen *undesigned life-history documents* of large family living. On the basis of these, an outline was formed which has been used in the present study.

2. Information on the large family system was secured from about one hundred and fifty persons, all of whom had lived as members of large families. Written life histories and oral interviews were the two chief methods used to secure information. In fifty-four families, it was possible to combine both of these methods.

3. The main reliance in this study has been to look at large families through the eyes of children who grew up in them. At least one child in each family contributed a case record of his family. These hundred were mostly mature adults, well

[4] Rebecca Reyher, *The Fon and His Hundred Wives* (New York: Doubleday and Co., 1952), p. 30.

distributed by order of birth, preponderantly women, and more frequently married than single.

4. The chief effort and interest of the study have been to develop insight and hypotheses, believing that these are the essence of primary research. No one particular technique of research has been followed: the emphasis being rather on securing all possible information and organizing it so as to give it the most possible meaning for the formulation of hypotheses for future studies.

· 3 ·

Subject: Children in a Hundred Large Families

THIS BOOK is concerned mainly with the children in the hundred large families, and with particular reference to selected aspects of their development. The present chapter seeks to summarize certain facts about them, such as their number, sex, age, make-up, and distribution by family size. Some attention is also given to types of large families and to a concept of family structure which it is believed is significant for family study.

THE CHILDREN: BY NUMBER AND SEX

A total of 879 children were reported as ever having been born alive in the hundred families of the study. Mathematically speaking, then, the average size was almost nine children per family. Of these 879 children born alive, 458 were males and 421 were females. This means that one hundred and nine males were born for every one hundred females, which is somewhat higher (by three points) than is true for all births in the population at large.

Of these 879 live births, a total of thirty-five were reported as having died in infancy, meaning in this case before they were a year old. This is an infant mortality rate of forty, meaning that the number of live-born children who died before they were a year old, per 1,000 babies born alive, was forty. Considering the age distribution of the families under consideration, and the prevailing infant mortality rates at the various times when the 879 children were born, this is a very low rate.

There is some reason to believe that the reporting of infant deaths in our families is not wholly accurate. This may have been due, for the most part, to the fact that when the informants were among the younger members of a large family they did not know of children born years before their own birth, especially if those children lived only a very short time. Several of the informants, youngest in order of birth, mentioned this possibility, saying that they suspected it, but that there was always a family silence when the subject was broached.

Of the thirty-five children reported to have died in infancy, twenty-four were males and eleven were females. Thus of the 844 children who survived infancy, 434 were males and 410 were females. Another fifteen of these were reported as having died before the age of fifteen years, and four more between the ages of fifteen and twenty. It is probable that these figures are accurate.

THE AGE DISTRIBUTION OF THE CHILDREN

In tabulating the children by age, the following procedure was followed. First, the ages of those who died in infancy were not included; second, the ages of those who died after the first year and before the twentieth are tabulated; third, all ages are tabulated as they were, or would have been, if living in 1950. This was done to reduce the children who survived infancy to the terms of a common denominator, and to conform to the age tabulation of the parents as presented in Chapter I.

Table 4 shows this age distribution, classified by five-year periods. Perusal of it will enable the reader to visualize the period of time over which family life and child development processes extend in the present study, and also the relative importance of successive periods. It will be seen that half of the female, and almost 45 per cent of the male, children were born since the end of World War I. Roughly speaking, then, half of our children were born before World War I, and

Subject: *Children in a Hundred Large Families*

approximately half following it. Reckoning in terms of years of growing up in their respective families, about two-thirds of the boys and three-fourths of the girls did all or most of their growing up in the period between the two World Wars.

TABLE 4

Age Distribution of 844 Children Surviving Infancy, as of 1950, by Five-Year Periods

Age Period	Number of Males	Number of Females
1–4	7	5
5–9	11	11
10–14	15	18
15–19	32	25
20–24	45	40
25–29	42	51
30–34	42	55
35–39	48	46
40–44	43	36
45–49	40	35
50–54	40	33
55–59	24	25
60–64	21	16
65 and over	24	14
Total	434	410

CHILDREN BY SIZE OF FAMILY

Attention is called to two facts concerning the distribution of the families by number of children. One is the range and distribution by number of differing sizes. Reckoning by number of children ever born, every number from six to sixteen is represented; counting by number surviving infancy, all of the ages save one are found. A second fact is that sixty, or three out of five, were families with from seven to eleven children each, surviving infancy, a size that might be thought of as typical large families in terms of size. That is to say, they are large enough to be large families in the commonly accepted sense of the term, but not large enough or too small to deviate, in some degree, from the popular concept of the large family.

TABLE 5

Children Ever Born, and Children Surviving Infancy, by Size of Families

Number of Children Ever Born, by Families	Number of Families	Number of Children Surviving Infancy, by Families	Number of Families
5	0	5	5
6	26	6	22
7	13	7	22
8	15	8	8
9	11	9	12
10	6	10	6
11	13	11	12
12	6	12	7
13	5	13	1
14	3	14	4
15	1	15	0
16	1	16	1
Total 879	100	844	100

SOME STRUCTURAL TYPES OF LARGE FAMILIES

The study of the family as a group, and particularly with relation to the factor of number of members, calls to attention the various ways in which families change their size. Families become large in several ways. Five of these ways were encountered in the present study.

First, a family may be large because several generations are living together. Early in the course of the study, a man presented himself, saying that he had learned of our project and that he was willing to coöperate. Asked how many children he had, he replied that he had one. He then went on to say that he lived with his father and mother, his wife, his son and his wife, his son's wife's sister (a widow), and her

Subject: Children in a Hundred Large Families 43

eight-year-old son. In other words, here were four generations living together, with eight persons in the household, but only one child. This is one form of large family, and, from the standpoint of the eight-year-old boy, has significance for child development. The lone child growing up in a household filled with adults is a distinctive type of family situation, not infrequently found in other cultures, but scarcely referred to in our own literature. This type of large family is not included in the hundred cases which constitute the basis of this study. The remaining four types were included, provided more than six children were born to one or both of the parents.

A second type of large family is one whose size has been increased by the inclusion of kinsfolk, servants, and/or other persons who are sharing continuously the common life of the household. In spite of the shrinkage of living facilities which result from present-day city housing arrangements, perhaps a minority of families, especially those with children, pass through the entire child-rearing period without the living in of persons other than parents and children. A study of four hundred and ten students in a large urban university, made by the author, revealed that only one hundred of the four hundred and ten had grown to college age in families which had consisted of parents and children only.[1]

Information on this matter was sought from the informants in the present study, and data of some value were secured for ninety-four families. Some of the information was complete and specific, stating the number of persons other than the parents and children who had lived with the family, their relationship to the family, and the periods of time they had lived there; in other cases, only the number of such persons was specified, and a word-designation of their status. A summary of the data from these ninety-four families shows

[1] For a complete report of this study, consult James H. S. Bossard, *Parent and Child: Studies in Family Behavior* (Philadelphia: University of Pennsylvania Press, 1953), chap. III.

that twenty-six report no other persons living with the family, twenty-four report one but never more, twenty-two report two but no more, twenty report three, and two report a total of four, at one time. One of the last named was a family of twelve children, born very close together, living with their parents, two grandparents and two servants, for a household of eighteen persons. A total of one hundred and thirty-six persons other than parents and children were reported as having lived at a given time with sixty-eight of the families. This indicates the overall increase in the size of these households that must be considered from the standpoint of the family as an interacting unit.

An analysis of the one hundred and thirty-six persons mentioned shows that relatives and servants account for all but twenty of them. The number of relatives mentioned was sixty-six; of servants, fifty; of other adults, fourteen; of roomers, four; and of nurses, two. Among the relatives, grandparents predominate, with aunts accounting largely for the remainder.

Two further comments on the data just cited should be noted. One is that the periods of time during which these other persons lived as members of the families studied varied a good deal. Most often mention of such persons was accompanied by statements like these: "My grandfather lived with us for five years," "My aunt stayed with us for a number of years," "We had a succession of servants when the children were small." A second comment relates to the completeness of the information on this point. Obviously, some children, accustomed to the complexities of a large household, would be inclined to forget the presence of other persons. Then, too, these are facts that might have varied a good deal on the basis of order of birth. Younger children might not experience the presence of servants; older children, the presence of grandparents. The child-rearing period in the history of a large family covers a good many years, and our informants entered and left these periods at differing times.

A third type of family is large because it combines several sets of children. Included here are cases where the father has two (or more) sets of children with two (or more) different mothers, or the mother has two (or more) sets of children with two (or more) fathers, or the familiar cases of "my children, your children, and our children." Two illustrations of the last named will be cited. One included a total of fourteen children. Of these, six were born to the father's first wife. After her death, he married a widow with five children, all of whom came to live in the same household. Three additional children resulted from this marriage. The second illustration is a family of but six children. To the father's first wife were born two children. Upon her death, he married a widow with one child, and this union resulted in three more children. Curiously enough, the father's stepchild, that is, the child born to his second wife with her first husband, and the oldest of the six children, was the father's obvious favorite.

This type of large family, in which several sets of children are combined in the same household, constitutes a distinctive kind of family situation, of great importance to the student of child development and of family relations as well. More will be said of this type later in the volume.

Finally, there is the family that is large in the commonly thought sense of the term, meaning a family consisting of a father, mother, and a relatively large number of children. Most of the families in this study are of this kind, with a specified minimum of six children.

THE FAMILY OF INTERACTION

Experience in this and other studies, and especially in dealing with the processes and problems of family interaction, has led the author to develop and emphasize the concept of the family as an interactive unit. Such a unit would include all the persons who live in the same household at a given time as a family group. The author has emphasized this idea elsewhere, primarily from the standpoint of child development, and has employed the term "family of orientation" to designate the family group in which and through which the child receives his orientation in the larger society. The term is used by way of contrast to the "family of procreation," which is confined to the procreative unit of parents and children.[2]

General sociological and anthropological theory has long recognized the basic idea involved. Both sciences have emphasized that the family is a social rather than a purely biological unit. Three lines of evidence in support of this viewpoint are usually presented. One is the fact, revealed by the anthropologists, that family groups exist in societies which do not understand the biology of reproduction. Apparently, there are societies whose members are not clear on the relation of the father to the process of reproduction, attributing impregnation to a fertile field, the position of the moon, or some other agent. Second is the universal rule which permits adoption into the family, a practice which admits the stranger and nonrelated person to the status of family member. Finally, there is the tracing of family descent through either the male or female line, and ignoring a large number of blood relatives, thus indicating again the triumph of social acceptance over biological bond.[3]

In determining the composition of the family as an interactive unit, two points need to be emphasized. One of them is that it implies the inclusion of parents, kinsfolk, children, and other persons who are living and interacting as a family. Thus two parents, one grandparent, an aunt, and six children would constitute an interactive family unit of ten persons.

A second consideration is that of time. Did the ten members of the family mentioned in the preceding paragraph all live together over any period of time? Did the six children

[2] James H. S. Bossard, *The Sociology of Child Development* (New York: Harper & Bros., revised edition, 1954), p. 55.
[3] James H. S. Bossard, *Parent and Child: Studies in Family Behavior*, chap. III.

live in the home at the same time? Questions of this kind are particularly important in the study of the large family. An illustration or two will serve to clarify and perhaps underscore the point.

Mr. and Mrs. King have been married for thirty years. Ten children were born to them, all of them living today. They are very proud of their large family and point to their five sons and daughters as evidence of what large family life can produce. In going over the history of this family, one learns that the oldest child is twenty-eight years old and the youngest one is six. The oldest child left home at eighteen, the second oldest at eighteen, and the third oldest at seventeen. All three of them left home before the youngest child was born. Before this tenth birth, the King household consisted of two parents and six children. In fact, only for a brief time did seven children live at home: most of the time the household consisted of five or fewer children.

Even more striking is the case of the Cutting family. This included eleven children, four of whom were born to the first wife and seven to the second. The age of its members permits a study of the Cutting family in terms of the arrival and departure of its members. The four children born with the first wife were all born within six years of the marriage of the parents. The oldest of the four, a boy, was "adopted" by the grandparents when a year old; the fourth born, another boy, was similarly taken after the death of the mother. Eight years after the death of the first wife, the father remarried. These four children, therefore, lived in two families in their earlier years, in each of which there were two children and two adults. The father had seven children with his second wife. When the youngest of these seven was born, the first-born child with the first wife was twenty-nine years old, was married, and had an eight-year-old son. At no time in the history of this family did more than six children live at home at the same time, and, most years, the number was five or less.

Finally, as an illustration of what may happen in a smaller family in this respect is the Iredell family. To Mr. and Mrs. Iredell were born six children. The youngest one was born when the oldest one was eighteen years old, and the second born was sixteen years old. In the entire history of this family, there were only four years, after the birth of the youngest, when the six children lived together. Due to the age differential in the birth of these children and other family circumstances, the youngest child is growing up virtually as an only child.

Opposed to cases of this kind are those where the children were born in rapid succession, and continued to live together, and with their parents, for many years. One such family was the Cartons, who had seven children in nine years, all of whom kept close to the family hearth until after their twenty-fifth year.

While a large number of our families were of the latter type, the basic insistence here is that for many purposes of sociological analysis, and particularly for the study of family interaction, it is not the parents and total number of children born to them that constitute the family unit, but the number of persons living together at any given time. A large family resembles in this respect the travelers on a transcontinental train, with passengers boarding and alighting at various points en route, and others making through passage. Or it partakes of the nature of many audiences which modern speakers face: the number is fluid and changes at irregular rates and times.

TIME INTERVAL AND SEX SEQUENCE OF BIRTHS

Supplementing the foregoing are other facts about the children in large families. These have to do with the time interval and sex sequence of their births.

In regard to time intervals, two groups of facts are important. One is the total time span between the birth of the oldest and the youngest child in each family. This is determined in part, of course, by the total number of children born. In most of the families in this study, the time interval between births is from one and a half to two and a half years. But the time interval between the respective births is also important. For example, in several of the families with six children, the number of years intervening between the first and the sixth birth exceeds that found in families with ten or even more children. As a rule, however, the larger the number of children the greater the time interval between the first and last births.

The time interval between particular births is also important and is often referred to by the informants in their interpretation of their own family situation. Most frequent are the comments of youngest children who are born a number of years after the next younger ones. An illustration of such a case and how it was interpreted is revealed in the following excerpt:

> I was born the youngest in my family. The next youngest one, a brother, was born eleven years before I was, and my sister was born twelve years before I was. All of the others (seven in all) were born a year or two apart. Because of this, I never knew my brothers and sisters as brothers and sisters. My father and mother were old when I was born. Only one grandparent was living, and she resided in another state.

A second kind of time interval that is stressed in the case material is that which appears between "clusters" of children. Illustrations of this kind are where one group of children were born, perhaps in rapid succession, to the first wife, and then, after an interval of several years, a second set were born to a second mother, or, the same situation may appear to the children of one father and mother. In one family case record, five daughters were born in due course of biologic time. Then followed a ten-year interval, during which there was every indication that the family was complete, only to be followed by the birth of three sons in the course of the next five years. The parents of this family, and their friends, repeatedly spoke of the two families which they had raised. This factor of time intervals between births is an important one in interpreting the life of large families, and especially of interrelations between the children.

Of equal importance is the sex sequence of the children. Mathematically, the sex ratio is nearly equal, but the exact order in which boys and girls follow each other is another matter. The pattern is unique for each family, and the sex constellation appears differently to each child. Considerable emphasis has been given to order of birth in studies of personality development, but there has been somewhat less appreciation of the sex sequence and its significance.

Table 6 presents the sex sequence and time interval between the births of the children in twelve families selected from our cases. The symbols "M" and "F" signify males and females, and the numbers combined with each indicate the age at the time the case record was obtained.

The number of possible combinations of age and sex of children in a large family is enormous, so that for purposes of analysis each family must be thought of as having a distinct and separate pattern. An examination of the accompanying table will show the wide range that exists. In the second family included, the oldest and youngest of six children were born twenty years apart; in the ninth family, nine children were born within seventeen years. Again, considering only sex sequence, in the third family, six daughters were born, followed by a son; in the eleventh one, there were six sons, followed by a daughter.

TABLE 6

Sex Sequence and Time Interval Between Births of Children for Selected Families

1.	F 27	–	F 26	–	F 24	–	F 23	–	M 18	–	F 16		
2.	F 21	–	M 16	–	F 14	–	M 13	–	F 6	–	M 1		
3.	F 64	–	F 62	–	F 61	–	F 60	–	F 57	–	F 55	–	M 51
4.	M 53	–	M 52	–	M 51	–	M 49	–	M 47	–	M 46	–	M 43	–	F 42	–	M 39	–	F 34
5.	M 66	–	M 65	–	M 63	–	M 61	–	M 60	–	M 58	–	M 56	–	F 54	–	M 52	–	F 48	–	F 46	–	F 44
6.	F 51	–	M 47	–	F 43	–	M 40	–	M 37	–	M 36	–	M 33		
7.	F 43	–	F 42	–	F 41	–	F 39	–	F 36	–	F 35		
8.	F 24	–	F 23	–	M 21	–	M 20	–	F 14	–	F 11	–	M 9		
9.	F 39	–	F 36	–	F 35	–	M 33	–	M 31	–	M 29	–	F 26	–	F 24	–	F 22		
10.	M 57	–	M 56	–	F 54	–	F 47	–	M 44	–	M 41	–	F 39	–	M 37	–	M 35	–	F 34	–	M 32
11.	M 36	–	M 35	–	M 33	–	M 32	–	M 29	–	M 27	–	F 24		
12.	M 37	–	M 35	–	M 34	–	F 30	–	F 28	–	F 27	–	M 22	–	M 20	–	M 18		

SUMMARY

1. A total of 879 children were ever born in the hundred families of this study, of whom 458 were males and 421 were females. This is a sex ratio of 109.

2. Of the 879 children born alive, thirty-five died before they were a year old, and fifteen more died between the first and the twentieth year.

3. Approximately half of the children were born before World War I, and half after it. Most of them, therefore, were full grown by the time the study was made.

4. By size of families, approximately three out of five came from families ranging in total number of children from seven to eleven, inclusive.

5. Families may be large by combination of several generations; by taking in of kinsfolk, servants, and other persons; by combination of several sets of children, as in the case of remarriage of parents; by adoption of a number of children; and by the birth of many children. Our families are chiefly of the last-named type.

6. Considering the family in terms of its interactive processes, size of the family means the total number of persons living as family members within the same household.

7. The time interval between births, and their sex sequence, are also of great importance. In this respect, each family is a separate and distinct pattern.

· 4 ·

Attitudes and Motives: How Its Members Regard the Large Family

THE FIELD of human motivation is a difficult one for the careful student of behavior. It is easy, to be sure, to impute motives to someone else; it is difficult to identify them correctly, even for ourselves to ourselves, for the human mind is prone to deceive even itself. This chapter, then, is tentative and suggestive only, dealing chiefly with expressed attitudes and possible interpretations and appearances. It is the purpose to consider: first, the sources and nature of the material obtained; second, the attitudes revealed; third, some light on sibling attitudes; fourth, the types that seem to appear; and fifth, some comments and interpretations.

SOURCES AND NATURE OF THE INFORMATION OBTAINED

Two sources of information were obtained on this phase of the study, and are summarized in this chapter. One was a series of interviews with parents of eighteen large families, ten of whom were in families included in the study and eight were not so included; the other source was the information obtained in written and/or oral form from the children who grew up in the hundred families. Chief reliance has been placed upon the second source; the former was gathered and has been utilized mainly for its supplementary value.

What was learned from the parents of large families will

be summarized briefly. The interviews with these persons were conducted in informal and discursive manner. In the case of the parents of large families not included in the study, no reference was made to such a study. The conversations ranged over the entire field of family life. They began, for the most part, with platitudinous professions of pride in their families. Then, as they progressed, it seemed quite clear, in one group of cases, that these professions were genuine and sincere; in other cases, further discussion tended to contradict them.

Parents in seven of these eighteen families stated that they had planned from the very beginning of their married lives to have large families, if at all possible, and there was every indication that this was true. In the case of one family, the parents had been sweethearts since school days, had planned a family of ten when they were married, and ended up with that exact number. In two other cases, one or both parents had lived abnormally lonely lives as children, and sought consciously to avoid such a situation in the families they formed. In another case, both parents were college graduates, had been impressed with their studies of differential birth rates, and sought to "do something about it." Another family made it abundantly clear that they owed the size of their family to their church and their country; while the parents of two families, blessed with adequate incomes, indicated that duty and pleasure had been satisfied in their cases.

Analyses of full-length interviews of the parents in the other eleven families were less convincing and favorable. The following case is illustrative of the ambivalent or true feelings that were revealed. Mr. and Mrs. Barber were more than perfunctory in their expressions of happiness and pride with their large family. The entire interview seemed firmly based on this assumption. Then, as the interviewer left the Barber home, Mrs. Barber walked to the waiting automobile at the front of the house. "Is this study you are making going to be published?" she asked. When assured that it would be, her last remark followed: "Well, I hope you'll find out something that will help men like Bill [her husband] to keep their pants buttoned."

Other interviews were similarly suggestive. One large family father, after participating in a lengthy and glowing account of his wonderful family, proudly exhibited an addition he built to their home, giving him his own sleeping room. It was near the end of the inspection of the new part of the house that he quietly remarked: "You know, that woman is insatiable." Another husband, who too was "very proud" of his large family, complained privately of his wife who became pregnant "every time I look at her." One mother of seven born during the depression decade indicated her religious philosophy when she said: "The Lord sends them, I always say, and the Lord will help us take care of them," while another mother of nine in a family that lived at a low economic level showed her blind optimism with the remark that "anything can happen in the next nine months." The proudest of all parents was a father whose five-feet-one height and menial occupation suggest an explanation which seems fairly obvious.

The other source of the information, chiefly utilized in this chapter, consists of that furnished by the sibling informants. As has been pointed out in the preceding chapter, each such informant was asked to describe the attitude of the father, the mother, his or her own, and that of other siblings. Some kind of statement was obtained from the sibling informant in each of the hundred families. A few consist merely of a phrase, such as "wanted," "a religious duty," "resented," "source of irritation," and the like; others were descriptive, evaluative, and showing good insight.

A study of parental attitudes toward family size, as seen through the eyes of the children in the families, is uniquely different from most other approaches. Certain inadequacies of such information will at once suggest themselves. What, the critic asks, do children know of the real attitudes and motives of their parents? Furthermore, children tend not to be aware of their parents, except in terms of their special needs of them, and hence one might again ask: What understanding do they have of their parents' motives, especially in so intimate an area of life?

Without denying at least a partial validity of these objections, certain facts may be pointed out by way of defense. The judgment which the child reports is one that has been formed on the basis of continued life experience with the parents, and in the area which is most vital to the child's needs. The informant is reporting a judgment based on behavior, not on verbal profession. Moreover, our informants are mostly of mature age, the majority of them are married and have had experience with their own families. Again, the informant's evaluation of the situation is as important as the objective fact, in the event that they differ. Particularly is this true in the present study with its emphasis upon child development. If the children *thought,* for example, that their parents' attitude toward a large family was one of shame, then so far as the children were concerned that judgment became a fact in their family experience. From the standpoint of child development, what the children thought the attitude of the parents was becomes the operative fact, not what the attitude may have been in reality. At any rate, the succeeding tables present the material gathered, summarized in specific categories for statistical treatment.

THE ATTITUDES REVEALED

The succeeding tables (7 to 13) present the attitudes toward large families of the fathers, mothers, and sibling informants. They are classified on the basis of the principal attitude indicated by the informant.

Table 7 indicates the attitudes of the fathers as seen by their children. Of these one hundred fathers, fifty-five are white Protestants; twenty-nine are Catholics, including the three fathers married to Protestant wives; eight are Jewish; and eight are Negroes.

TABLE 7

Attitudes of Fathers Toward Their Large Families as Reported by Their Children

	Total

Wanted it so . . . .
   15 Protestants, white
   4 Catholics
   5 Negroes
   1 Jew
	25

Happy and proud . . . .
   10 Protestants, white
   3 Catholics
   3 Negroes
   2 Jews
	18

Economically desirable . . . .
   3 Protestants, white
   1 Catholic
	4

Acceptance, with some overtones of resignation . . . . .
   10 Protestants, white
   7 Catholics
	17

Sense of duty, religious, civic, or social . . . .
   5 Protestants, white
   6 Catholics
   1 Jew
	12

Annoyance, irritation, resentment, shame, etc. . . . . . .
   10 Protestants, white
   3 Jews
	13

Parent termed irresponsible . . . .
   2 Protestants, white
   1 Catholic
   1 Jew
	4

No information given . . . . 7 Catholics	7
	100

Table 8 presents the attitudes of the mothers as indicated by the sibling informants. In the cases where there was more than one mother, the attitude of the natural mother of the informant was tabulated. A comparison between Tables 7 and 8 reveals significant differences in attitudes, and to ascertain the number of families in which such conflict of attitudes existed Table 9 was constructed. This presents a classification

TABLE 8

Attitudes of Mothers Toward Their Large Families as Reported by Their Children

	Total
Wanted it so	18
10 Protestants, white	
4 Catholics	
4 Negroes	
Happy and proud	5
4 Protestants, white	
1 Catholic	
Economically desirable	3
2 Protestants, white	
1 Negro	
Acceptance, with some overtones of resignation	21
14 Protestants, white	
3 Catholics	
2 Jews	
2 Negroes	
Sense of duty, religious, civic, or social	15
6 Protestants, white	
9 Catholics	
Annoyance, irritation, resentment, shame, etc.	27
18 Protestants, white	
4 Catholics	
5 Jews	
Parent termed irresponsible	5
2 Protestants, white	
2 Catholics	
1 Negro	
No information given	6
2 Protestants, white	
3 Catholics	
1 Jew	
	100

of the families on the basis of such conflict between the parents, as reported by their children.

Tables 7, 8, and 9 amply support the contention advanced earlier that the attitude toward family size is not a family attitude but an individual one.

TABLE 9

Conflict of Parental Attitudes as Reported by Siblings

	Total
No conflict reported	50
25 Protestants, white	
16 Catholics	
7 Negroes	
2 Jews	
Conflict reported	37
23 Protestants, white	
6 Catholics	
1 Negro	
4 Jews	
3 Mixed marriages	
Not clear	10
6 Protestants, white	
3 Catholics	
1 Jew	
No knowledge	3
1 Protestant, white	
1 Catholic	
1 Jew	
	100

Table 10 summarizes these cases of conflict between the parents of attitudes toward size of family by racial and religious groups. The number of cases for Jewish and Negro families is too small to be significant statistically. The number of Protestant and Catholic families is larger, and a comparison between the two reveals a marked difference in frequency of conflict. Each of the cases of mixed marriage reported conflict between the parents over size of family.

TABLE 10
Conflict in Attitudes of Parents Toward Family Size, by Racial and Religious Groups

	Conflict	No Conflict	Not Clear	No Information	Total
Protestants, white	23	25	6	1	55
Catholics	6	16	3	1	26
Jews	4	2	1	1	8
Negroes	1	7			8
Mixed marriages	3				3

Information on the attitude of the siblings toward the respective size of their families was also secured. In most cases, the informant expressed only his own attitude; in a few cases, that of the other siblings was also presented. Table 11 presents in summary form the attitudes of the main informants.

A comparison of the attitudes of fathers, mothers, and sibling informants toward their large families suggests some interesting conclusions. In Table 12 these attitudes are grouped, in so far as possible and in as many cases as this can be done, into three categories: friendly, acceptance, and critical or qualified. While each group is represented in each specified attitude, in general it will be seen that fathers are preponderantly friendly, mothers are more largely submissive and/or critical, and the sibling informants are mostly critical.

In how many families, then, were both parents and sibling informant agreed that their large family life was good, and without qualifying or critical comments? The question naturally presents itself at this point. For its answer, every record was carefully examined with this question in mind, and thirty such families were found. Eighteen of these were Protestant white families, nine were Catholic, two were Negro, and one was Jewish. In addition, there was agreement in four more families, two Protestant white and two Catholic,

TABLE 11

Attitudes of Sibling Informants Toward Large Families

	Total
Happy to have it so	28
14 Protestants, white	
11 Catholics	
2 Negroes	
1 Jew	
Think large family is desirable, but should conform to economic and health circumstances	26
15 Protestants, white	
5 Catholics	
4 Jews	
2 Negroes	
Acceptance, without comment or with overtones of resignation .	11
7 Protestants, white	
2 Catholics	
2 Negroes	
Critical, resentful, ashamed, or disliked *	34
21 Protestants, white	
9 Catholics	
2 Jews	
2 Negroes	
No information	1
1 Jew	
	100

* Ten more passed through this stage, chiefly of experiencing feelings of shame, but changed their minds as they became older.

TABLE 12

Attitudes of Fathers, Mothers, and Sibling Informants

	Friendly	Acceptance	Critical	Total
Fathers	47	29	13	89
Mothers	26	36	27	89
Siblings	28	11	60	99

who indicated that their attitude was due to the fact that their families had adequate economic means, and that if that had not been the case their attitudes might well have been different.

SOME LIGHT ON SIBLING ATTITUDES

An analysis of selected facts about the sibling informants throws considerable light on the reasons for their attitudes toward the size of their families, tending to show that such attitudes are the products of their past experiences. First, of particular interest is the question of the role of the religious background. Is it true that large families are invariably approved of by Catholic siblings, and that Protestants tend to be largely critical or unfriendly? Table 13 presents the siblings' attitudes, classified by racial and religious groups. It is obvious that all kinds of attitudes are found in all of the groups, but the Protestant informants clearly tend to be more cautious and critical than do the Catholic ones. The differences, however, are not pronounced.

TABLE 13

Attitudes of Sibling Informants, by Racial and Religious Groups

Attitude	White Protestant	Catholic	Jew	Negro	Total
Happy to have it so	14	11	1	2	28
Desirable, but limit to prevailing circumstances	15	5	4	2	26
Acceptance	7	2	—	2	11
Critical, resentful, ashamed, or disliked	21	9	2	2	34
No information	—	—	1	—	1
Total	57	27	8	8	100

Order of birth seems of distinct importance in determining the attitude of sibling informants. Of the eighteen informants who were first-born children, only four (two Protestants and two Catholics) look with favor upon large families, and it is interesting to note that they are from families of six children. Eight of the eighteen were resentful or rebellious in their attitudes, four favored limitation of size on the basis of economic circumstances, one was ashamed of the family size, and one was impressed with the difficulties that were inevitable between the children in a large family. The informants who were the last born in their families, and there were eighteen of these, showed a more favorable attitude on the whole. Eight liked or accepted their family size, and another eight thought it all right if limited to economic means. Only one youngest child was definitely resentful, and one expressed no attitude at all. The sixty-four informants who were inbetween children showed a wide range of attitudes: twenty-seven approved or accepted their family size; fourteen favored it, but thought limitation for economic reasons desirable; eleven were ashamed; and twelve were critical or resentful. Those who were ashamed or critical generally ranked in the upper third on the basis of order of birth.

The marital status of the informants is not without its apparent influence. Those who are married point out most often that family size should be limited to economic circumstances, and especially is this true of the married males; or they indicate critical attitudes or feelings of shame: these are mostly married women. The informants who were single, and especially the single women, reported attitudes of happiness, pride, or acceptance of the large families in which they were reared, and in which they may still be living.

Changing the approach and analyzing by groups with similar attitudes, one finds that those who emphasize the need for adjustment of family size to economic circumstances were siblings who were now married, were in the twenties and thirties on an age basis, and fall heavily in the lowest third in order of birth. Those who were bitter, critical, or resentful were mostly women born in the first third in order of birth, were married, and are now in middle age. Those who were ashamed of their large families were chiefly women born in the first third by order of birth. Informants whose attitudes were favorable to their large families were largely single women and married male Catholics. Almost half of them fell in the twenty to twenty-nine-year age bracket.

In concluding this analysis of the facts about the informants, it should be emphasized that no evaluation is made of their attitudes or of the sincerity of their convictions. Attention is merely called to a fact which became clear long before the study was concluded: namely, that certain backgrounds and types of family experience seemed to produce certain attitudes toward the size of the families in which the informants had been reared.

SELECTED TYPES OF LARGE FAMILY ATTITUDES

The foregoing analysis of attitudes and motives in regard to large families has been a piecemeal one, considering separately attitudes of fathers, mothers, and siblings, and with special reference to the background factors which may have influenced these attitudes and motives. Perhaps it would be even more revealing to present selected types of large family situations, showing the combination of these respective attitudes in a family unity. Eight types will be summarized briefly.

1. First are the families in which the parents have a conscious ideal of family life which involves a goodly number of children and where the emphasis is upon the cultivation of family bonds and family values. Some of these are families with ample or moderate financial means; others have upheld a familistic ideal in the face of economic stress and strain.

The Scott family is an excellent illustration. Mr. and Mrs. Scott were childhood sweethearts. They became engaged while in high school, but waited to marry until Mr. Scott had completed his college training. Both came from large Protestant families, with strong familistic traditions. Both wanted a large number of children, and in due course of time they achieved the number they had originally agreed upon. Early in the life of the family, they moved to an outlying part of the town, gradually building a house designed for large family living, and surrounded by six acres of land. Children and parents lived, played, and worked together as a family. Financially, there was a family treasury; many problems were considered and decided in family council. Later on, as the children grew older, the problem of their education was planned as a family, and financed on a common basis until ultimately all goals had been achieved. World War II scattered some of its members to faraway places, but constant communication between all members is maintained. Several years ago, the parents and children all combined to stage a public exhibition of their creations in their chosen artistic field, developed originally as a family recreational project.

2. A second type, akin to the first, is where strong family values and traditions are combined with definite religious convictions concerning the size of the family. Such families are found among Catholics; Protestants, white and Negro; and Jews. The case selected for illustration is a Catholic family.

Mr. and Mrs. True both are devout Catholics. They were graduated from the same university, met and were married in the Catholic chapel of the school. They have eight living children. Both parents and the children consciously approve of their large family. "My husband and I," writes the mother, "have tried to build our family life on a striving for a humble acceptance of God's will, and a perfect faith, hope, and trust in His love for us. We believe if we teach our children to first love and serve God above all other things, and second, to love their fellow men, all else will fall into line. The longer we live together the more congenial my husband and I become. Our children seem to reflect this growing closeness by also becoming more congenial.

"This matter of happy family life is not an easy matter, but one that must be constantly thought about and worked on. We feel it is not a question of material things, but of attitudes. . . . This does not mean that we haven't had problems; that would be dishonest, but we try to solve our problems before they become serious or cause unhappiness.

"I think the aspect of 'togetherness' should be explored in any family study. It is this banding together of its members that makes for closeness in family life. We have consciously worked to develop this aspect in our family life. We always try to have dinner together around our big dining-room table. . . . We pray together. . . . We work together, as my husband is a great believer in family enterprises. . . . We go places together in our family car. . . . We play together, and have our own family customs that we carry out together as such. We feel that in doing all these things together, we have drawn bonds of close affection around our family that will endure and serve as an inspiration and guide to our children in the development of their own families."

3. There is another type, found among both our Catholic and Protestant families, where religious factors are dominant but where the response is one of fear or reluctant acceptance rather than of a conscious upholding of the social and spiritual values involved.

Mr. and Mrs. Roger have thirteen children, born within a span of fifteen years. Both of the parents are highly religious. They regard children as being sent by God, and think that it would be very sinful to do anything to limit the number of such gifts. Married life involves sex relations and children are the inevitable result. Mr. Roger emphasizes constantly the grave responsibilities and burdens which this family places upon him, and shows many signs of annoyance with the children. Mrs. Roger appears submissive, speaks of her children as God's blessings, but gives every indication, quite manifest to the older children, that she thinks Heaven has been somewhat more than generous with these blessings.

4. In a majority of the hundred cases, there were some members who were critical of the size of their families. It is only in a minority, however, that all of the members seem to be so minded.

Mr. and Mrs. Provost had eight children. Both parents had been born in Europe but came to this country at an early age. All of their children were born and reared in the United States. The father's family had lived comfortably in Europe, but he had never made a good adjustment here. Moreover, the latter half of his large family appeared during the depression decade. His children seemed an extreme annoyance, and he vented his frustrations upon them and their mother. The mother, weighed down with the responsibilities of her family, focused her resentment upon the father and, in part, upon the children. The children, in making the transition from the culture of their Old World parents to that of urban America, directed their resentments against their parents. A part of this resentment was against the size of the family. Tensions in this family seem to have been constant, and tragedy occurred in more recent years. Despite its Old World traditions, every member seemed to resent the large size of this family.

5. References to feelings of shame about family size appear frequently in the case material of this study. In some cases, it was the parent who had such feelings; in others, it was the children. Often, this sense of shame was an adolescent phase, replaced in time by acceptance or feelings of pride; but in others, no reference is made to its passing. Older daughters appear to be particularly ashamed of their mothers' pregnancies.

The Mellicks lived in a small community in which everyone knew everyone else, and where gossip was relentless and often salty. After the Mellick family reached a certain size, the father was teased a good deal about the size of his family. Apparently his sensitivity to this banter was such that he became very much ashamed of his family, and avoided being seen with them. He would drive his children to church, but not go in with them. When he drove to town, the children would cry to go with him, but he would refuse to take them. Mrs. Mellick seemed to welcome her first four children, but was ashamed when the later ones appeared. Almost twenty-five years separated the birth of the last from the first one: she was so ashamed with her last three pregnancies that she did not leave the house during most of these three periods. The older children, too, shared in this embarrassment. They were teased by the other children at school as the younger ones kept appearing, and one day one of the girls was asked if her parents "didn't know anything of the facts of life."

6. One of the combinations encountered a number of times in the course of the study was that of an expansive, baronial type of father and a submissive type of woman as the wife. These are the men who like to be surrounded and followed by their brood, who see their large families as an expansion of themselves, and who consider their wives as necessary means to this end. When these men become grandparents, they quickly essay the role of patriarch.

Mr. Hughes combines an independent income, a good position, and a flair for the dramatic. He likes to do things with a flourish, and in the grand manner. He seems to like nothing better than an audience. If he goes to prune a rose, at least four of the children will be drawn into the operation: more extensive jobs call for correspondingly greater dramatic personnel. At one time, he maintained three automobiles, so that when the family went anywhere the three cars might follow each other with the Hughes family members comfortably seated and spaced in them; in fact, there were times that the entire family had to go for no other reason apparently than that the show might be put on. Mrs. Hughes is described as a quiet, mousy type, meekly submissive to her husband.

7. A number of the parents are described by their children as lacking in responsibility, with implications in some cases that this was a reason for the family size; in others, that it was a factor in the internal life of the family. One combination was where the father was lacking in these respects, with the mother as the responsible one; in other cases, the situation was reversed; in still others, both seem irresponsible to the sibling informant.

The Tome family is an unhappy one, and seems always to have been so. Mr. Tome is a skilled worker of a type that is always in demand, but he is unemployed often, drinks a good deal, and spends much time berating his wife and many children. One of the chief complaints about his wife is that all she has to do is to look at him and she becomes pregnant. Mrs. Tome says she is proud of her husband, that he is a very handsome man, and besides, "anything can happen in nine months." The older children refuse to give any money to their mother to run the house because "she doesn't know what to do with money if she has it." The older daughters quarrel heatedly with each other over who is to give up "what part of whose earnings." All of the children have left home as soon as they were able.

8. Finally, there were the families in which the references were clear as to the advantages which it was hoped to gain from a large family.

Mr. and Mrs. Koster are pictured as hard-working persons who reared a large family on a large farm in an agricultural area noted for its fertility. The informant emphasizes that both parents wanted children and welcomed them as helpers in the common family tasks. "A large family was for us a sensible arrangement, we had lots of things to do and lots of space in which to do it. I never heard or saw any indication from either of my parents or from any of us children that there were too many of us."

CONCLUDING COMMENTS

Certain general conclusions concerning parental attitudes and motives became increasingly clear as the study progressed, and these will be summarized briefly by way of conclusion of this chapter.

1. The large family may be planned, just as the small family often is. The term "planned parenthood" has been used so largely to mean planning for a small family that it seems necessary to emphasize this other phase of the planning process. A number of the large families contacted during the six-year period of this study may be said to be planned, not necessarily for a specific number of children, but for general size. Such planning may have grown out of family pride, values of family life, religious beliefs, possession of wealth, economic gain, or personal philosophies or inadequacies, but they were planned.

2. It seems very clear that the way a parent rationalizes a fact after it has taken place is quite different from that parent's wishes before its occurrence. Parents who were ashamed, critical, resentful, or indifferent before a child was born subsequently were "happy," "proud," "pleased," "thrilled" with the addition of that child later on. Such subsequent reactions may be genuine or obviously compensatory for feelings of guilt. Mr. Blank, for example, was known throughout his community for his agitated unhappiness and resentment during each of his wife's pregnancies, and his great delight after the child had been born and reared out of the baby stage. Attitudes are not static, nor are they always definite, or obvious.

3. Some large families are neither planned nor unplanned. They are incidental to the marriage of persons of all kinds of aspirations, ideas, beliefs, fertility, and contraceptive sophistication. In other words, they just happen, and parents, and siblings as well, react to them in varying ways. The motif of acceptance runs through and between the lines of much of the material on which this study is based. "Life sits on the back of all of us," runs an old African proverb, "and we cannot shake him off." It applies equally well to many large families.

4. The facts presented in this chapter emphasize that there is an individual rather than a family or husband-wife attitude toward family size. It seems necessary to stress this point because much of the past literature seems to assume that it is the attitude of the married pair which constitutes the unit for study, due perhaps to the fact that past investigations have dealt largely with small families in which some degree of family planning is accepted by both parents. In this study, one is impressed with the differences, and often decided ones, in the attitudes of the two parents, and the siblings, toward family size.

The differences between husband and wife in these respects are a subject that seems to us never to have been fully explored. One came to sense various degrees of differences between the parents of many of the one hundred families. At times, such differences led to tensions, which found expression now in specific disagreements, now in recurrent verbal sniping, now in sullen resignation. In other cases, there was sharp disagreement, with bitterness, frustration, and perhaps patterns of partial aloofness in relations. One particularly revealing interview recorded during the course of the study was with the relatives of the mother of eight, who castigated the "unreasonable demands" of the father as much as the "Christian resignation" of the mother. Outwardly, neither parent had given indication of such an issue between them.

Moreover, the attitudes of the father and mother combine in a unity which is a new emergent. The Lesters are an excellent illustration. Mr. Lester is a very conscientious and God-fearing man who considers it a sin to make any contraceptive effort. Mrs. Lester is described as a lazy, irresponsible woman. This combination produced a child approximately every year over a number of years. As the family grew in size, Mr. Lester spent more and more time away from home to devote himself to business, in order to meet conscientiously the increasing obligations of his family. Mrs. Lester, on the other hand, spent much of her time in visiting about, leaving her children, under the supervision of the two oldest daughters, to shift as best they could.

5. All that was learned in this study fostered a healthy skepticism of those studies of motivation in family size which take the form of a statistical exercise in the identification of some specific factor. It seems much more in accordance with the facts to say that the motivation involved in bringing human beings into the world involves the projection of a person's philosophy of life into the future. This philosophy, whatever its nature, is the product of one's past experience, plus one's hope of the future. Life unfolds in terms of the whole rather than as particles making up an aggregate. All life is dominated by a dynamic cohesiveness, in which the past, present, and future are indivisibly related.[1] It is quite true, of course, that the working out of this philosophy depends upon the technical aids known to a person. In this case, this means his degree of contraceptive sophistication.

In the development of this personal philosophy, many influences are operative. One's cultural background is important. This includes, for example, the national and religious values of one's group. They may be a part of one's family traditions. In some families, it is assumed as a matter of

[1] Marshall C. Greco, *Group Life* (New York: The Philosophical Library, 1950), chap. II.

course that there is to be little or no family limitation, at least not until a good-sized family has been established, just as it is assumed in some families that the children will go to college or in others that they will take the practical courses in school and go to work as soon as the law allows. As one is able to get into the "inside" of families, it is amazing how definitely some of these matters are a part of the family pattern, passed on from one generation to another. Considered objectively, the assumption that a family will be large is perhaps just as natural as that it will be small and limited to a long-range program for the development of its members.

Again, the background factors may be temporal in character. That is, they grow out of the prevailing circumstances of an age. In the course of the study, one noted that families that were large, with many small children during the depression, developed critical attitudes toward families of their own size. Impressed with the ruggedness of their own experiences, these children have grown up and taken very cautious attitudes about desirable family size. This was noticeable even in Catholic families where depression-reared children were highly critical of large families. On the other hand, in families where the children are younger and have grown up during the lush war and postwar years, the attitude toward large families has been much more friendly. In some of these large families, three, four, or more members have gone into the armed forces, have risen in rank and income, while the parents have been pleased with the tax exemptions gained through the younger children.[2]

But the philosophy of parenthood and motivation for family size is highly specific and individual. It combines a person's experience in the family in which he was reared and how he came to evaluate it; his personal version of the general cultural background; his personal traits; his own needs, psychological and emotional, as well as economic. Finally,

[2] For a frank statement of these points of view, the reader is referred to Don Rose, *Full House* (Philadelphia: J. B. Lippincott Company, 1951).

there is the sex version of all of these, i.e., how the male and the female define respectively these background factors and experiences. One of the overlooked facts in the study of culture is the deep-seated and often fundamental difference between the male and the female culture in any given society.

SUMMARY

1. Information on the attitudes toward large families, and on possible motives, was obtained from the parents of eighteen large families and from the sibling informants in the hundred families.

2. Attitudes of fathers, and of mothers, as reported by siblings, vary greatly, from extreme pride to deep resentment.

3. In half of the families, fathers and mothers appear to agree in their attitudes; in the other cases, there was conflict or lack of necessary information to form a judgment. Conflict seems more prevalent in Protestant than in Catholic families.

4. Attitudes of siblings tend to be more qualified or critical than those of the parents.

5. First-born siblings tend in particular to be critical or qualified in their attitudes; the youngest ones tend to be more favorable. Inbetween children show a wide range in attitudes.

6. Married informants tend to emphasize the relationship between family size and economic circumstances. Single women are relatively more favorably disposed toward the large families in which they were reared.

7. The main types of large family situations, so far as attitude toward their size is concerned, are: (a) those with a conscious ideal of the large family as the socially desirable family life; (b) the religiously inspired large family, either in combination with consciously held family ideals or inspired by fear; (c) the family, often of recent European vintage, where the social aspirations of the members conflict with Old World traditions; (d) families in which members are ashamed

of the numerous progeny; (e) families where the "expansive-minded" father, often married to a "submissive-minded" mother, have a large number of children to please the father; (f) families with irresponsible parents; and (g) parents who see economic advantages to a family labor force.

8. Large families may be consciously planned; they may be welcomed, on the basis of after-the-fact rationalizations; they may just happen; they may grow despite the objection of one of the parents.

9. The motives involved in bringing children into the world do not result as a rule from the operation of some countable factor, but rather of the life philosophy of the parents.

· 5 ·

Interaction—Personal Relations Within the Large Family

WHAT IS LIFE within the large family like? Are large families happy families? What are some of the basic factors and problems in large family living? Questions of this kind present themselves, especially as a sequence to the survey of attitudes and motives presented in the preceding chapters.

Before turning to the material of the present study, two general facts about family living need to be emphasized. One of these is the relationship of size to the complexity of family life; the other is the peculiar nature of intrafamily relationships. Following this, selected data from the one hundred families are presented under the following headings: happiness in a hundred large families—the data; selected variables in large family relationships; large family happiness; the unhappy families; and the medium-happy families.

FAMILY SIZE AND FAMILY RELATIONS

Contemporary students in the social sciences are devoting considerable attention to the analysis of the human group, how it behaves, and how the characteristics of the group affect the behavior of its individual members. The study of the effects of the size of the group in such areas as classroom teaching, discussion, and family interaction has been particularly promising.[1]

[1] James H. S. Bossard, "The Law of Family Interaction," *American Journal of Sociology,* January, 1945, p. 293; *The Sociology of Child Development* (New York: Harper & Bros., 1948), p. 146; and *Parent and Child: Studies*

Two laws of family interaction, developed at the University of Pennsylvania, relate directly to the size of the family group. One of these is the author's law of personal relationships, which emphasizes the fact that every increase in the number of members of a family (or other primary group) results in more than a corresponding increase in the number of personal interrelationships. The law has been stated as follows: With the addition of each person to a family or primary group, the number of persons increases in the simplest arithmetical progression in whole numbers, while the number of personal interrelationships within the group increases in the order of triangular numbers. The mathematical formula for this is as follows:

$x =$ the number of personal interrelationships
$y =$ the number of persons in the group
$$x = \frac{y^2 - y}{2}$$

---

in *Family Behavior* (Philadelphia: University of Pennsylvania Press, 1953), chap. VII. Robert F. Bales, *Interaction Process Analysis: A Method for the Study of Small Groups* (Cambridge, Mass.: Addison-Wesley Press, 1950); "A Set of Categories for the Analysis of Small Group Interaction," *American Sociological Review*, April, 1950, pp. 257-63; Robert F. Bales, et al., "Channels of Communication in Small Groups," *ibid.*, August, 1951, pp. 461-68. Herbert Goldhamer, "Communication and Social Solidarity," notes of a course given in the Department of Sociology, University of Chicago (Society for Social Research, University of Chicago, 1948, mimeographed). Alexander Paul Hare, *A Study of Interaction and Consensus in Different Sized Discussion Groups* (Chicago: University of Chicago dissertation, 1951). George Homans, *The Human Group* (New York: Harcourt, Brace and Co., 1950). William M. Kephart, "A Quantitative Analysis of Intragroup Relationships," *American Journal of Sociology*, May, 1950, pp. 544-49. Carol M. Larson, "School Size as a Factor in the Adjustment of High School Seniors" (Pullman: State College of Washington, Bul. No. 511, November, 1949). Carl Murchison, "Experimental Measurement of a Social Hierarchy in *Gallus Domesticus*; Time Function in the Experimental Formation of Social Hierarchies of Different Sizes," *Journal of Social Psychology*, February, 1936, pp. 3-17. Georg Simmel, *The Sociology of Georg Simmel*, trans. by Kurt H. Wolf (Glencoe, Ill.: The Free Press, 1950). Herbert A. Thelen, "Group Dynamics in Instruction: Principle of Least Group Size," *The School Review*, March, 1949, pp. 139-48. *American Sociological Review*, Vol. 19, December, 1954.

The other law is spoken of here as the Law of Potential Intragroup Relationships. This recognizes the fact that there are relationships within a group other than those between any two persons. There may be a relationship between one and all the other members singly and in all possible combinations; or between any combination of members with any other combination of members. Our colleague, Dr. William M. Kephart, has presented this second law. "Although the number of potential relationships increases disproportionately as the size of the group increases, such relationships are never indefinite in number, the quantity always being mathematically determinable."[2] The total number of potential relationships that can exist in a given group is represented by the following mathematical formula:

$$P.R. = \frac{3^n - 2^{n+1} + 1}{2}$$

What these two laws mean in the study of the family becomes evident when the formulae are translated into numbers. The series follows:

Number of persons	= 2	3	4	5	6	7	8	9	10
Number of Personal Relationships	= 1	3	6	10	15	21	28	36	45
Number of Potential Relationships	= 1	6	25	90	301	966	3025	9330	28,501

In other words, in the family of seven interacting members, the smallest unit in this study, there are 21 different personal relationships and a total of 966 potential relationships. If the number is extended to ten members (two parents and eight children) there are 45 sets of personal relationships and a total of 28,501 potential relationships. Truly a large family presents an almost incredible web of interrelationships.

[2] Kephart, *op. cit.*, p. 546.

THE PECULIAR NATURE OF FAMILY INTERACTION

Family living involves a unique and distinctive kind of social interaction. To begin with, a family is a set of peculiarly intimate relationships, such as one finds nowhere else in human relationships. Its intimacies are of many different kinds and degrees. They are mostly continuing in character. They exist regardless of the degree of harmony within the family; in fact, family discord and tensions precipitate their own distinctive forms, as well as the varieties of their expression.

A second peculiarity about family interaction grows out of the composition of the family. Comprising the family group are units dissimilar in age, sex, and experience, yet bound together by bonds of affection, kinship, and mutual interests. No one has described this phase of family life better than Bosanquet, writing more than half a century ago:

As with all organic wholes, its parts are admirably fitted by nature to subserve each other's needs, and to supplement each other's efforts. The need of the weak for protection finds its correlative in the pride of the strong in protecting; the clinging appeal of the child for affection elicits a response which might otherwise remain dormant forever. The authority which all adults like to exercise finds a beneficent outlet in guiding the action of immature wills; and children who weary when left to the caprices of their undisciplined natures, find strength and contentment in a rule which is autocratic without having the impersonal rigidity of external law. And the man, again, who would prefer solitude to the constant clashing at close quarters of his own will with that of another man, finds it completed instead of thwarted when its functions are supplemented by those of the woman.[3]

Third, there is about family interaction this additional dis-

[3] Helen Bosanquet, *The Family* (New York: The Macmillan Co., 1902), p. 242.

tinctive feature: its naked incisiveness. One can dissemble only little in most phases of family interaction. Indeed, from more than one aspect, family interaction is a brutal process, the more so because of the very likenesses of the family members and the intimacies of the relationships between them. Here again it is worth while to quote Bosanquet at some length.

> A plain person finds no attraction in a mirror; and a person sensitive to his own defects of character may be inexpressibly jarred by seeing them reflected in another. I have known mothers whose irritation at the faults of their children was greatly enhanced by the fact that they recognized them as merely the faults of their own childhood recurring once again. And we fear no critic as we do the critic of our own Family, for has he not the key to all our weaknesses within himself? The stranger may be hostile and severe, but we can always console ourselves with the thought—which in nine cases out of ten will be perfectly true—that he does not really understand us. It is not being misunderstood which hurts most; it is being understood at our weakest, just as what helps the most is being understood at our best. And the member of our Family understands us literally "down to the ground," for it is the same ground upon which he himself stands.
>
> Here, too, we may perhaps find an explanation of the strange bitterness which so often seems to attach to differences of opinion between members of the same Family. When an outsider differs from us we can accept it as something to be explained away by differences of experience, of surroundings, of education, above all of inherited temperament and disposition; in a sense it is possible to think of each being so far right that his opinion is the natural outcome of the sort of person he is. But when our brother differs from us there is no such escape from discord; this, we feel uneasily, is the same sort of person as ourselves, his opinion proceeds from the same nature as our own, and we cannot see any reason for the conflict. It is as if one's own judgment were divided against itself.[4]

[4] *Ibid.*, pp. 249-51.

HAPPINESS IN A HUNDRED LARGE FAMILIES

Each of the informants in the present study was asked to rate the family in which he or she had grown up for its relative happiness. Was the general tone of the family in which you were reared happy, medium, or unhappy? This was the specific question that was asked. No attempt was made to define the term "happiness," the assumption being that each person was able to answer the question in the light of his own experience and understanding of the term. Replies were received for each of the hundred families, and Table 14 presents the replies received in summary form.

TABLE 14

Family Happiness, as Reported by Siblings

Happiness	Number	Per Cent
Happy	50	50.0
Medium	36	36.0
Unhappy	14	14.0
Total	100	100.0

The question at once presents itself: how does this compare with other studies which present data on family happiness? Several such studies are available. Professors Burgess and Cottrell reported these facts for 526 Illinois couples, largely from Chicago. They used a five-degree classification of very happy, happy, average, unhappy, and very unhappy. For purposes of comparison, these may be reduced to happy, average, and unhappy. Thus summarized, the percentages are as follows:

Per Cent
Happy — 63.1
Average — 14.4
Unhappy — 21.5
No reply — 1.0

Since 71 per cent of these cases had been married from two to four years, and the cases in the present study were married for much longer periods of time, the comparison is not wholly proper.[5] Another study by R. O. Lang of 8,263 couples married for from one to sixteen years is subject to the same comment. This study showed 64.9 per cent were happy, 19.2 per cent were reported as average, and 15.8 per cent were termed unhappy.[6]

Terman's study of 792 couples is that of an older group, married from one to twenty-seven years. The average age of the husbands was 38.8 years and that of the wives was 35.8. Reducing the seven-degree ratings which he utilized to happy, average, and unhappy, he found that of the 792 husbands 82.6 per cent reported that they were happily married, 12.9 as about average, and 4.6 as unhappy. For the wives, the percentages were 85.2, 9.2, and 5.6, respectively.[7] Popenoe, on the other hand, citing data on 8,370 marriages secured from several hundred mature adult students in summer school classes at several institutions, reports that of the childless couples 59 per cent were happy in marriage; of those with one child, 62 per cent were happy; of those with three or more children, 71 per cent were happy; and of those with five or more children, 69 per cent were happy.[8]

Various other studies dealing with data on happiness in marriage have been made, each of value in respect to some specific purpose, but not comparable to this study. Our data

[5] Ernest W. Burgess and Leonard S. Cottrell, Jr., *Predicting Success or Failure in Marriage* (New York: Prentice-Hall, 1939), pp. 21, 32.
[6] R. O. Lang, *A Study of the Degree of Happiness or Unhappiness in Marriage as Rated by Acquaintances of the Married Couples,* unpublished M.A. thesis (Chicago: University of Chicago, 1932).
[7] Lewis M. Terman, et al., *Psychological Factors in Marital Happiness* (New York: McGraw-Hill Book Co., 1938), p. 78.
[8] Paul Popenoe, *Modern Marriage* (New York: The Macmillan Co., 1940), Appendix VI. See also Robert B. Reed, "The Interrelationship of Marital Adjustment, Fertility Control, and Size of Family," in "Social and Psychological Factors Affecting Fertility," *Milbank Memorial Fund Quarterly,* October, 1947, pp. 383-425; and Judson T. Landis, "Length of Time Required to Achieve Adjustment in Marriage," *American Sociological Review,* December, 1946, pp. 666-77.

are unique: first, in that they are confined to large families; second, to families that have been in existence for many years; and third, in that the ratings are furnished by the children rather than the married pair.

A final word about the more tragic side of unhappiness in the hundred large families. Only two divorces are reported: one, that of a Catholic father; the other, that of a Jewish father. Also, one Jewish father committed suicide. One of the divorces involved a man given to excessive alcoholism; the suicide, in addition to family unhappiness, was seriously involved in the depression of the nineteen-thirties.

SELECTED VARIABLES IN LARGE FAMILY RELATIONSHIPS

Two further questions are apt to arise in the reader's mind concerning the happiness rating of our families. One is the variation on the basis of racial and religious groupings; the other, on the basis of family size. Table 15, which presents

TABLE 15

Happiness Ratings, by Racial and Religious Groups

Group	Happy NUM-BER	Happy PER CENT	Medium NUM-BER	Medium PER CENT	Unhappy NUM-BER	Unhappy PER CENT	Total NUM-BER	Total PER CENT
Protestants, white	26	47.3	23	41.8	6	10.9	55	100
Roman Catholics, white	16	61.5	7	27.0	3	11.5	26	100
Jews	2	25.0	2	25.0	4	50.0	8	100
Negroes	6	75.0	2	25.0	—	—	8	100
Mixed Marriages	—	—	2	66.6	1	33.3	3	100

the data classified by racial and religious groups, is of significance chiefly for the comparison it affords between white Protestants and Roman Catholics. The number of Jews and Negroes, while included in the table, is too small in each case to be significant statistically. It would appear from Table 15 that children reared in Roman Catholic large family homes reported, in our limited number of cases, a higher rate of happiness than children reared in Protestant large families.

Table 16 presents these ratings of family happiness by the number of children who survived infancy. Because of the small number of cases, the families are grouped into four categories.

TABLE 16

Happiness Ratings, by Number of Children Surviving Infancy

Number of Children	Number of Cases	Happy NUMBER	Happy PER CENT	Medium NUMBER	Medium PER CENT	Unhappy NUMBER	Unhappy PER CENT
5, 6, or 7	49	22	44.9	18	36.7	9	18.4
8 or 9	20	10	50.0	9	45.0	1	5.0
10, 11, or 12	25	16	64.0	8	32.0	1	4.0
13, 14, 15, or 16	6	2	33.3	1	16.6	3	50.0
	100	50		36		14	

An examination of Table 16 suggests at first glance that, barring the very large families, happiness in large families increases as the size of the family increases. A careful reading of the case records suggests another explanation, and that is the role of the time interval between births. In the case of the "smaller" large families, i.e., those with five, six, or seven living children, the time interval between births averages three to four years. In some of these families, each child may be separated by three or more years from the next one; in other cases, there may be two or more sets of children, with a considerable period of time between the sets. In the larger large families, especially those with ten to twelve children, the children tend to follow each other in rapid succession, with time intervals of a year to a year and a half. More will be said about this in the chapter on sibling relationships; suffice it to say here that one of the hypotheses formed in the present study is that, from the standpoint of family happiness, particularly as seen through the eyes of the children, short intervals between births are more desirable than longer ones.

LARGE FAMILY HAPPINESS—SELECTED ASPECTS

Further insight into the factors making for happiness in large families may be gained from analyses of the happy and unhappy families. Turning first to the fifty happy families, what do the informants mention which might throw light on the reasons for their happiness?

1. Is the type of the community in which the family lives a factor? This question was raised invariably by persons with whom the study was discussed. An analysis of the data shows little to support this view. Eighteen of the fifty happy families grew up in towns, villages, or farm villages, exactly the same proportion that families from this type of community formed in the total number (36 out of 100). The same is true for farm families and small-city families. In both cases, the percentages of such families in the happy group equal their percentages in the total number. Only in the case of big-city and suburban families do the numbers show any disproportion. Of the total number of eight suburban families in the study, six are in the happy group; of the twenty-four big-city families in the study, only nine, instead of the twelve that mathematically should have appeared, did so. In both cases, however, the number does not seem large enough to be definitive.

2. Is happiness in the large family the result primarily of a friendly attitude toward its size? In other words, is the family happy in those cases where the parents wanted a large family, and unhappy when the reverse is true? No unqualified answer can be made to these questions. There are a number

of families where both parents and siblings welcomed a large family and were happy in their family experience. This was particularly true in those cases where the entire group had a strong sense of familism, as a matter of family tradition or religious belief or both, and where all of the members were mutually devoted to each other. But the attitude toward family size is an individual one, and there were only thirty families in which both parents and the sibling informants agreed in their friendly attitude toward a large family. Not all of these families were rated as happy families, and many were rated as high in which there were members with critical attitudes toward the size of their families. Brief summaries of selected cases will indicate these contrasts. In Family X, everyone liked the idea of a large family, but the father was so domineering that there was much unhappiness in the family; while in Family R, the difficulty was with the ineffectiveness and irresponsibility of the mother. In Family Y, the father wanted a large family, the mother obviously did not, but the financial means the family enjoyed permitted family arrangements which all of its members seemed to have enjoyed. In Family K, the father resented the coming of the children, and drank a great deal, but the children rallied around the mother, and, with the resilient spirits of youth, had an enjoyable family life. Finally, there is Family W, where the mother died, the father was overwhelmed by his responsibilities, the depression complicated the lives of all, yet the informant, after polling all of the other eight children, reports the unanimous rating of a happy family life.

3. In a recently published work, the author has advanced the theory that family rituals are a relatively reliable index of family integration and a conserver of family values.[9] The term "family ritual" is used to mean "a prescribed formal procedure, arising out of a family interaction, involving a

[9] James H. S. Bossard and Eleanor S. Boll, *Ritual in Family Living* (Philadelphia: University of Pennsylvania Press, 1950), chap. 9.

pattern of defined behavior, which is directed toward some specific end or purpose and which acquires rigidity and a sense of rightness as a result of its continuing history. Thus defined, ritual develops in connection with many aspects of family life, but clusters chiefly about such things as holidays, anniversary days, meals, vacations, religious worship, and collective ways of using leisure time." [10]

Are happy large families given to the development of family rituals? Do such rituals appear to be a factor in the happiness of large families? No specific questions pertaining to family rituals were included in the large family study, so that the answer made to the foregoing questions rests wholly on information on rituals volunteered by the informants. This gives such information added value, but it means also that the role of ritual will tend to be understated rather than the reverse.

Forty-six of the hundred case records contain references to aspects of family living which come quite clearly within the meaning of our term of family rituals. A few of these refer to the family's observance of religious or racial rituals; the others picture coöperative forms of family activity centering around birthdays, holidays, family reunions, vacation activities, winter evening recreation, and the like. Of these forty-six families, thirty-seven were rated as happy families. In other words, of the fifty families rated as happy, informants in thirty-seven of them went on to illustrate their happiness in terms of common participation in family rituals. The other nine family records that contained references to rituals were families rated as of medium happiness. It is clear, both from the frequency with which happy families describe rituals, and the context in which they are presented, that rituals are generally associated with family happiness. Conceivably, others of the happy families practiced rituals, even when their scant records made no mention of them.

[10] James H. S. Bossard and Eleanor S. Boll, "Ritual in Family Living," *American Sociological Review*, August, 1949, p. 464.

4. Does happiness in large families just happen, or is it most often achieved by conscious and intelligent parental effort? This supplements the preceding question about rituals, for family rituals do not just happen but usually their development involves parental leadership and promotion. The present question therefore raises a larger issue—that of the role of parental efforts of all kinds to promote happiness in large families. To answer this question, the case material on the fifty happy families was read with this in mind, and the answer of the facts was decisive. In all but two of them, the sibling informants point out that their parents "worked at" the happiness of their families. In thirty-seven of them, as already pointed out, family rituals were emphasized; in a number of these, and in eleven more families where rituals were not mentioned, the parents were described as making efforts consistently to organize their children in group activities, to devise group projects, to furnish facilities for group efforts, and to organize family efforts in many different directions. It seems very clear, by way of summary, that large family happiness does not just happen, but that it is an achievement. Happy group participation apparently is a form of learned behavior. An illustration or two will suffice to underscore this point.

The Bakewell Family. "Our house was—and is—full of books, which were read and loved. We always had a piano and any other musical instruments within reach which someone wanted to 'learn.' We sang and played together, and did a lot of family reading together. Sunday afternoon was often the time for the latter, and any time was good for singing, and as we all had a good ear, we did not need to buy music we wanted to sing. We listened, and then harmonized it ourselves. Some of the nicest, coziest times were when, during the winter, we 'picked the apples,' sorting from the barrels those that needed eating or cooking, to keep from spoiling—and we sang and sang. We still do, when we get together. A family custom that we always maintain is to waken the birthday child with music early in the morning. Now, because so few of us are at home, it is a favorite record or the playing of a favorite hymn, but even those of us who are away from home get this greeting on our birthdays, and we know we are being serenaded on our natal day."

The Wister Family. "When we were children we were carefully supervised. We had a playroom in the house, and in summer Daddy pitched a tent in one corner of our lawn for us to play in. Not only did we play in our yard, but so did the whole neighborhood. We were the only children who had a tent with cots, table and chairs, doll beds, dolls, dishes, etc. And here it was that we had our tea parties."

The Marlyn Family. "Mother and Dad were relatively young when the first five of us came along and they played with us, and we all loved it. Dad used to chase Mother with a mop and she used the broom to get after him. We all squealed with delight for we knew that it was all in fun. People who came to the house to sell things often doubted the presence of Mother because of the great shrieks of laughter and accompanying noises that came from our house. In the summertime, we enjoyed many parties in the playhouse. If a cake 'fell,' we had a party, and we used to pray that the cake would fall. Every birthday was a grand occasion, presents or not. Everyone always had a cake. In November, we have five birthdays plus Thanksgiving, and our parents' anniversary, but each one has a cake. They are special ones, too. Mine was always chocolate with white icing, red teaberries, and pink candles."

The Hylan Family. "Our family life was very happy. We got along well together. My father skated with us, took us to the horse and dog shows, gardened with us. Mother let us have pets—sometimes three dogs and a dozen lesser creatures. We had a great deal of family fun. I can remember only two fracases. Once my youngest brother had a tantrum, and at another time there was some uproar over teaching my eldest brother arithmetic."

5. Does one parent stand out as of particular importance in the promotion of happy family life? The evidence here is impressive and clear-cut. In twenty-six of the fifty happy families, the role of the mother is singled out for special comment or emphasis—this without benefit of suggested questions on our part. Selected statements from these comments show the variety of functions that the mother served.

> Mother was the peacemaker in our family
> Mother was the shock absorber
> Mom always had good insight
> Mamma was the well-balanced realist
> She had such good sense
> Mother had our complete confidence
> Mother was very sharp and always knew what was going on
> Mother was wise, lovable, and always patient
> She had tremendous ability and capacity
> She had such a keen sense of humor
> Father died and mother really raised us. We all loved her
> We all liked to be alone sometimes with Mother

This emphasis upon the role of the mother should not be regarded merely as expressions of sentiment and filial loyalty. The more one reads the case material of this study, the more one sees the mother as the peculiar key figure in large family living. First she must bear the children, which means that other duties and responsibilities must be carried along with the strains of repeated pregnancies and confinements. Next, she is to manage the household. She is the ever-present adult in an active, complex, and often hectic domestic establishment, in which many persons of different ages, duties, interests, and traits have to be coördinated if the whole is to function properly. It is in the home that the minutiae of living center. There is a good deal of food to be prepared; a lot of clothes to be washed, mended, bought, and altered; many beds to be made; much straightening out to be done; many unforeseen crises to be met—all in the face of the time schedules of its various members. The mother's administrative and managerial ability is very important. If she has it, it is fortunate for the family. A good mother in a large family must be a good organizer and administrator.

Problems of adjustment are constantly arising. Who washes the dishes this week, who makes the beds, when do the shifts change, what substitutions are to be allowed, how are infractions to be dealt with? For settlement of many of these issues, the mother is looked up to; when they reach a point of seriousness, they may be carried to the father. Father tends to serve the role of court; mother is the agent who settles matters out of court. Mothers do this constantly in many families. A good mother is a good personnel officer.

The mother of a large family has many and varied emotional needs to serve. One mother of six has put this very well. "Every time I walk through the house," she said, "I have to be six different kinds of a mother. My 16-year-old boy needs one kind, my 15-year-old girl another, my 13-year-old boy another, and so on down to the baby. Then, at night, when my husband comes home, I must be a supervisor to see that all is quiet and peaceful in the household. Each of these seven needs me, and each for different reasons."

The reader who keeps in mind the range and complexity of large family living will not only appreciate the vital role of the mother in the promotion of family happiness, but also the nature of the critical comments directed at mothers who are inept and ineffective. These will appear in the discussion of the unhappy large families, to which we now turn.

THE UNHAPPY FAMILIES

Fourteen families were rated as unhappy by our sibling informants, and all the supplementary information of their case records confirmed this judgment. In analyzing these records, four factors are emphasized most frequently.

1. First in order of frequency are the families that were unhappy because of the father's misbehavior. Excessive drinking by the father was mentioned in four cases, and in two of these this led to the termination of the marriage. In two cases, it was the father's temper and domineering habits that were constantly disturbing.

The case records of these six families make rather pathetic reading. In one case, the son writes: "The death of my father came as a distinct relief to all of us." Another writes: "When my father drank, he was out of humor. Then the children would be the victims, and he was without mercy." A daughter writes: "Such upsets in the life of a family caused emotional strains never before dreamed of, created tormenting mental conflicts and exhausting tensions. His drunken rages, his fits of cruel temper, and his unkind treatment of my mother, make it difficult to write about."

2. Complementary to drunken and domineering fathers are the references to ineffective mothers. In four of the unhappy families, this seems to be the chief, or an important, source of difficulty. More adequate consideration will be given to this factor later in this chapter.

3. Next are the families where the parents were foreign born and the children were native born, with a resultant conflict between the two generations growing out of differences in ideas, values, and aspirations. This is a type of situation well known to students of the family, and the five cases in which this factor is emphasized fully confirm the scholarship of the past. The situation, briefly stated, is as follows. The parents cling to their Old World ideas and ways, the children accept those of the country of their birth. The parents think their children are difficult and ungrateful; the children think their parents are incompetent, old-fashioned, and unreasonable. Moreover, they tend to be ashamed of their parents, and the parents come invariably to realize it. Sometimes one

parent or child appears as the chief offender in the eyes of the other generation, but the problem is far broader than the personal clash it seems at times to be.

Basically, the clash is a cultural one, between that which the parents retain and that which their children accept. This is further emphasized by the fact that these conflicts do not appear in all cases where the parents are foreign born, but only in those cases where the parents migrated from countries whose culture patterns are distinctly different from those of this country.

4. In four families, all or much of the unhappiness was attributed to the death of one parent, the remarriage of the other, with the result that two or three groups of children were reared in the same household. The problem of the stepparent, and the unhappiness of the stepchild, is proverbial: when there are two sets of children, the difficulties are increased. Most complicated of all are the well-known cases of "my children, your children, and our children." Not that unhappiness in all of these cases is inevitable. A total of thirteen remarriages are reported in the hundred families, and in at least three of the cases the step-parent seems to have been loved more than the natural parent. Many circumstances are involved in these cases of remarriage—the inheritance of wealth, economic pressure, and the relative social effectiveness of both the deceased and the second parent. The family in which Abraham Lincoln was reared is not the only one that improved with the coming of a stepmother.

In many of the unhappy families, it was one of the foregoing factors that was held responsible for the family's unhappiness, but in other cases, two or more would be combined. In the Koster family, for example, the father drank excessively, perhaps because of his wife's gross incompetence in their home with its six children. In another family, an immigrant father, rejected by his children and his wife, sought solace in drink. In other families, other factors were involved, and these will be touched upon in the succeeding section of this chapter.

THE MEDIUM-HAPPY FAMILIES

The thirty-six large families that reported medium happiness are significant chiefly for the light they throw on the factors making for unhappiness. In most of these cases, the basic family situation was sound, the family should have been happy, and apparently would have been, save usually for some one or more "flies in the ointment." The factors making for family happiness that have been identified in the happy families are present often in the medium-happy ones: it is their very presence which throws into such clear light the counteracting factors. It is these latter aspects that call for more extended discussion.

1. Economic pressure is mentioned more frequently (in fourteen out of the thirty-six cases) than any other factor. This covers a wide range of circumstances—business reverses, the depression, unemployment, irregular employment, too many mouths to feed, and the like. Since the economics of large family living is considered in another chapter, comment here is confined to an acknowledgment of the frequency and pervasiveness of this factor.

2. Fathers seem to cast a shadow over the happiness of a number of our families, and not as a rule because of their addiction to the common masculine vices. Drunkenness and apparent unfaithfulness are mentioned, but most references are to the overly stern and domineering father. Many of these fathers are pictured as hard-working and good providers, but as lacking in other traits which enable a father to be a happy family maker. "Our home," writes an intelligent son, "was very much of the type called patriarchal. The pattern and code throughout was set by my father. He was very strict, and at times there was too much of the Spartan about him.

As children, this often irked us." A grown daughter writes: "It is around my father that our family revolves, yet any outsider can see that it is my mother who holds us together. It is she who sees to it that we don't say or do anything that would make my father angry. He has little or no patience, and he is always right. It is impossible to ever talk anything over with him. Now that I am older, I can see that he has neglected to give us the one thing we need most—fatherly love. Although my mother tries hard, she cannot be expected to fulfill the emotional needs of six children alone." In another case, one of eleven children writes: "My father was almost indifferent to us. He never drank, but he was a big man, and he would discipline us, often severely, whenever there was noise and confusion." Since this family with thirteen members lived in a four-room home, one can muster some understanding of the father's excessive irritability with which his daughter charges him. Another informant writes: "Father was strict and high-tempered. He had a strong voice and bellowed out his commands. Mother stood by quietly, apparently cowed by father, abiding by the orders and trying to work them out with the children. Father had a dominating personality and everyone in the household was afraid of him. As a result, a family that would otherwise have been very happy was only medium so." Then, there was a mother of three children who, when contributing the case record for the family in which she was reared, turned around and looked furtively at the doorway each time she spoke of her father. The pattern in her family had been that of an unreasoning, domineering father, compensated only in part by a sweet, gentle, and loving mother. Finally, there is the case record presented by one informant with this laconic summary: "Family medium happy. Mother submerged, father dominant."

3. What has already been said about the pivotal importance of the mother in the large family is amply reinforced

by the comments made about mothers in the medium-happy families. If, on the one hand, there are families in which the mother's qualities soften the harsher domestic features, there apparently are many others where her ineffectiveness and irresponsibility are manifest to her children. Comments of this kind appear in ten of the case records of the thirty-six medium-happy families, and in twenty-three of the one hundred cases.

Criticism of mothers appears on a variety of scores. Statements that mothers were too easy-going and allowed others to take advantage of them are found here and there. In other cases, the mother was submissive to a domineering father, but took out her resentment in various quiet ways. One informant writes: "I do not think mother was a companion to any of the children. Physically, we were all well cared for, but emotionally this was not true. I do not believe that mother created a warm parent-child relationship." One of a very large family, who writes appreciatively of the other members of the household, spares no words in attributing their difficulties to "the constant nagging and screeching of our mother, who, incidentally, is sweetness personified in the presence of guests." Still another mother is criticized because "she never went anywhere with us. She saw to it that we got to church and school, but she never went anywhere herself. Before she was married, she was very active in church and school work, but apparently she was ashamed of having married a man so much older than herself and with so many children." More serious is the complaint of a sibling who says: "During the early years of my life, my mother's temper caused me to be the brunt of many unkind actions, such as knocking me on the floor and kicking me when I was down. I may have deserved some punishment, but never so harsh, nor committed in such violent anger. I used to go upstairs and try to hang myself, but I never quite had the nerve or power to do so. After I left home to go to work, I became more and more rebellious toward my mother, and now, ten years later, I still wake up shuddering from dreams in which I have bitter conflict with my mother."

Too easy-going, too submissive, too unloving, nervous, irritable, high tempered—these are qualities of parents that children thought it necessary to emphasize in accounting for a lack of happiness in their home life as children. But most frequent of all are references to or implications of the mother's lack of ability as a manager. The mother who was a poor manager of household finances, who could not organize the tasks of the household, who could not coördinate the labor of her children and the family chores, who never seemed to know what was going on or why—these mothers seem to have been a trial to their children. One of eleven children speaks for all such children when she said: "My mother seemed confused much of the time. She just never seemed wholly to know what it was all about. Perhaps there were times when she was too tired to know or care."

One final kind of mothers who lessen the happiness of their families are those who interfere with the educational plans of their children, and particularly of their daughters. Much has been written in recent years of mothers who project their ambitions upon their children, and thus interject themselves into the formal educational process in which their children are involved. They insist that a son go to medical school, or that a daughter go to college. But cases of this kind are typically found in the contemporary small family. The large family at times presents a variant of this. These are the cases where the mother is reluctant to see her children educated beyond her own level. Especially is this true with her daughters. The chief aim of girls should be to get husbands and have children, like the mothers. Such mothers realize that they got husbands without much education, and why should the case be different with their daughters? Jealousy may develop here, often below the level of consciousness, on the part of mothers, especially against the older daughters.

This was well illustrated in the Dulane family. Mrs. Dulane was an attractive but relatively uneducated woman who married a man of cultural attainments and interests, to whom she bore ten children. The oldest child, a daughter, "took after" the father. She was an excellent student, and has continued her educational progress throughout the years. She married a product of a well-known university and graduate school. From the beginning, the mother has shown animosity toward this daughter, and the longer the daughter's educational progress has continued the greater has been the mother's animosity. Mrs. Dulane says that her daughter is an ungrateful and unnatural child; her favorite is a daughter who functions on the same biological and cultural level that she does.

4. Informants in one out of five families (twenty-two out of one hundred) speak of favoritism as a disturbing element in the general pattern of family living. It is mentioned in families that rate themselves as happy, unhappy, and of medium happiness, but most often, relatively, in the medium-happy families, and is characterized as the factor which is responsible for the family not being rated as a wholly happy one. Eight of the medium-happy families speak of it in this light.

Charges of favoritism are of different kinds and degrees. First, there are those where the father is said to favor the girls and the mother is wound around the fingers of the boys. Resentments in such cases tend to be mild, although there are two cases where the boys came to be rather bitterly disposed against the father. Second are the reverse cases where the sexes stick together, the father lining up with the boys and the mother with the girls. This happened in certain farm families, and the closeness of feeling seemed to be associated with constant coöperation in tasks. But there were the cases, too, where this same sex cleavage existed because the father, a first-generation American, retained his Old World adherence to the masculine tradition. In these cases, the girls, sensing a difference in regard to this tradition in this country, tend to resent the father's attitude.

Favoritism is more serious when it is confined to one or two of the children. These are the cases where one daughter ("because she looks like mother") has a special drag with father; or where a son, because of his reliability, is given special authority; or where one child has the privilege of "talking back" and the others do not; or where "all the children know that if they want anything it is wisest for Jane to ask for it"; or where mother has her special pet who dare not be disciplined "by father or any of the others." In certain cases, there is not one child but two or more, as in the Seton family. "The children early learned to gang up against two of the children who were special favorites of our mother. In her opinion, neither one could do any wrong. Mother persistently played favorites so far as they were concerned." Finally, it should be added that at times there were curious selections in this process of favoritism, as in the Nixon family, where the father's obvious and pronounced favorite was the daughter of his second wife, whom she had with her first husband—this in the face of his children with his first and second wives.

5. In a few cases (eight in number) the chief disturbance of the family harmony was a troublesome child member. "The only family contention of any seriousness in our family," writes one informant, "was caused by my oldest brother, lazy and spoiled by his war experiences. Finally, after years of drifting, he got a job with the federal government, and seems to be able to hold it. This permits him to pursue his kind of life." Another points out that the "only trouble in our family was caused by the oldest boy who was in constant conflict, not only with his parents but also his brothers. I [his sister] had almost no contact with him." In another family, the chief problem was "our lazy member. He doesn't get along with the family as a whole the way the other children do. When

any work is suggested for him to do, he either argues or retires to a room by himself. Either way, he doesn't share in the activities and pleasures of the others." Then there is the case where "the only fly in the family 'ointment' is the animosity between the father and the youngest son. The latter feels that father is unjust to him, and he retained his resentment as long as father lived. None of the rest of us feels that way about father, who was a quiet man, with a great admiration for books, learning, and children." Finally, there is the family where one child "whined and complained all the time, although the rest of us saw nothing to whine and complain about."

6. The existence of cultural differences between husband and wife, and the role of such differences in family life, is just beginning to be explored, and it is doubtful whether we know what facts to look for or how to assess the ways of their operation.[11] Perhaps the chief exceptions to this are interreligious marriages, although even here their significance in areas other than the religious life of the mates has not been fully considered. Three such marriages are included in the hundred cases, and in each one this difference between the parents looms large in the minds of the informants. Perhaps the best statement of the issue in our material is contained in a case record that was obtained in the course of the study but not included in the hundred cases tabulated. The informant writes:

Two differing philosophies set the scene for life in our family: that of my father, a Protestant and a conservative, and that of my mother, a Catholic and a liberal. The two were far removed from each other both in their thinking and in the people they liked and wanted to associate with. My father was, as a result of his experiences, inclined to be straitlaced about our relations with boys. My mother, as a result of her extremely circumscribed way

[11] For a pioneering study in this connection, see Bossard, *Parent and Child: Studies in Family Behavior*, chap. IX.

of life as a young girl, was inclined to be more liberal. My father wanted us to be educated, even though we were girls. Education was an investment and increased the value of his children. Education for us was a must. Mother wanted us to go to parochial school and then to go to work. Whenever we were naughty, she would say to my father, "Let them go to work." The fact that all of his six girls ultimately graduated from school shows how completely my father was victorious in this matter. Not many friends came to our house, and those who did were papa's friends. Mama always hated their coming because she knew that they were not on her side. Papa was completely imbued with the belief that a man could control and direct his own destiny. Individual success, education, literacy, all were up to the person to accomplish what he wanted to. Mama, on the other hand, had an inferiority complex. Life was too much for her. She was always giving up. There was, she said, no reason to keep up with the Joneses. One of the big battles in our home was about father's Bible, a large 12 by 14, that was about seven inches deep. Papa wanted it kept in the living room where it could serve as a symbol of religious respect. My mother objected to it because it was the King James version. Certainly there must have been some way of settling this that would have satisfied father and mother's church, but my mother had a complete lack of tact.

My father said you should say Yes, Sir and No, Sir when speaking to your elders, but my mother opposed it vociferously and usually won out. There was constantly a struggle between them; they didn't agree on anything, and particularly on anything that pertained to bringing up the children. My mother said that it was because my father wanted to cuff the children around, and my father claimed it was because my mother just didn't know anything about how to train children. It led to endless battles that colored every detail of our family life. At first when there were disputes, as children we always held my father responsible. There was no reason for it except that he was a man and mother was a woman, and besides, his voice sounded thunderous. We chided mama for taking it and said what we would do if we were in her place. In later life, I learned that my mother was wrong many times and was not only stubborn as my father said, but downright cussed at times. It is true that she worked endlessly and got no apparent thanks for it, but it is also true that like many another wife and housewife she did not organize her work or schedule her time. When my father said this, as he often did, there always followed one of those headache affairs at our house. At least the children were on her side, she said, and as time went on she worked this for all it was worth. In fact, my father was a veritable outsider in his own home, and his only redress was to express his misery to his friends outside. One great source of displeasure to my father was the fact that he was never appreciated by his children. With the exception of myself, all of the other children's attitude was patterned after my mother. When I got to be older and saw through things and began siding with my father, I became the sore thumb for the family.

But cultural differences of other kinds appear implicit in many cases. These referred to or implied differences that contemporary social scientists are including under the term "social class." Not that the words were used by any of our informants, but in at least eighteen additional cases such differences may be assumed safely as related adversely to family happiness. In fourteen cases, the father was married to a woman of obviously lower social status; in four cases, the reverse was true. What this came to mean in family life, as emphasized by the informants, may be gathered from the following excerpts:

Father and mother never seemed to speak the same language.

Father was an intelligent man who loved his books; mother not only did not care for them, but seemed to be jealous of them and us when we shared them with father.

Mother seemed often not to fit into our life with dad; she was indifferent and submissive, and acted as though she felt inferior.

My father was an uncouth man, given to drink and salty interests. He worked steadily and supported his family, but he never shared our life with mother. His life seemed to be made up of work, liquor, and sex.

7. Shame of its size is widely prevalent among the members of large families. The data on this for the hundred cases were summarized in Chapter 4, and it will be recalled that there were only thirty families in which neither parent nor sibling informant was recorded as having been ashamed of the large number of children. Undoubtedly, if all the siblings could have been polled for their attitudes, the number of shame-free families would have been even smaller.

The question that now presents itself is this: What is the importance of this factor in the unhappiness of large family living?

A careful reading of the case material reveals, first, that one must distinguish between the happiness of the family and that of the informants. Informants frequently recorded themselves as having been unhappy or as having passed through periods of unhappiness because of the size of their families or their mothers' repeated pregnancies, and yet stated that the general tone of their family life was happy. Feelings of shame on the part of the informants are most common among the older children, and when they are in the teen-age period. The remarks of their friends and schoolmates seem to have been particularly distressing. "Don't your parents know the facts of life?" "If it isn't the cat at your house, it's your mother." "I didn't know you were Catholic." "Where do you all sleep? Do you hang on hooks?" It is in the adolescent years that comments of this kind sting as perhaps they never will again.

It is when the parents are ashamed of their large families that the whole tone of family life is apt to suffer, for coupled with shame is rejection of parenthood, of its duties and responsibilities, and a lack of those conscious efforts at promoting good family living that have already been emphasized as of such high importance. Moreover, the children realize or sense the attitude of the parents in these cases, and come to feel their own rejection. The child's rejection by his parents has been much emphasized by contemporary students, and children in large families where the parents are ashamed of the size of their families constitute a specific phase of this kind of problem. One could not but be impressed during the course of the study to note how informants, now in middle age, related in detail instances of family life which involved the parents' shame of their children and the latter's poignant experiences which resulted.

It should be noted, however, that in only a few cases are such attitudes of parents emphasized as the chief cause of the family's unhappiness. Rather is this factor cast in the role of an accessory, lurking in the background, casting its depressing and humiliating shadows.

SUMMARY

1. The size of the group is of marked significance in determining its behavior, and particularly the interactive processes that develop among its members.

2. Family interaction is a unique and distinctive kind of social interaction, both because of the make-up of the family population and the naked incisiveness of its continuing interrelationships.

3. Sibling informants, in rating the families of the present study for general tone of family relations, identified fifty of them as happy, thirty-six as of medium happiness, and fourteen as unhappy.

4. Family happiness varied from one racial and religious group to another and by size of family.

5. In analyzing the happy families, type of community and a friendly attitude by parents toward large families were not found to be significant *per se*, but the cultivation of family rituals, conscious efforts of parents to promote family group life, and especially administrative and managerial ability on the part of the mother, were revealed rather clearly as important factors in the development of happy large family living.

6. A study of the unhappy large families emphasizes the importance of the father's misbehavior, such as drinking and vile temper; the mother's ineffectiveness; the disorganization that appears in immigrant families because of intergenerational conflicts; and the death of a parent, followed by the subsequent remarriage of the other parent, with additional "flocks" of children.

7. The medium-happy families were those where the basic family situation was sound, and the family would have been completely happy but for some disturbing factor. Such factors include economic pressure, domineering fathers, ineffective mothers, favoritism toward some one or more of the children, the antics of some one troublesome sibling, cultural differences between the parents, and feelings of shame about the size of the family.

6 ·

The Vulnerability of the Large Family

"MY OVER-ALL ATTITUDE toward the large family," writes one of nine children, "centers around one major impression: the large family is vulnerable. This vulnerability will achieve some broader meaning as the anatomy of my family unfolds. The main weak spot in this particular situation appeared with the death of the mother when the oldest child was sixteen, followed by the death of the father seven years later. Such a combination of events is the worst that could happen to growing children who must meet the tests of maturity far too early."

To bring a large number of children into the world, perforce in rapid succession, is to give that many hostages to fortune. If fortune smiles through the years ahead, well and good; if fortune does not, the circumstances in most large families will be such as to present some serious problems. It seems proper therefore to follow the chapter dealing with personal relations in the large family with one dealing with some of the crises that are apt to arise. No systematic effort was made to gather data on this, since the whole study has been slanted in other directions. This means that the material presented here appeared for the most part in an incidental way. While this gives the evidence an added value, it does mean too that the chapter presents a picture which is in some ways an understatement of the facts. Specific topics dealt with include: (a) divorce in the large family, (b) extra-marital relations of large family parents, (c) drunkenness of parents, (d) death of the parents, (e) resulting problems and adjustments, (f) the impact of the depression, (g) war and the large family, (h) sibling sacrifice, and (i) "sticking together."

DIVORCE IN THE LARGE FAMILY

The presence of children is recognized generally as a deterrent to divorce. To this it might be added that the larger the number of children the less the probability of divorce. At least, this seems to be supported by our case material. Of the one hundred families, only two were broken up by divorce, and in both cases as a final step in a lengthy period of domestic unhappiness. In one of the two cases, divorces came after twenty years of married life, during which the husband drank heavily, deserted a number of times, and misbehaved in various other ways. In the second case, divorce came after almost twenty-five years of marriage. A glimpse of what may have been involved here appears in the following comment by one of the children: "Neither father nor mother had any conception of family responsibility or sound family living. Neither was mature enough at marriage to take on a large family group. None of the children was planned for."

In spite of the long periods of married life, both divorces involved children when they were quite young. In each family, there were three children under fifteen years of age at the time of the divorce. Since the minimum period of separation before divorce is possible was two years in the two states where the divorces were granted, these children would be correspondingly younger by at least that period when the separation of their parents occurred.

EXTRAMARITAL RELATIONS OF LARGE FAMILY PARENTS

No effort was made in the course of this study to gather information on extramarital relations of the parents, and what is recorded here is what was mentioned incidentally in the discussion of other matters.

There were three families in which one of the parents was so much involved with a lover outside of the marriage bond as to be evident to the children and to be emphasized by them in their analyses of their own development. In two of the cases, the offending spouse was the husband; in one, it was the wife. In two additional cases, such extramarital relations may be inferred, although no specific charge to that effect was made.

The significance of these situations, so far as the children were concerned and as pictured by them, is invariably the same. The parent was neglectful of parental responsibilities, family relations were strained, financial resources of the family (in two of the cases) were squandered, and children were embarrassed or weighed down by an awareness of the situation.

DRUNKENNESS OF PARENTS

Informants for seven of the hundred families mentioned drunkenness of the father as marked and extending over a period of years, and to the degree of interfering seriously with the life of the family. References to drinking by parents were made in other cases, but it was only when such drinking was noted as a family hazard that it was included in this summary.

The facts noted in these cases usually are the same: father drank; money thus spent could be ill spared by the large family; father was cruel when drunk, often beating the children "unmercifully," or being "sadistically cruel," or "highly irritable." In three of these cases, father also "took up" with bad company when drinking. It might also be added that fifty-four children lived in the seven families where the father was drinking excessively. It is this involvement of a large number of children in a relatively small number of families which is one phase of the problem of family vulnerability.

DEATH OF THE PARENTS

By far the most frequent and most serious of the hazards of the large family is the death of a parent. In thirty-one of the one hundred families, one or both parents died, leaving children under the age of fourteen years. For purposes of the above enumeration, only families in which as many as four children (or three if there were only six children in the family) were under fourteen were included.

1. In two of the families, both parents died, leaving nine children in each case. In one case, the mother died first; in the other, the father. In both cases, the interval was seven years. In one case, the mother died ten days after having given birth to twins, leaving also a four-year-old, an eight-year-old, a ten-year-old, a twelve-year-old, and a fourteen-year-old. The other two children were sixteen and seventeen, respectively, at the time. Seven years later, the father died. Meanwhile, the depression of the nineteen-thirties had affected adversely the family's financial position. In the second case, the father died first, leaving nine children, aged one, three, four, six, eight, nine, eleven, thirteen, and sixteen, respectively. One of the children had a serious physical defect. Nine years after the father's death, the mother died. The time was during the depression. In both of these cases, the burden of the family fell upon, and was carried by, one or more of the older children.

2. A second group consists of those families where the father died, leaving the mother and young children in varying ages. There were seventeen such families. In two of the seventeen, the mother remarried. In one case, the widow, with six young children, married a widower with five of his own, and then had three more with her second husband. The

other widow, left with ten young children, remarried and bore one more to make it eleven.

In the remaining fifteen cases, the mother did not remarry, but maintained a home for her family. In only two of the fifteen cases did there seem to be financial resources sufficient to cushion, to some extent, the impact of the father's death; in one case, the mother's lover apparently came to the rescue. In four of these fifteen families, the father suffered from a long, disabling illness before death ensued, thus adding to the economic and other complications. In two cases, the father died before the birth of the last child, thus leaving a pregnant wife and (in both cases) a number of children all below the age when full-time employment is permitted.

A total of one hundred thirty-seven living children was included in these seventeen families where the father died.

3. The third group consists of twelve families where the mother died, but not the father, during the dependency of the children. All but one of these fathers remarried, two of them marrying three times. Of the eleven who remarried, two married widows with children of their own. In both cases, there were children with the second wife, so that there resulted families with "your children, my children, and our children." Six of the widowers who remarried were married to women with no children but with whom they had a "second flock" of children. Three fathers who remarried had no children with their second wives. A total of one hundred fourteen living children was involved in these families.

In summary, it is clear that the premature death of parents presents a major problem for the large family. Combining all of the cases where one or both parents died, and including the two cases of divorce, a total of thirty-three families is found to fall into this category. The total number of children in these families was two hundred eighty-one. This is a third of the 844 children in the hundred families who survived infancy. In other words, one out of three large families loses one or both parents before the children are grown, and one out of every three large family children lives in these broken-up families.

RESULTING PROBLEMS AND ADJUSTMENTS

Certain stock phrases come to be applied to family situations of the type just described, but the specific problems and patterns of adjustment that follow show a great variety of kind and degree. Some of these will be described briefly.

1. One separate group is those families where the death of a parent improved the family situation, at least in some respects. Most of these are cases where the father is the parent who died. There are seven such families. In five of them the father is described as drinking heavily, being very cruel to his wife and children, spending money on liquor that was much needed elsewhere, associating with evil companions, and creating constant contention in the home. Reference has already been made to the role of drunkenness in the study as a whole. In two cases, long, disabling illness of the father occasioned severe strains on their families, both financially and otherwise, with death coming as a relief in certain respects. In all of these cases, the sibling informants emphasized the improvement in the general tone and character of the family life, following the death of the father, and in spite of other difficulties that might have been created.

2. The most obvious problem is that of the step-parent. It has been shown that this most often is that of a stepmother rather than a stepfather. Fathers left with large families are able to find wives; mothers so accompanied seem less inclined or able to do so. Far from being the stereotype that the stepmother is represented to be, the eleven found in this study present an interesting array of different types. Two of them, for example, came to be loved more than the real

parents, and the testimony of the children is that the family life improved after their coming. One of them, personally known to the author, was a truly remarkable woman. She married a widower with eight children, raised them all, came to be loved by them, and in time was doted on by a considerable number of grandchildren. A striking woman in physical appearance, with an amazing capacity to deal effectively with people, she held the entire kinship group together long after her husband's death. The other stepmother of this type married a man with twelve children, and ten years later the father complained that he had no family because the children loved their stepmother more than they did him.

Other stepmothers represent somewhat modified versions of these two. One of them, at the quite opposite end of the scale, frankly declared that she did not love the father nor the children but married for the sake of getting a husband. The family history, given by one of the children, while restrained in tone, is replete with references to "this unromantic figure," her "demanding ways," and the "antiparental code" among the children. The father in this case was "a gentle, even-tempered man," who permitted his second wife to "wear the pants" with firmness and vigor.

Then there is the stepmother who is shrewd and designing, like Mrs. Carver. She loved her stepchildren "so very much" they were encouraged to stay at home, or if older, "to come home at any time." However, at the end of ten years, all of the first flock of children found themselves living elsewhere than at home, and, if they came home, it just never suited for them to stay over mealtime or overnight. Or there is Mrs. Gowan, who managed things so adroitly that the children of the first wife did all the housework, and her children got all the new clothes. Or there is the Curtain family where the father inherited a goodly sum of money from his first wife, and his second wife managed to spend most of it on her own children.

Finally, there is the stepmother who married a man much older than she, with eight children, and bore four more of her own. "She was easy going and never complained. She accepted life on the surface but underneath showed very strong feelings of resentment, feeling dominated by her older, dogmatic husband. . . . Mother treated all of us alike. She saw to it that we got to church and school, but never went anywhere herself. Before she was married, she had been active in both church and school work, but apparently was somewhat ashamed of her marriage to this older man with his eight children, and wouldn't go anywhere because she did not want to expose herself to cutting remarks." The impact of community gossip, particularly in a small town, is one that many a young woman who married a widower or divorced man has had to contend with: apparently it can be quite pronounced if the man has a large number of children to boot.

3. The remarriage of parents with children often makes it necessary for two, and later perhaps three, sets of children to live together in one household. The problems here are those of adjustment not only of one individual to another but also that of group to group. Many factors are involved, and the situations that result vary a great deal. Much depends on the fairness and administrative ability of the mother, who is called upon to deal with many of the details of household life, and mothers differ materially in these respects. The age and sex make-up of each group, and the relation of each to the other, can be very important. In one family, for example, a widow, with a number of children and some economic means, married a widower equally blessed with children but not with economic means. The latter's children, who came to the new home owned by the widow, were older than the widow's children who had always lived there, and soon attempted "to take over." This naturally created a good deal of friction.

One kind of situation that may arise in such families is well illustrated in the following case. A man who was left a widower with six children met up with and married a widow with four of her own. In due course of biologic time, they had four more of their own. One day a neighbor passing by heard the father call to his wife. "Oh, Mary," he shouted, "your children and my children are beating hell out of our children."

The problem of financial resources tends to be a troublesome one in cases of remarriage, and especially so if there are children. The problem is apt to become keener as the children grow older, and the line between "my money" and "your money" and perhaps "our money" grows less distinct. One of our families, where intrafamily relations were bitter from the very beginning, consisted of a widower with children and money, who married a widow with children and money. More wealth was accumulated after the marriage, as also were a few more children. Just how much should each set of children derive from the common pot? The question has not yet been settled satisfactorily, nor may it ever be so settled, according to the children.

4. The remarriage of parents creates emotional problems for the children. Sometimes they may be very disturbing. Jane, one of our informants, writes of her own experience as follows. "When my mother went away for a vacation, she always took my oldest brother and youngest sister, but when my dad went, he took me. When my mother was away, I was the mistress of the house with supervision. . . . My father died suddenly early in my thirteenth year. It was as if I had lost half my life. We had always been pals. A year and a half later, my mother remarried. I was bitter, resentful, and hurt. I couldn't understand how she could put anyone in the place of my father. And then, on top of everything, she became pregnant almost at once. . . . I became ill just after my father died, and the doctor who visited me said I had

The Vulnerability of the Large Family

heart trouble because I had grown too fast. . . . I became very nervous, cried easily, and fainted at times."

In another case, the mother died, leaving nine young children. The father was completely overwhelmed. Although he did not remarry, he seems "to have developed a shell about himself emotionally. He provided for our material needs, but did not show us the emotional side of his personality. He refrained from joining us on picnics and other social affairs to which we went. Our report cards were all he discussed with us about school. . . . We were adults before we realized that he loved us." Nine children, no mother, a father who did not show "the emotional side of his personality"! Small wonder that "we still are very affectionate with each other."

5. Going to live with relatives is one of the solutions utilized when the parent of a large family dies. The procedure and resultant pattern are generally the same. The father or mother dies, leaving a large family. A number of the children are quite small. The remaining parent and the older children unite to "try to work things out" while one or more of the younger children are taken over by grandparents or other kinsfolk. This means that they are reared by older, often much older, persons—a fact whose significance is analyzed in the chapter on child rearing.

Mrs. Tryon died at the age of twenty-six, leaving four small children. Her husband seemed to be overwhelmed by his family responsibilities and a large farm to manage. His deceased wife's parents, then in the middle fifties, took the oldest child, aged five, to raise; the father's parents took two of the others. Aided by a servant, he retained the baby of the four. Later he remarried, but the oldest son remained with his maternal grandparents.

Mrs. Garson, a young widow with five children, returned to live with her parents and sister and brother who had never married. The mother did not remarry, and she and her children lived there until both the parents and the sister and brother died. The oldest child remained with the family until he was forty-one years old, when he left home to marry.

6. Economic pressure is the overshadowing problem in most large families. This leads to a variety of adjustments. There is a great deal of wearing of clothes of older children. Often the hand-me-downs do not fit. This may be serious, particularly in the case of some articles of attire, such as shoes. The difficulties of wearing shoes two sizes too large or one size too small are not wholly physical. Children tend to be cruel to each other. School children are much given to make comparisons. Children who are ill-clad or shabbily dressed are made very much aware of it. One is impressed again and again with the references to this in the case material. One comes to see, too, how these very facts create a strong bond among the children in large families. Their bond is that they are all poor together, and thus they try to find compensations with each other.

The father of a large family has stated the reality of economic pressure in simple terms:

> The only formula for maintaining a large family on a small pocketbook is to learn and study how to do without the things that don't really matter. We have done without them, and now we find that we have not really missed them. A minor secret of success is to distrust and avoid the installment plan, except for the absolute necessity of buying a home. We have steadily resisted the tempting appeal of "Only five dollars down" and the rest some day. In our house there is no such thing as "only five dollars." When you pay cash you buy what you need; the installment plan is a temptation to buy what you do not really need, and most people use it to get what they want and not what they must have. It is simpler and safer to discipline your wants a little and do without.[1]

While the present study does not concern itself with the

[1] Don Rose, *Full House* (Philadelphia: J. B. Lippincott Co., 1950), p. 105.

The Vulnerability of the Large Family

economics of large family living, reference to it appears constantly both in the interviews and in the written materials contributed by the informants. Virtually every sibling and parent with whom this study was discussed emphasized the basic importance of an adequate economic base for large family living, and the variety of problems that arose when such a base did not exist.

Because most large families have little or no financial reserve, the death of a parent, and particularly that of the father, creates serious problems. Some of them are directly economic by nature; others constitute what might be termed secondary sequelae. Several illustrations will clarify this latter concept.

Mr. Hoskin's death left his widow with eleven children. Various adjustments were made, but the third youngest sibling was left with one outstanding recollection: "Mother was always so overburdened with cares and responsibilities that she had no time to consider us as individuals. I do not think she was a companion to any of the children. Physically, we were all cared for; emotionally, I think we were all deprived."

The Termans lived very comfortably with their seven children. There were servants, usually two of them, vacations were regular and liberal, recreational facilities at their home in an attractive neighborhood were wholly adequate. Mr. Terman's ample income ceased when he died suddenly, and a financial surplus that would have sufficed for a family of two or three was now wholly insufficient. Sharp readjustments in the scale of living had to be made at once. The two older children withdrew from school, and hopes for their professional careers were forgotten. Servants were discharged, the home was sold, and two younger children were withdrawn from private school. Mrs. Terman and her children have not been in want, but they have reduced markedly their whole plane of living.

Other sequelae can be summarized in briefer form. "We

had no money for medical care." "We wore each other's clothes two and three deep." "We never had allowances like the other children." "I was the only girl that didn't have a new dress for commencement." "After father's death, all the beautiful family unity disappeared, and it became every man for himself."

THE IMPACT OF THE DEPRESSION

Raising a large family during the depression decade was a doubly difficult task. A number of our families were adversely affected by it, and refer to the adjustments which became necessary as a result. A careful reading of the case histories which refer to the depression reveals recurring mention of the following results:

> Father's work and income became irregular.
> Compelled to change residences.
> We had no allowances. Nickels and dimes could not be spared.
> Children working at odd jobs.
> Children wore hand-me-down clothing.
> Could not afford a doctor.
> We had no toys.
> We went to work as soon as we could.
> Our parents negated all our desires.
> We lived in very limited quarters. (In one case, thirteen lived in four rooms, with no conveniences.)

The depression decade witnessed a large-scale reversal of the population movement from country to city. Among the many who now returned to the country were a number of our large families. There are frequent references among the families whose children were small during the thirties of "moving to the country," "daddy tried to combine farming with another job," or "we went to live on grandfather's place in the country."

This moving to makeshift quarters or to the property of relatives was not always a pleasant experience for the children. Nor is it difficult to understand the reasons for this. Adjustments involving a family of three may not be easy; the difficulties of accommodating as many as ten or more are somewhat greater. What this may mean to a young child appears in such excerpts of case records as these: "Father was a big man with a deep voice. He became very irritable when we were noisy, and living as we did in such small quarters, we could not help but get into his hair." Or there is the sibling who writes: "For four years we lived in a tenant house on the ———— Farm. We did not like it there because we were constantly being told by the owners to stay away from this, and not to touch that, and not to go here or there. It got so that we dreaded seeing them."

WAR FOLLOWED THE DEPRESSION

A decade of depression was followed in our history by a period of military activity and spending. As a result, there were millions of families, whose children had felt the pinch of the depression, to whom the decade of the forties brought undreamed-of prosperity. This was particularly true of a number of our large families. As one reads their histories, it is apparent that World War II, whatever else it brought, was an economic windfall in many cases. As the older children in these families arrived at permissible age, they entered military service or war work, in which financial compensations were both large and regular. Three or four sons and daughters in the service, or in war work, made for swollen family fortunes.

The point is frankly stated by an author and father of a large family. Don Rose, father of twelve, writes:

In the past, I may have grumbled some about paying income taxes, but not now. At present we seem to be on the receiving end of the pipe line to Washington. Five of the boys have done time in the armed forces of the United States. Jack's training alone, as an officer of the Air Force, is supposed to have cost somebody about $20,000. All five boys have collected mustering-out pay, and rebates on their military insurance. Four have received a bonus. Two got a complete college education out of the war.[2]

The Rose family is not one of the hundred large families included in the present study, but the Rose family experience is typical in this respect of a number of our families.

SIBLING SACRIFICE

When misfortune overtakes the large family, is its impact distributed evenly among its members, or do some bear an unequal share? What resources are there within the family that come to be relied upon and utilized? Who bears what part of the burden?

The answer is written large and repeatedly in our material. It is the older children who most often carry the major part of the burden. Of the thirty-one cases where one or both parents died while the children were small, in twenty of them a younger sibling informant emphasizes this sacrifice of the older child or children. Sometimes it is one sibling, usually the oldest or second oldest; other times it is the two or three oldest ones that are identified as having been the main reliance. In some cases it is the economic support they contributed which is stressed; at other times, it is as an emotional surrogate for the parent that the older brother or sister is mentioned. Excerpts from the case studies tell their own stories.

A. My father died when he was still a young man (forty). He literally worked himself to death supporting a family of eight. Because of his death, our financial difficulties were very great. My older brother, then eighteen, took over. We looked up to him for guidance and advice. He developed a very protective attitude toward us. He was the disciplinarian of the family. He did not

[2] Rose, *op. cit.*, pp. 105-6. See also James H. S. Bossard, "Adolescents in Wartime," *The Annals of the American Academy of Political and Social Science*, November, 1944, pp. 33-43.

The Vulnerability of the Large Family 121

marry but stayed at home until he was in his thirty-seventh year, helping mother rear the family.

B. At the death of my father, my oldest brother took over the family reins. He was very sober and solemn. We and my mother asked his advice in everything. He was very good to us, and helped the younger members of the family to get an education. We had always thought of him as destined for the priesthood, although he never openly expressed the wish. I always felt he had given up his chance to help the rest of us. He did not marry until we were all grown and mother had died.

C. My sister was the oldest of a large family. After my father's death and my mother's remarriage, the entire responsibility of the large house became hers. Instead of going to dances, parties, and playing basketball, as her friends were doing, she was at home, keeping house, doing the laundry, and watching over her younger brothers and sisters. When mother went to the hospital, she and I were left in charge altogether. The baby cried routinely every night, but still we got up and saw that the family had breakfast and were ready for school. Often my sister would miss school.

D. The economic situation in our family was due to the death of my father at the age of forty, when the oldest boy was sixteen and the youngest was one year of age. There was no social security nor insurance for occupationally incurred diseases in those days. After my father's death, my sixteen-year-old brother seemed suddenly to mature. On the day of the funeral, he turned to my mother and said: "Don't cry, Mom. I'll take care of you." And to this self-imposed task as head and breadwinner of the family, he gave himself with all the eagerness of youth. . . . He never married. He lived with his mother until his death. His life was short, he worked hard, but I am sure he had more satisfaction than others who live only for themselves.

E. My oldest sister was the strongest personality in our family. After father died, she became mother's executive officer. She was in charge of finances, she would buy the food, and handled much of the discipline. It was she who put me through college and medical school. She was the legal guardian of three of the children. She has never married. She is a teacher and is very active in community affairs.

Enough has been said to indicate the general features of these situations. The parent dies, leaving a large breach. The oldest child, or several older children, step into this breach. Their labor contributes to the support of the family, they become the family counselor and disciplinarian. They do not marry, unless late in life. They give up their own plans and careers. They are the family sacrifice on the altar of need.

"STICKING TOGETHER"

If the large family is peculiarly vulnerable, frequently developing situations in which there are marked economic difficulties, it also calls forth adjustive traits among its members that enable them to surmount their problems. Economic necessity may be a stern taskmaster, but it does develop the resourcefulness of its "victims." Case histories of large families, where death struck down a parent prematurely, where long, disabling sickness ensued, where economic depression found its subjects, are also replete with references to the family coöperativeness that made it possible to surmount the difficulties. The references to this, while often brief, are nevertheless quite clear and positive.

A careful reading of the hundred case studies shows that in forty-eight of them some relatively serious crisis arose which created unusual economic difficulties. In thirty-nine of these the informants stressed the fact that one of the saving elements in the situation was the way in which the members of the family stuck together to weather the storm. Some excerpts will indicate the nature of these comments:

> Despite all this, we made out because we children were a closely knit group. We never had any serious quarrels and we were careful not to create problems which might embarrass the

others. We kept in close contact with each other down to this very day.

After father died, we all worked and hung together. This feeling is still very strong. . . . In my family, we developed a very strong attachment to each other, and I suppose this was due to my father's early death. We helped each other through school, and today we have a strong interest in each other's welfare. We constantly correspond with each other and tell each other what happens to each.

The early hardships we endured after father's death in no way interfered with the seven of us from having a normal childhood. We were early taught the value of coöperation. Each one of us took an active part in caring for the younger members of the family and helped with the chores.

We have often been glad that there were so many of us. First we were left fatherless, then motherless. One of us is permanently crippled. We were left in this condition during the depression. Things looked very black for us, but we decided to stick together, and to stay together, and to help each other. All kinds of contrary suggestions were made by relatives and other persons, but our choice was to stick together. And it was this sticking together that brought us through.

There are, to be sure, some few contrary cases—the exceptions that prove the rule. Two excerpts suffice to set the tone here:

In our family, lack of funds created competition among the members of the family. Each child began to look after himself as soon as he was old enough to do anything.

It was during this period of our lives [following the death of the mother] that the motto became "every man for himself." All the wonderful family feeling that mother and dad had built up among us was gradually disseminated as our thoughts and feelings were exploited by the adults we knew. Instead of drawing closer to each other as brothers and sisters should, our efforts were concentrated on making a good impression on the grown-ups, or they would really make things tough. If one member of the family was unfortunate enough to get outside the pale of approval—"too bad, but we can't jeopardize our position for your sake."

SUMMARY

1. The large family is vulnerable. To bring a large number of children into the world is to give many hostages to fortune.

2. Divorce and extramarital relations of parents of large families are noted, but only in a few cases.

3. Drunkenness of large family fathers is more prevalent, and has serious repercussions for the children. Drinking fathers tend to be harsh and cruel parents, especially when drinking.

4. Death of the parents is the most serious hazard. In two families, both parents died; in twenty-nine, one or the other parent died while as many as four of the children were under fourteen years of age.

5. In some cases (seven) the death of a parent was reported as improving the family situation. In other cases, it created the problem of the step-parent, made it necessary for several sets of children to live in the same home, created emotional problems for the children, led children to be raised by relatives, and in general intensified economic pressures.

6. Economic pressure is common and persistent in many large families. The death of a parent tends to intensify this.

7. The economic depression of the nineteen-thirties adversely affected a number of the families in this study. Their very size made the impact of the depression all the more serious.

8. World War II and its aftermath, with its opportunities for military service, war work, and postservice educational opportunities, came as an economic windfall to many large families.

9. Crises in the large family fall with particular heaviness upon the older children, many of whom are sacrificed to the common need.

10. "Sticking together" on the part of the children is a common device in the large family for weathering family crises.

· 7 ·

Child Rearing in the Large Family

CHILD REARING is coming to be recognized, even by students of behavior, as the essence of personality formation in the next generation. Properly understood, child rearing is the most pervasive and important educational task that man assumes. It involves a continuing process of teaching, some of it formal, like that of the schools, but most of it informal, unconscious, and so minutely incidental that both pupil and teacher are largely unaware of what is going on.

In regard to this teaching process, much is said, as is always the case in educational procedures, about the pupil, his ability to learn, his attitude toward instruction, the progress he makes, and the methods of instruction that are most effective. Somewhat less is said, as is also the case elsewhere, about the teacher, and the most elementary facts about him. Who is he? A man or a woman? Old, middle-aged, or young? What is his attitude toward the child? What is the nature of the relation between teacher (i.e., parent) and pupil (i.e., child)?

Amazingly little study has been made of family processes of child rearing. Who rears the children in a family? What differentials exist among those who do, beginning with such simple facts as age and sex? What is the significance of these and other differentials? Questions of this kind arise as one turns to a study of child rearing in the large family as revealed in the case records of a hundred large families. The present chapter presents a brief analysis of what are considered to be essential facts about those who do the rearing, and then presents the material found in the case records as it pertains to these and other selected aspects of the child-rearing process.

THOSE WHO REAR CHILDREN: SOME BASIC DIFFERENTIALS

One of the most obvious and important differentials among those who rear children is that of chronological age. On this basis, three main groups may be identified. One consists of older persons, such as grandparents, great-uncles, great-aunts, and overage parents. Here the time span between children and those who rear them covers two generations. A second group, but one generation removed, consists of parents, customarily in the middle-age period. Finally, children may be reared, wholly or largely, by other children, usually their own brothers and sisters. Age differences here tend to be slight.

Each of these age groups can be subdivided and on several bases. The rearing elders may be male, such as one finds in the traditional patriarchal form of the family, or female, such as appears in the matriarchate found often among American Negroes. They may be classified, too, on the basis of past experience. Some old folks look back on a happy past. They may have been persons of distinction themselves, whose achievements have added to the family name, or they have been associated with such persons. In either event, life has been good, and the past which witnessed it appears in happy retrospect. Other elders look back on an unhappy or tragic past. Examples could be found among the refugees of recent years, or among the less privileged segments in society. Excellent illustrations of elders among the latter group who reared grandchildren can be found in Ethel Waters' book, *His Eye Is on the Sparrow,* or in Richard Wright's *Black Boy.*

The degree of kinship of the older person who acts as disciplinarian is also important because it is related to the child's conception of the right of the older person to discipline. A grandparent thus would fall into a different category from a great-aunt or a distant cousin. This is perhaps part of the larger problem of the relationship of the older person to the family whose children are being disciplined. Many details of family living are involved here. Is the family living with the older person, or is the older person living with the family? If the latter, does this involve inconvenience or an economic strain for the children in the family? Is the older person, when disciplining, interfering with others, or assuming a responsibility not otherwise carried?

All of these distinctions are important in the study of child rearing. Normally one would expect elders to make for conservatism in the process. At least their emphases tend to be slanted toward the past. Past ways and values become the central core of the process, even as the past experience of the elders determines the color of the process. Where that experience has been happy, the past will be presented with overtones of glorification. Old values are good values, to be cherished; traditional ways are good ways, to be maintained; old landmarks are stable guides, to be cherished and followed; old days were good days, to be repeated in the lives of the young. But where the past was unhappy, full of frustrated hopes and bitter experiences, other emphases and insights are transmitted.

Child rearing by the old tends often to be authoritarian, for age has learned and is positive about many things, which makes for impatience with childhood and youth, and their eagerness to learn and experiment with life. Age may be disillusioned, too, for time teaches the futility of many dreams, while youth alone knows better than the verdict of the centuries. There is this, however, in favor of elders, that long experience shows many of the problems of the young to be transitional, phases of the growing-up process, to be taken in patient stride, like measles and the chicken pox. And elders tire more easily, especially nervously, and are inclined to accept adjustments which make for peace. Age loves the quiet, which has its exactions as well as its opportunities for youth.

Much depends, in the last analysis, upon how elders operate. They may be authoritarian, dogmatic, insistent, impatient, intolerant, and domineering. They may have developed a pathological distrust of people and of life, seeking to force this attitude upon the young or trying to manage the children's social relations on the basis of that distrust. Such attitudes tend to create rebellion in their charges, and a rejection of authority as it is personified for them. But if elders are happy and patient and tactful, they can bring the best of the past into close rapport with the eagerness of youth. The time span between two or three generations is not an easy one to bridge: much depends on how the task is approached and in what spirit.

Parents in the middle-age span, constituting the second group who rear children, reveal most of the distinctions that have been pointed out about elders, but many of them exist in lesser degree. The basic fact about this group is that they stand at a different place in the life cycle, and hence view many things from a different vantage point. Moreover, they are still striving. They are the present possessors, not the former manipulators. They are striving for themselves, and usually even more so for their children. Life is still an unfinished book, and the next chapter must be an improvement over the present one. To this end, the past is incidental. The wisdom of yesteryear is horse-and-buggy lore. The ways of the grandparent are rejected; the pediatrician, the psychologist, the psychiatrist know far better. Child rearing is sidewise and competitive, to be measured by what the neighbors do. "The man on the radio says." Children are put under pressure, especially by middle-class parents. Comparisons with other children are constant; impersonal aids rather than loving hands constitute the main reliance.

Finally, there are the children who rear other children.

This is a type of child rearing that obtains in many large families and in societies where life is relatively simple. Sometimes siblings share an authoritarian control with elders; in other cases they carry the major or sole portion of the responsibility. In either event, the sibling share makes for a kind of child rearing that is above all realistic in essence. The young understand the young, they see the problems of their charges through the eyes of youth, they measure them by the criteria of their own needs. They know, too, what measures are effective and what methods are to be avoided. Because children have confidence in the judgment of their peers, they are responsive to their discipline. Peer discipline is effective discipline because it is determined and administered by peer standards.

The day that this is written, two incidents occur within one city block to illustrate the point under discussion. A mother hastens down the street with her daughter, perhaps six years of age. The child's shoe laces open, her shoe is partly off. She falters, tries to fix it. The mother does not look, but yanks the child's arm, half dragging her along. The child limps, with her shoe flapping on the pavement. Another hundred yards down the street, three children are walking together. One of these, too, has "shoe trouble." Here all three children stop. They sit down on the pavement. With considerable laughter and talk, they take off the troubling shoe, put it back on the foot, and then resume their journey. When children are together, they have the license to be children and to "enjoy" the problems of childhood.

Only the merest mention has been made of sex differences among those who rear children. Of what importance is this in the process of child rearing? How does the role of the grandfather, father, and older brother compare with that of the grandmother, mother, and older sister? With children of the same sex? With children of the opposite sex? Recent studies have said a great deal about the Oedipus factor in the love life of the child, but very little is known about its meaning in the field of discipline and other aspects of child rearing. Yet mention of the sex of the family disciplinarian, and in relation to that of the child who is disciplined, appears frequently in the case material of the hundred families. This suggests a fruitful field for future study.

WHO DISCIPLINES THE CHILDREN IN LARGE FAMILIES

Who disciplines the children in large families? Each of the hundred case records in our study included material sufficent to answer this question in rather specific fashion. Table 17 presents this information in tabular form.

TABLE 17

Who Disciplines the Children: A Hundred Large Families

	Number of Cases and Per Cent
Both parents shared equally	26
Mother, chiefly or wholly	27
Father the stern front, mother the actual administrator	5
Father, chiefly or wholly	22
Siblings, chiefly or wholly	20
Total	100

It will be noted that in thirty-two cases, virtually one-third of the total number, the mother was identified as the chief or sole disciplinarian of the family. The only modifications to this appeared in five cases where the father was said to take matters in hand if the breaches of behavior were very serious. This total, together with the twenty-six cases where the mother shared equal responsibility with the father, means that in fifty-eight cases, or virtually three out of five, the mother had a major role in the disciplining of the children. The large family makes this a natural arrangement. The home inevitably becomes a busy center in such families, and reference has already been made to the fact that this places large administrative responsibilities upon the mother. From meeting these administrative responsibilities in the home, it is an easy and somewhat inevitable step to discharging also many of the disciplinary responsibilities.

The supplementary information furnished in these cases throws added light on the child-rearing process. "Mother was a shrewd manager." "Father was too mild." "Father was helpless with so many girls." "Father was away a great deal of the time." "Mother was hot-tempered." "Father was quiet and studious."

Certain facts about the sex order of birth of siblings seems important in this connection. Of twenty-one families where the mother was undoubtedly the disciplinarian in the family, and the father was living, in fifteen cases the first child was a female and in twelve of them the first two children were females. It may be that when the oldest children are girls, the mother seems the more natural parent to "take over" the disciplining of the children. Once the pattern is established, it tends to be maintained with the children that follow, regardless of their sex.

Fathers who dominate the disciplinary process in a large family seem to be a distinctive type or series of types. Some of them are authoritarian-minded, believing that a family needs a boss and that it is the right of the male head to act in that capacity. Most often, they have a patriarchal conception of the family, and in several cases were aided and abetted in their domineering by a similar-minded grandparent, grand-uncle, or aunt. In other cases, drunkenness was a besetting vice, and liquor inflamed their sadistic bent. In still other instances, they are described as stern and forbidding figures. About half of the mothers in these families are described as weak, ineffective, and/or submissive.

The twenty families in which some one or more siblings acted as the chief or sole disciplinarian reveal a variety of family situations. There are the cases where the death of the father threw major responsibilities on the shoulders of the children, and in a majority of these cases the mother was incapable or unwilling to act as directive head of the family. There were the two cases where both parents died during the dependency of the children; there were three cases of stepmothers, overly hesitant in stepping into the breach. Finally, there were at least seven families in which both parents were so ineffective that the older children found it necessary to rise to the occasion.

INTERFERENCE IN DISCIPLINE BY RELATIVES

Table 17 presented data on the chief disciplinarian in the hundred families. One additional group of persons who participated in the disciplinary process needs to be identified. These were the relatives who lived with the families and who interfered with matters disciplinary. There were twenty-four families in which the informants made reference to such situations, and a total of thirty-three relatives were so identified in these families. Table 18 presents this information in tabular form.

TABLE 18

Relatives Living with Families and Interfering with Discipline of Children

Degree of Kin	Number of Families	Number of Relatives
Grandmother	7	7
Grandfather	4	4
Grandmother and grandfather	3	6
Aunt	3	3
Grandparent and aunt	2	4
Great-aunt	1	1
Uncle	1	1
Grandparent and uncle	1	2
Both grandparents and uncle	1	3
Uncle and aunt	1	2
Total	24	33

The reactions of the children to this interference by relatives living with the family have also been noted. Of the thirty-three persons involved, the reactions of the children were specified. In the case of sixteen, or two-thirds of the twenty-four, the children resented such interference; in nine cases, relations with the interfering relative were accepted without adverse comment. Typical critical comments were as follows: "Grandmother was very bossy." "Relations with grandfather were very strained." "My grandparents were very troublesome." "My aunt talked into everything." "My great-aunt prodded my father into extra firmness."

METHODS OF DISCIPLINE AND CHILD REARING

Two facts stand out clearly concerning the case material on methods of discipline and child rearing. One of these is the nature of the impressions which the informants contributed. Apparently one of the things which people remember most vividly about their childhood is how they were treated by their parents, especially in those "crises situations" which are involved in behavior problems. Most of the informants were quite vocal concerning this phase of their family life, and for the most part spoke and/or wrote about it with considerable objectivity. It will be recalled that all but four of our informants were over twenty years of age, and that a majority are now married, and with children of their own. Their comments, in addition to being relatively objective, often revealed considerable insight into the psychology of parenthood and its meaning in child development.

A second fact which stands out is the very great difference in discipline and child-rearing practices from one family to another. In one family the informant uses the terms "child rearing" and "physical beatings" as though they were synonymous. In the next family, children were reasoned with on problems of discipline and physical means employed only as a last resort. In another family, "we were whipped constantly, and by both parents"; in the next one, "father was indifferent, mother was a nagger, using her reputed illness as a weapon"; in a third one, "we were never whipped, we respected our parents and did what we were asked to do." As one reviews the material, it is like moving from one world to another. Here is a world of conflict, fisticuffs, wild threats, and impulsive, angry beatings; the very next case is one of serenity, respect, politeness, and mutual consideration.

Table 19, which presents in tabular form the main methods of discipline in the hundred families, must be considered therefore as a slightly arbitrary summary. The specific categories stated in the table correspond with the main ideas expressed by the informants, but, as has been indicated, each family has its own more or less distinct version of these.

TABLE 19

Main Methods of Discipline and Child Rearing

Method	Number of Families
Physical punishment, largely or extensively	9
Physical punishment to some extent, combined with other measures	26
Occasional severe physical punishment by father, coupled with fear of father. Mother cowed, and/or seeking to soften temper of father	10
Severe physical punishment when father was drunk, coupled with fear of father	2
Some physical punishment by father, coupled with love for mother	4
Slight physical punishment, with effective supervision, management, and talking things over	17
Occasional physical punishment, but mostly deprivation of things and withholding of privileges	4
No physical punishment, but other methods used effectively	17
No physical punishment, not much discipline of any kind	11

THE USE OF PHYSICAL PUNISHMENT

The hundred families in this study show a wide variation in their reliance upon physical punishment as a form of discipline and child rearing, as well as in the extent of its use. A careful reading of the case material indicates the existence of four types of families in this respect. One of these is the type in which discipline for any offense that is more than trivial means physical punishment. The child misbehaves, it is slapped; the misbehavior is serious, it is given a liberal dose; the offense is a major one (and the parent makes this decision, often on a temporary whim), and a severe beating follows. In most, but not all, of these cases, the father is the disciplinarian. In some cases, this policy is born of the immoderate use of alcohol; in some, of ill health; in others, from emotional upsets; and in a few, it represents a conscious policy of parenthood.

In a second type of family, physical punishment casts its continuing shadow. It is not the main method that is used, it may not even be the principal one, but its possibility is consciously and constantly kept in the background. One is reminded here of one of the families which had the custom of "kneeling under the whip." Writes the informant in this family: "A sawed-off broom handle with leather straps hanging from the end hung close to the door in the kitchen, and whenever mother felt that we needed to be straightened out, she would make us kneel under the whip, which meant that we lost our freedom. The place where the whip was hung was a strategic one. Kneeling close to the door gave us a good opportunity to see our sisters and brothers at play." In this second type, there was strong reliance upon fear as a factor in child rearing and upon physical punishment as its inspirer. In a few of these families it was the mother who administered the punishment; in several cases, it was both parents; but in the majority of these families, mother was the informer and father the administrator.

In the third type of large family, physical punishment was a kind of last-resort method. It might be reserved for major offenses. Or it might be utilized on sporadic occasions when parents were out of sorts. The chief reliance, however, was on other methods. Finally, there were the families, twenty-eight in number, in which physical punisment was not used, either because other methods of discipline were utilized exclusively or because there was very little discipline of any kind.

OTHER METHODS OF CHILD MANAGEMENT

All parents have ways of dealing with children and their behavior other than the physical laying on of hands. These comprise a variety of methods, many of which are identified in our case material. In four families, the customary device employed by the parents was to deprive the children of things or privileges which were much prized. This might mean the withholding of allowances, refusal of permission to play with the other children, absence from the movies, and the like. In ten families, the informants stressed the careful supervision and strict management by the parents, most often by the mother. Such management might be quite pervasive, to the point of being smothering, and was so described in several cases. The comments of the informants about their mothers in these cases are interesting. "She always knew what was going on." "She understood us better than we did ourselves." "Mother was a darned shrewd manager and manipulator." "Mother possessed that fortunate faculty of bringing about a desired result without seeming to use force or being possessive."

Akin to the emphasis upon management were the references to the organizing abilities of one or both parents. Illustrative of this was a family with thirteen children. Here the parents stimulated active participation in school, church, and community activities, channelizing the energies of the entire family group in these directions. In addition, a strong sense of family pride was fostered, with the result that two informants from this family insisted that there had been no disciplinary problems in it. Child rearing in this case appears as incidental to the functioning of a well-organized family life.

Emphasis upon a parent's capacity for leadership, expressed by the informants in eight families, is perhaps but another way of referring to the type of situation that has just been described. "My mother," writes a member of an intellectual family, "was not only an excellent manager and housekeeper, but she often was the leader in our activities and discussions. Mother was well read, she had a deep sense of understanding, about all kinds of things. True, she could be very critical of our friends, and several times forbade us to associate with persons we brought home. Yet withal, she had great confidence in us, and in turn we trusted her judgment."

Respect for parents was expressed by a number of informants, and emphasized as the key to parent-child relationships in seven families. "When papa spoke," writes one of a large Negro family, "we all listened and obeyed, for we all respected him." "My mother," writes another, "was more than loved and respected: she was admired." "Between parents and children," says one of eleven, "there was mutual respect and affection. We were taught ready obedience to our parents and respect for each other. Loyalty among us was intense." "We respected father both for what he achieved and what he did for us," says an oldest son. "It would never have occurred to us to displease him."

Love of parents is mentioned in a number of case records as influencing the behavior of the children. Sons tend to use the word "respect" in speaking appreciatively of their fathers, and the word "love" for their mothers; daughters apply the term "love" to both fathers and mothers. Love cannot be separated from respect, admiration, and other feelings of appreciation: we are here merely reporting the term used by our informants. There are thirteen case records where love of parents is emphasized as an important factor in child rearing, but reference to love of one parent, as distinguished from the other, appears in a good many more. Fathers who rage and bluster and bully and whip and otherwise alienate the affections of their children should read our case records to see how the children turn to their mothers for comfort and love and sympathy, and, finding them there, obey the dictates of love rather than the thundering demands of fear.

COOPERATION BETWEEN PARENTS CONCERNING CHILD MANAGEMENT

This matter of the agreement or difference between parents in regard to child management was a subject on which information was generally volunteered by their children who coöperated in the study. There was every indication that the informants thought of this as an important point. Table 20 presents this information in summary form.

TABLE 20

Coöperation Between Parents Re Child Management

Relations	Number of Families and Per Cent
General agreement	50
Disagreement	28
Not stated or pertinent	22

In exactly half of the families, siblings reported general agreement between the parents concerning child management. This includes the twenty families where the parents shared responsibility equally, as indicated in Table 17, and an additional thirty families where one parent takes the lead, but with the apparent approval and coöperation of the other. The most customary form of the latter, and apparently the most successful one, is where the mother takes the lead, with the father standing in the background ready to give his support.

The twenty-eight families in which there was disagreement between the parents constitute quite a different story, with a number of well-defined variations. There is the family where father is violent and mother is cowed and resigned; or where the father is loved, managing his children with quiet persuasiveness, while the mother is explosive, irritable, and always ready to depreciate the father. In another case the father, aided and abetted by his aunt, lords it over the children, while the mother plays the role of a sullen servant, bogged down with pregnancies and housework. Or there was the mother who played up to the children after the father punished them, seeking to draw them close to her; and the mother who calmed the irate father, or comforted the children when he dealt with them too harshly. There was the father, "always so high tempered, so that we flew to mother for shelter," and the father "always considerate while mother was forever nagging at us." Finally, there were the parents "who never could agree," as well as those who both administered punishment but for quite different offenses. Apparently these lacks of consistency and harmony were never lost on the children, nor were the efforts of one parent in these families to "undercut" the other, with the children.

SELECTED ASPECTS OF CHILD MANAGEMENT IN LARGE FAMILIES

Many of the problems of child management are much the same in all families, regardless of size; others tend to be affected by the number of children per family group. Precise determination of changes in the nature and intensity of such problems as related to changes in size awaits specific studies directed to specific problems. Such studies could be of tremendous value in various fields of human behavior. We can record here only certain tentative conclusions, based on materials in the case records.

1. Increase in the size of the group seems to increase the tendency to manage by rule rather than by decision in an individual case. Whereas, in a family with one child, all kinds of problems can be dealt with on their individual merits as they arise, in a family of thirteen there is a greater necessity and tendency to make rules from which deviations are not tolerated at all, or with relative reluctance.

The case of dietary management is an illustration in point. Section 18 of the questionnaire utilized in the study will be recalled. It reads as follows:

The study is particularly interested in the dietary habits which prevail in large families. How much were dietary whims and dislikes honored in your family, and to what extent were menus standardized, with little or no attention to likes or dislikes of an individual member? To what extent were special dishes prepared for such persons?

Few questions asked in the course of the study elicited such prompt and decisive responses, and Table 21 presents this information in tabular form.

TABLE 21

Standardization of Menus Served to 100 Large Families

	Number of Families
Meals standardized, with no provision for individual likes and dislikes	73
Meals standardized, but with some provision for individual likes and dislikes	22
Very little standardization of meals, and with much provision for individual preferences	5

The statements of the seventy-three constituting the first group in this table reveal a clear-cut attitude. It is as follows. We ate what was put on the table. If any one of us did not like it, that one kept quiet and ate, or went without. To prepare meals for ten, twelve, or more people day after day is a big job. Dietary whims and food idiosyncrasies cannot be recognized. One conformed or else, and the "or else" meant going without food. Special dishes, if prepared at all, were confined to doctor's orders or a spell of sickness.

The twenty-two informants in the second category in Table 21 also emphasized the fact that the same foods were served to all members of the family, but were less insistent about the lack of exceptions. An analysis of these families showed that they were families that (a) lived on farms and raised much of the food that was consumed, (b) had servants to prepare and serve the food, or (c) consisted of only six or seven children.

Similar were the circumstances in the five families that reported considerable pandering to individual preferences in food. Two were farm families, smaller in size; two were well-to-do, with several servants; and one mother was "a slave to her children."

2. A second aspect of large family living which early comes to impress the student is the tendency to take many crises, especially minor ones, in stride. This is much more true than in small families, perhaps for two main reasons: one, the fact that crises occur so much more frequently, and second, that they are shared in by so many more persons. For example, the spilling of ink on a tablecloth becomes in the small family a major crisis, with father, mother, and child involved. All three work on the mess, with the parents doing the major part. The same incident, in a large family, leaves father undisturbed behind the evening paper and mother intent on her sewing. The child who spilled the ink wipes it up, aided perhaps by another child. The point is even more dramatically illustrated in the remark of a Cuban mother of twenty-five. A woman of wealth, living on a large plantation, she was accustomed to sitting on the veranda of her palatial

home and dealing with the problems that involved her many servants and numerous offspring. One day a servant rushed up in great alarm. "Carlos," he said, "has fallen into the well." Carlos was one of the twenty-five. "He'll get out again," said the mother, continuing with her managerial duties. The point to be noted is that in large families so many minor anxieties and crises arise that the parents, and the children too, develop an immunity against all but major casualties. Things are always happening in large families, so that one comes to live with all which that implies.

3. Seeing a succession of children grow up gives one a sense of perspective about their problems and the ways of dealing with them. Students of child development have shown that the young go through a series of stages each with its own peculiar problems, many of which are temporary in character as incidental phases of growth. The small family parent, encountering a particular problem but once, tends to be greatly concerned about it, and may rush the child to a clinic or professional practitioner in the child development field, thus complicating the problem by the very anxieties which are manifested. The mother of ten, on the other hand, having seen a similar problem develop, and pass, in at least eight of her children, comes to be not only more patient but also more understanding and reassuring. Other siblings, too, having gone through the same stage, also are more helpful in their own distinctive ways.

4. There is considerable reason to believe that child-rearing emphases and practices differ between the older and younger children in large families. About one out of every six informants made some reference to this. One reason is that parents alone tend to rear the older children, whereas parents and older siblings rear the younger ones. Another reason is that parents have gained much from their experiences with the older children, and these older ones are

present, not only to advise and intercede perhaps, but also to remind the parents of what failed or succeeded in their own cases. Then, too, parents mellow as they age, and become less insistent and positive about many matters. Time tends to wear a person, even a parent, to a certain smoothness which makes for greater ease in social relationships. This softening of discipline tends to be most pronounced in the case of the last one or two children in large families. Often the second last one is expected to be the last one, and may be the favored one, like Joseph in the Old Testament, rather than the youngest one.

5. The sex distribution among the children poses some problems of child management in large families. A common arrangement in our families is for the mothers to take the daughters in charge and fathers the sons, but additional factors operate. The case records are replete with references to daughters who turn their fathers around their fingers, and sons who are the obvious favorites of their mothers. Perhaps the most frustrating of all situations growing out of sex distribution is where most or all of the children are girls. In these cases fathers are rather hamstrung. If they do seek to discipline the girls, especially in any vigorous way, they tend to have "beehives swarming about their heads." This is complicated by the fact that fathers with a number of grown daughters often become quite apprehensive about their social activities. After all, being a man, father knows what the boys want when they come acourting, and a father with five or six daughters and no older son to aid him may not be at ease until all of them are safely married, and for several reasons. This is a real, even if seldom identified, problem in selected large families.

TWO REQUISITES FOR SUCCESSFUL PARENTHOOD [1]

From repeated readings of the case material, two conclusions concerning the requisites for successful parenthood stand out quite clearly. One of these has to do with a selected group or complex of personal traits that are basic in human relationships. The relationship between parent and child is similar in many respects to the relationship of any two persons, so that the traits that are important in personal relationships *per se* are equally pertinent here. These involve respect for the other person, consideration for his physical presence, tolerance of his views, and appreciation of his interests and needs. Parents who lack these traits do not deceive their children, even though conscious recognition of that lack may be long resisted or variously disguised. Parents who assume that the very fact of their parenthood compels respect for them are deceiving themselves. While virtually every child in our culture absorbs some emphasis from others on the respect that is due to his parents because they are his parents, no child can close his eyes indefinitely to personality defects in his parents that everyday family life reveals.

But successful parenthood calls for more than certain personal traits. Parenthood is a technique, or perhaps it would be better to say an art, which must be learned. Experience keeps a dear school, and nowhere is this more true than in a school of many children, of one's own children, and a school that is in almost constant session. Other schools operate on a limited schedule and there is the relatively rapid turnover of pupil personnel. The school of family living has neither of these features. The problems in child management presented to a parent are constant and continuing. Meeting these problems successfully is not merely a matter of appropriate atti-

[1] This discussion should be supplemented by the reading of the excellent study by A. L. Baldwin, J. Kalhorn, and F. H. Breese, published under the title of "The Appraisal of Parent Behavior," *Psychological Monographs,* Vol. 63, No. 4 (1949), p. 387.

tudes, but also what is popularly spoken of as "a know-how." It is in this connection that a certain intellectual objectivity is important, not so much in adhering to an acceptable policy as in maintaining an experimental mood. Parenthood that follows a policy of child rearing, however rational it may be, is apt to become dogmatic, especially in a large family. Children differ, decidedly, from each other; large families multiply these differences. The rational mind in parenthood must be an open mind, bent on finding ways that work.

SUMMARY

1. Those who rear children may be divided into three age groups: the old, the middle-aged, and the young. Each tends to develop its own emphases and values. Another difference is between males and females.

2. In the hundred large families of this study, twenty-six reported both parents sharing equally in matters of discipline; thirty-two identified the mother as the chief disciplinarian; twenty-two so reported the father; and twenty said that it was the siblings rather than the parents who were most important in this connection. In twenty-four families, older kinsfolk interfered appreciably in the processes of child rearing.

3. Physical punishment was used extensively: in thirty-five cases, to a considerable extent; in twenty-eight cases, not at all; in the other thirty-seven families, its use was occasional.

4. Other methods of child management included deprivation of things or privileges, strict supervision, organization of family activities, parental leadership, and love and respect for parents.

5. In only half of the families was complete agreement (between the parents) in matters of child management noted by the sibling informants.

6. Increase in the size of the group seems to increase the tendency to lay down rules of conduct. Dietary management

illustrates this in the large family. Meals in most large families are standardized, with scant consideration for individual tastes.

7. Other aspects of child management in large families include a tendency to take mishaps and crises in stride, a sense of perspective about child problems and ways of dealing with them, a frequent difference between the treatment of older and younger children, and an obvious complication of problems by the sex distribution of the children.

8. Two requisites for successful parenthood are (a) certain traits important in interpersonal relationships, and (b) willingness to learn the technique of good parenthood.

· 8 ·

Interaction Among the Siblings

ONE IMPORTANT ASPECT of the whole child-management and child-rearing process in the large family has been omitted thus far. This concerns the part played by siblings in their relations with each other. Obviously, when a number of children live together, especially within the intimate framework of family life, they are bound to affect each other in many ways, so that any disciplinary relationship is only a part of the larger story of social interaction among them. It is to selected phases of this interactive process that the present chapter is devoted. These include: (a) child discipline and management by siblings, (b) siblings as surrogates, (c) sibling sacrifices, and (d) the "oldest" child as a type.

CHILD MANAGEMENT BY SIBLINGS

In ninety-one of the one hundred families, reference was made by the informants to the role of siblings in the management of the children, principally in matters of discipline; and in eighty-two of them, the references were of a nature as to identify such sibling participation as an important aspect of the child-rearing process. These eighty-two cases are taken, therefore, as constituting the material on child management by siblings.

But first a word about the eighteen families that are not included. In two of them, no information on sibling participation was given; in three additional ones, family discipline seems to have been at a minimum; in two other families, there were servants who operated in the absence of the parents. In the remaining eleven families, there were parents and other elders who sharply insisted on keeping all disciplinary matters in their own hands. In four families, for example, there was an autocratic father who was profuse with disciplinary measures and expansive in matters he sought to control; in two families, the mother acted similarly, brooking no competition; and in five families, there were grandparents, uncles, and/or aunts who participated in such a pattern. It is noteworthy that in families where older relatives were present to participate in child management the discipline was pervasive and severe, with much physical punishment. The children in these families were governed by fear, and allowed no, or very little, control over each other. In several of these families, it seemed evident that resentments which the elders felt toward each other were being "taken out on" the children. Much child discipline may be thus inspired, in large and small families alike.

Turning to the families in which sibling participation was emphasized, the first group consists of those where some one or more of the children was the chief or sole disciplinarian. Reference has been made in Table 17 in Chapter 7 to twenty families in which this was the case, as well as to the family situations which prevailed in these cases. For the most part, these were families in which one or both parents died, or where the father was given to drunkenness, or where one or both parents were ineffective. In addition to these twenty cases there were seven more where, for some extended time during the life of the family, one or more of the siblings were obliged to assume the chief or sole responsibility for the management of the siblings living at home. These would include such obvious cases as extended illness of a parent, absence from home over a long period, and the like.

Which of the siblings is chosen to assume this major role in the management of the other children? Considering the twenty-seven families just referred to, the following facts appear. In nine cases, it is the oldest daughter; in eight, it is the oldest son; in one, the second oldest daughter; in one, the second oldest son; and in two cases, the oldest brother and sister shared the responsibility. Thus in twenty-one of the twenty-seven families, the oldest child, daughter and/or son, is specifically identified in the case history. In three of the remaining cases, the informants speak of the control of the younger by the older ones; and in another three, it is the group as a whole that is specified. As one informant put it, "We were father and mother to each other."

The second group where sibling participation in child management was emphasized consisted of fifty-five families in which the children played a supplementary role to that of the parents. The extent of sibling participation seems to have varied considerably in these families, but two features were emphasized in all cases regarding the role of the siblings. The informants agreed that the role was important but that it was supplemental to that of the parents or other elders.

On the whole, two types of arrangements prevailed in these cases. One was where the older children discipline, lead, supervise, or are given protective custody over the younger ones. Thirty-two of the fifty-five were of this kind. In some families, this meant that two or three of the older ones looked after the younger ones; in others, there was a lock-step of age seniority in which each one lorded it over the one immediately below in the age ladder. The other type of arrangement was where one or two of the older children functioned as assistant to the parent. In most cases, this parent was the mother, and the assistant chosen was usually the oldest daughter.

In some of these families where siblings played a supplementary role, the children were encouraged to assume responsibility, not only for themselves but also for their younger brothers and sisters, as evidence of their own relative maturity. In the larger number of cases, however, such responsibility was forced upon the older children because of the ineffectiveness of the parents or their unwillingness to carry a full share of their parental responsibilities.

Interaction Among the Siblings

One question which presents itself at this point is how children regard this role of one of their own number. Information was obtained in seventy-five cases where siblings played the chief or an important role in the discipline and management of the other children. Table 22 presents these reactions in tabular form.

TABLE 22

Reactions of Children to Sibling Discipline

Reactions	Number	Per Cent
Noted as satisfactory	34	45.3
Noted as very satisfactory	9	12.0
Sibling much loved and respected	9	12.0
Accepted, no further comment	15	20.0
Resented by some siblings	8	10.7
	75	100.0

Selected excerpts from the case records reveal how definite many of these reactions were. "My oldest sister," says one, "was really the disciplinarian in our family ever since I can remember, and I would obey her sooner than my parents. She was very unselfish and disciplined us not for her own pleasure but for the help it was to my mother. She bathed us, helped sew for us, and assumed a great deal of the burdens and responsibilities of the family. Even after she was married she would call on the telephone and tell us to do so and so. She thus disciplined us from afar. She has always been concerned with the welfare of mother and the family. She would help me with the chores in order to save mother. I always obeyed and respected her, and loved her more than the rest."

There were a number of cases where the role of the dominant child rested not so much on powers of discipline as upon elements of leadership. This is indicated in the following excerpts. "My oldest brother was our pioneer. He managed to find interesting things for us to do each day. He acted as our protector and adviser. He saw to it that we found new and interesting ways to go to school and come back. In our spare time, he would take us for a wagon ride or a sleigh ride, as the case might be. He would organize games for us." Another informant reports: "My oldest sister had a way with her of handling other people. We all obeyed her because we all sort of looked up to her."

One factor which undoubtedly made for good relations between siblings in these cases was the fact that the leadership or authority of the dominant one came about in many cases as a result of intrafamily developments. Father or mother died, parents were ineffective, mother was sickly, father was away, someone had to take over, and it was natural for the older one to do so. In almost half of the families, as noted in Table 22, such assumption of leadership was accepted without comment, as if to say: "It was necessary, he (or she) was the oldest, we acted accordingly." Here, then, is another evidence of that acceptance of life as it is, which seems so characteristic of large family living.

The eight informants who resented the role of older brothers and/or sisters form an interesting study in themselves. All of these rebellers were girls. In most cases, they rebelled against the dominance of boys. This might occur in a family of relatively recent foreign extraction, in which the masculine tradition was very strong. Or there were the families where an older brother actively supervised the courtship of his sisters, to the end that their conduct might be above reproach. Finally, there were the cases where there were personality clashes between the informants and the particular sibling who had top rating among the children.

How do reactions to discipline by siblings compare with those to parental discipline? To answer this question, the case material was examined specifically for expressions of resentment to discipline. Remembering that the overwhelming proportion of our informants were mature persons, a considerable objectivity of comment may be assumed. The result obtained seems highly significant, perhaps one of the most significant facts in the entire study, for it showed that whereas 10.7 per cent of the informants (eight out of seventy-five) rebelled against sibling discipline, 44 per cent (forty-four out of a hundred) voiced some resentment or disapproval of discipline by parents.

Another and related point of comparison between sibling and parental discipline involves that of methods utilized. The methods employed by parents have been set forth in the preceding chapter. Over against these are the data on sibling discipline. In three of the seventy-five cases, physical punishment was reported. In two other cases, mention was made of "light slaps." In all the other cases, seventy out of seventy-five, the methods involved reliance upon leadership, good will, counseling, group pressure, boycott, and appeals for coöperation. A few excerpts will indicate the nature of the comments on these methods.

Family A. The children disciplined each other to a considerable extent. It was mostly unauthorized discipline, and came about by one or more trying to put another in his or her place. For instance, one time when the youngest sister was to have the dinner ready and she hadn't even started the meal, the next two proceeded to prepare the dinner and talked about her all the time she was hiding behind a door and heard the unkind things that were said about her. She never did let that happen again.

Family B. The older ones in our family were expected to discipline the younger ones, and did so. The thing worked out something like this: each one had his or her share of the work to do. If a younger child did not do what was expected of him, he was left behind when the rest of us went to fish, swim, skate, or play.

Family C. As the oldest sister, I did much of the disciplining of the other children, especially those four years and more younger than myself. Rarely did I use physical punishment for fear of receiving the same from my parents. I attempted to discipline my younger brothers and sisters by verbal threats or withholding privileges.

Family D. Our parents were never consistent nor intelligent in their discipline, nor were they ever able to act together on anything that affected us. The result was that we children acted as father and mother to each other. Each felt responsible for the other's progress in society. Each took an interest in the other's educational advancement and the forwarding of our careers.

Family E. The oldest daughter disciplined the first group of children, and the oldest son disciplined the second group. This discipline was largely a matter of pressure, and involved the use of threats to tell father or mother. The oldest brother was the strongest disciplinarian of all. He particularly exerted strong pressure on the sisters because he wanted them to be ladies and to be above reproach.

Family F. My sister was going around with a boy whom we disliked. We didn't think he was good enough for her. Father stepped in, forbade him to come to the house, and threatened Ella with punishment if she persisted in seeing him. She did see him, meeting him away from home. Finally, my other sister and I told her that if she went with him, we did not want to be seen with her. That ended it very quickly.

A final question concerns the relative merits of sibling discipline, as viewed by siblings. This was seldom mentioned specifically, but much could be gathered by inference in the course of interviews with large family members. Four facts stand out from the written contributions and our own comments on the oral interviews.

First, siblings feel that they understand each other and each other's problems, and that often they do so better than the parents. They know why Mary is moody and Jim is stubborn and why Katie neglects her chores to stand in front of the mirror. Family relations are very naked and incisive, with little chance of successful dissembling, and nowhere is this more true than in the relations between the children.

Second, siblings have a better judgment often as to what constitutes misbehavior. Adults judge child behavior by adult standards, children judge it by child standards. This means that discipline imposed by children on each other will seem more reasonable and have more meaning. Behavior, and misbehavior, to be properly assessed, must always be related to the situation which precipitates them, and these underlying situations often can best be understood and evaluated by the children themselves.

Third, sibling discipline often is more effective than adult discipline, and for several reasons. One is that the approval and disapproval of other children have more meaning often than that of adults, particularly in certain age periods. Again, in the case of sibling discipline, the siblings are constantly present. One lives constantly with one's discipliners. Also siblings know what kinds of discipline are effective. They know that a sound spanking, while it may hurt for the time being, may have far less meaning than not being allowed to go fishing with the others. It may be argued here that children often are very cruel to each other, and this certainly is true. Perhaps the real reason for this is not what adults assume it to be, but because children are realists. They know what matters and what hurts.

Finally, there is the question of what all this may do to the older siblings who are charged with responsibility and who do the disciplining. This is largely an unexplored field in psychiatric research—this problem of what power and the exercise of power do to people, and at different age levels. Two phases of it were emphasized repeatedly in the case material: one that it hastened maturity, and second that it fostered habits of responsibility. One illustration will suffice.

Mary K was known casually to the author before this study began. She impressed one with her bearing, her behavior, her sense of balance, and her perspective on life. She had a commendable war record, and had risen to an unusually high rank, and at an early age. Subsequently it was learned that she was the oldest of a large family, and she consented to supply a family record. Excerpts from this record follow. "The entire responsibility of the large house became mine a good deal of the time. I was thirteen years old at the time. . . . Mother went to the hospital soon after. I was combining the third and fourth year in high school. I was in charge with some help from my stepsisters. The baby cried routinely every night, but still I got up and saw to it that the family had breakfast and were ready for school. I often had to miss school, but I managed to maintain an average of over ninety. . . . I have often wondered if my sense of responsibility is not one of the causes for the good positions I have held." [*]

SIBLINGS AS SURROGATES

Older siblings not only share in the discipline and management of younger children, but serve as parental surrogates in various other ways which constitute important phases of the child-rearing process. A number of the informants identified an older brother or sister whom they accepted as a parent substitute. Many aspects of this relationship appear in the case material. In one family, for example, an older brother fathered the youngest sister, thirteen years younger than he, practically throughout her minority. He took her to school, helped her with her lessons, advised her on all kinds of problems as she was growing up, and later on bought most of her clothes. The sister scarcely knew her father, and in all matters turned to her older brother as a child ordinarily turns to a father.

In many cases, deep affectional ties develop between older and younger siblings. The problem of affectional satisfaction while growing up is a problem for children in large families. There are many children, the parents are tired and weighed down with cares and responsibilities, they may not have the time, inclination, energy, or affectional resources to satisfy the respective emotional needs of their children. In such cases, it is natural for children to turn to other persons; and often this means other siblings.

[*] Author's Note: Cf. statement, in almost similar words, from a quotation by her younger sister, in chap. 6, p. 121.

This is particularly apt to happen where there are many children and there is considerable time span between the older and the younger ones. An eight-year-old child may find a twenty-year-old brother or sister a more "natural" parent than the forty-eight-year-old parent. The older sibling not only is older and wiser and more experienced, but also has the advantage of being a peer rather than a parent. While this affectional relation often develops between children separated by a number of years, it may also develop between siblings next to each other in order of birth. Instances appear in the case material where an older brother and sister form a partnership which virtually excludes the other children.

At times, the attitude of a younger child toward an older sibling turns into a kind of hero worship. Ten such cases are mentioned in the family histories. One is reminded here of the attitude of the Father of His Country toward his older brother. George Washington was a member of a large family. His father, Augustine, had four children with his first wife, and five with his second. Lawrence, the second-born and oldest surviving child born to the first wife, was destined to be an outstanding influence in the life of George, the first-born child of the second wife. Lawrence was educated in England, being given a long and careful schooling there, so that when he returned to Virginia at the age of twenty he had a grace and bearing and manners that quickly fascinated George. The latter "quickly made a hero out of Lawrence and began to emulate him. . . . For the enlargement of George's mind and the polishing of his manners, Lawrence was almost an ideal older brother. . . . He was everything an admiring boy wanted to be. . . . Best of all, he had an affectionate interest in George, whose abilities he may have sensed." [1]

This interest of older siblings often takes the form of economic aid. Older boys and girls, remembering the lack of

[1] Douglas Southall Freeman, *George Washington* (New York: Charles Scribner's Sons, 1948), Vol. I, pp. 58, 77, 95.

things in their own childhood experiences, utilize their earnings later on to purchase such items for their younger brothers and sisters.

Margaret is the oldest of ten children. She has always been a very attractive girl, but, until she became self-supporting, was handicapped by a lack of clothes. One such lack that rankled in particular was that she had to wear an old and not too becoming dress when she was graduated from high school. Subsequently she obtained employment and within a few years was receiving a liberal salary. For almost ten years, a considerable proportion of this salary went to buy clothes for her younger sisters.

Sarah was the oldest in a large family which consisted of "my children, your children, and our children." As soon as she was old enough to obtain employment, she helped to clothe her brothers and sisters. "They took it for granted that this was my responsibility. I did it willingly, and with no expectation that I would ever be repaid."

SIBLING SACRIFICE

Thus far references to the older children in large families have emphasized the services which they contribute to the parents and other siblings. It seems pertinent now to consider these situations from the standpoint of the older children, and particularly of the oldest child. To what extent do the older children carry the burden of rearing the younger children, and to what extent does this interfere with their own childhood and youth? Is it true that one child, usually the oldest one, is called upon to make a great many sacrifices while sharing parental duties and responsibilities?

To answer those questions, the twenty-five most complete case records were selected for analysis. The answers obtained were unmistakable. In nineteen out of the twenty-five families, it was quite apparent that one or two of the older children were called upon to carry a large part of the responsibility of rearing the younger ones, and did so at a sacrifice, often considerable, of their own interests and desires. In seventeen out of the nineteen families, it was the oldest sibling; in one, it was the two older ones; and in another, it was the three oldest ones. In five of the cases, it was the informant who so identified himself; in the other cases, younger brothers and sisters paid this tribute to their older brothers and sisters. In eight cases, it was the oldest son; in nine cases, the oldest daughter; in two cases, both older sons and daughters shared the responsibilities.

It is unfortunate that not all of the case records were complete enough to permit a statistical summary for the entire hundred families, for references to this aspect of large family living appeared repeatedly in the course of the study. One of the strongest impressions that the author received was that the large family system involved quite generally the exploitation of some one or more of the older children.

Few of the comments indicating such exploitation were of a complaining nature. Most of the references appeared incidentally, as part of the family story, and as indicating an adjustment, now conscious, now unconscious, to the necessities of the situation. Usually it appears as a kind of inevitable acceptance and adjustment, necessitated by the death, illness, or inefficiency of a parent, or by the sheer heaviness of the burden. At times the burden fell upon one because he was more competent; at other times it was easier to let one take over than to organize a group project.

Possibly the best way of presenting much of this phase of large family life is to quote from the informants' own words.[2]

(a) "For as long as I can remember," writes the oldest daughter in a family with nine children, "I helped with the dishes and then was given the responsibility of other tasks as I grew older. . . . There were eleven of us eating every day. Life seemed to be one eternity of dirty dishes after another. . . . It was my job to make the chocolate cup cakes for five school lunches that were carried, pack the lunches, and set the table for breakfast. I was

[2] See also case studies cited in Chapter 6.

in disgrace with my brothers and sisters if I failed to get up in time to make the cakes and I was too poor a baker to make them good enough to be edible the next day. I learned to bake bread and to iron before I was in high school. I have a faint recollection of washing, feeding, and caring for the baby when I was seven years old. I was 'mother's little helper' in so many ways for years. Mother certainly needed me. When we went visiting, it was my responsibility to see that the younger children did no damage or did not get hurt. My household tasks gradually increased until I was doing more of it than mother was. Her last baby was born at the beginning of Christmas vacation of my last year in high school, and I was put into complete charge including mother and the baby. Being the oldest girl in a large family meant that many of my own desires remained unfulfilled."

(b) "From the time that I was five," writes the oldest of eight, "I can remember taking care of the children. I used to lie on my mother's bed and push my little brother back and forth in his carriage until he fell asleep. Mother kept on having babies. Many problems beset us. By the time I was in third grade, I was always helping mother while the others played with the neighboring children. This made me old beyond my years, serious, and quite responsible for all that went on in the household. . . . Each Saturday, my mother went in to the city six miles away for the groceries and stayed for the day. In the evening she and dad visited friends and came home at about midnight. From age fifteen to nineteen, I found myself responsible for seeing that the housework was finished, cooking lunch and dinner for the children, and caring for the newest baby. At night, I bathed six children, washed their heads, and tucked them into bed. Saturday nights continued like this until I rebelled. I wanted to have time for dates like other girls had."

(c) "As time went on," writes one of seven, "my older sister more and more took on a double role: a substitute for the head of the house and a big sister to whom all would look and whose judgments and decisions all came to respect. Thus my mother and sister came really to be copartners in the operation of the house. As it was, mother referred most things to my sister. In consequence of all this, she was robbed of a normal teen-age and early twenty development. And, too, because of her exalted position, she gradually became a little managerial in her attitude toward her brothers and sisters."

Reference has been made to the fact that it is usually the oldest child upon whom this undue share of the family burden falls. There are large families, however, where it is the younger son or daughter who emerges as this particular type. Consider, for example, the Devers family, consisting of eight children, the first two of whom were girls. The oldest daughter was ill a good deal of the time as she was growing up and came to utilize her illness to escape responsibility in the household. The sister next to her, a year younger, was healthy, active, and shrewd. Very early in the life of the family, it was the second daughter who was considered the responsible older child, both by parents and siblings. By sharing some responsibility with the oldest of the sons, born next to her, she retained a definite control of the family which has continued down to the present time, when she and this same brother are conducting a business which employs the other siblings.

In another family, the oldest son is a moody type, roams about by himself, and shows little interest in his family. The second son, born a year and a half later, steps into his place as the leader of the siblings and their responsible caretaker. In still a third family, the oldest child, a daughter, is the father's special favorite and becomes the family social butterfly, while her two younger sisters develop into parental surrogates. In other words, while it usually is the oldest child who assumes or accepts a role of leadership and responsibility in any particular family, unusual circumstances place this crown upon a second or even a third child. The type, however, remains relatively the same.

THE "OLDEST" CHILD AS A TYPE

Whatever the sex and exact order of birth, these older siblings tend to encounter similar situations and develop definite trends of behavior. Some of the more characteristic outlines will be mentioned briefly.

First, they tend to be put under unusual pressures from an early age. From being put under pressure by others, they proceed to put themselves under pressure. Thus habits are formed which crystallize into patterns of responsibility. We agree here with the findings of an English psychologist who studied behavior among children in miners' families, average slightly under six per family. He says:

There is little doubt that in working-class families eldests in childhood and adolescence have to bear more responsibility than their siblings. Also they have to be aware of tensions and strains in the family, to mediate between the adult and child worlds and generally to sharpen and develop their capabilities. This tends to set them apart from the others, and to encourage a feeling of "difference" from and soon, probably, some superiority to "the kids." As a result of family position and experience they are likely to become more individualistic, better fitted for competition, scholastic or other, than their siblings. Nevertheless, they are far too often compelled, in part by their developed sense of responsibility, to forego, if not to sacrifice, opportunity in order to meet family needs they know to be real. They tend to leave school at the earliest possible moment and to find themselves at work, under the compulsion of conscience and family, augmenting the family income. So their difference from their siblings is reinforced and also their conviction of superiority. This in turn may lead to unconscious resentment of any movement of the others towards equality.[3]

One of our own informants put it this way: "Ever since I was a young man," he writes, "I got up ahead of the others.

[3] J. P. Lees, "The Social Mobility of a Group of Eldest-Born and Intermediate Adult Males," *British Journal of Psychology*, July, 1952, p. 216.

Interaction Among the Siblings

I took the lead in the day's work and responsibilities. I looked after my younger brothers and sisters. I helped them with their studies. I got them out of trouble when they got into it. I heard their gripes, I advised them as best I could, and I straightened out their quarrels with each other. As a result I developed very early in life an understanding of many things. I learned to listen rather than to talk, I learned to keep my problems and troubles to myself, I saw the follies and weaknesses of the younger ones. By the time I was twenty-five I looked at life in a rather objective way. Becoming a sort of second father meant that I became a man very early in life, perhaps too soon."

Patterns of sacrifice and service also manifest themselves early in life. Being the oldest means doing for others, and sacrifice can be as habit-forming as selfishness and aggression. Lees notes this tendency among the eldest in the study just referred to: "Once they had entered the Scholarship Scheme, the eldests seem to have been inclined to 'get on' only if their siblings had already done so; the intermediates all either 'got on' or wanted to do so, whether their siblings had or not." [4]

The matter is well put by a younger brother in a family of nine children who writes about his oldest sister as follows:

There is something about being the oldest that means too much responsibility. . . . My sister practically ran the house. She took over much of the responsibility from my mother, and when my mother went away on trips or for other reasons, she took complete charge. She was our second mother. She developed her own methods of discipline. She was extremely capable. She has always shown herself as a capable woman. She was one of the first women in our community to drive a car. And much of her life has been a giving of herself to others. After she finished school, she worked in a children's hospital. Then she took a children's clinic in charge. She has waited upon and spoiled her husband and two children. She was aware of the fact that she

[4] *Ibid.*, p. 215.

carried undue responsibilities at home as a young girl, but she has been quite proud of it and has felt that it prepared her for the kind of life and activities that she engaged in later on in life.

This comment was contributed by an informant who is a mature man, and professionally equipped as a student in the field of human behavior.

Reference has already been made to the insight into many aspects of life that older children obtain, resulting in the early development of a rather detached and objective viewpoint. Opportunities for obtaining such insights are numerous and begin early in life. Oldest children see themselves dethroned early in life, and then see the process repeated with the coming of each new child. They see their mothers become pregnant over and over again. In some families, they may attend in the delivery of the new baby, and help to care for mother and child. They hear the parents say the same sweet things to the younger children that once were said to them until perhaps, as one oldest one put it, "you feel an emotional numbness that won't wear off." If the eldest is a daughter, she will bathe and feed and help to rear the younger child. Many aspects of sex are no mystery to them. Sometimes these early contacts with the "realities" of life are shattering, as the following case suggests.

The oldest daughter was eleven when the youngest boy, the eighth child, was born. The practical nurses afforded by the community in those days were not interested in taking a maternity case where "there were all those children," and the parents decided that if they had to get rid of the children in order to be entitled to nursing care the eleven-year-old daughter could do nearly as well as a practical nurse. Four of the older children were sent to visit with relatives during the confinement, and the eleven-year-old managed the household and ministered to her mother's needs. Daughter "minded" the two children left, attended to household chores, as well as the "waiting" on mother and baby. Daughter was young and emotionally not prepared for such an experience, and did not understand until years later what it was all about.

Interaction Among the Siblings

At the time she did the things required, and built in her mind fantastic tales of horror about what had taken place. She brooded over the things she did not understand, and decided very definitely that she was never going to marry and go through the "awfulness" of having babies. She resolved that she would be an "old maid" and maybe keep house for her father. Her attitude toward marriage and babies persisted for the next ten years, keeping her mind singularly closed to any awareness of the companionship and interest in boys.

Other aspects of the eldest child as a type will appear in subsequent chapters, particularly in those dealing with the family formation process among children reared in large families, and the differentiation in personality types among siblings.

SUMMARY

1. A substantial part of large family living consists of the interactive processes between the children.
2. In all large families, much of child rearing and child management accrues from what the children do to, for, and with each other. Ninety-one informants refer to this and eighty-two treat sibling participation as an integral part of the child-rearing process.
3. In twenty families, one or more of the children acted as the chief or sole disciplinarian; in seven more families, such was the case for some considerable part of the life of the family.
4. In fifty-five families, children played a supplementary role to that of the parents.
5. The reactions of the children, as voiced by the informants, show a high degree of acceptance of the older children as disciplinarians. Apparently four times as many held this as similar attitudes toward discipline by the parents.
6. Older children act not only as disciplinarians but often as leaders, counselors, and protectors.

7. Older siblings serve as substitutes for the parents in many families. This is especially true when there are many children and their birth is extended over a long period of time.

8. Many older children are exploited by being called upon to aid in the rearing of the younger children to the point where their own life plans are interfered with in varying degrees.

9. The older child tends to develop definite behavior trends in the direction of early maturing, habits of responsibility, and patterns of service to others.

· 9 ·

Interaction Among the Siblings (*continued*)

THERE IS more to large family living than child management and discipline and the responsibilities of older children. Children in large families play together, work together, learn to live together, quarrel with each other, form factions among themselves, and the like. It is to these aspects of sibling relationships that this chapter is devoted.

PLAYING TOGETHER

A number of children growing up in the same household would be expected to play a good deal with each other, and that such play would constitute a major phase of their younger years seems a normal assumption. Information on playing together was solicited as a part of the study, and informants who were interviewed were encouraged to discuss fully this aspect of their home life. Of the hundred case records, seventy-seven contain some information on this matter. Of the seventy-seven, only five indicated "very little" or "not much" playing together. The nature of these comments suggests some of the reasons for this:

> We played on the street with other children. Our home was unattractive, small and unpleasant.

> The six of us were so widely spaced at birth that we preferred to play with children at school who were nearer our own age.

> We tried to get away from each other and cultivate our own friends. We never did get to know each other until after we were married. We played on the street with other children.

We had different interests and were of different types. Then, too, mother was so neurotic that we were ashamed to bring children to our house. We tried to leave home as much as possible and find friends elsewhere.

Informants in seventy-two of the seventy-seven families reporting, then, indicated that the children in their families played together to a considerable extent. Forty of them used such terms as "all of the time," "nearly all of the time," or "most of the time." The other thirty-two said they played together "a lot of the time," "to a considerable extent," or "much of the time."

Most of these references to playing together were happy in tone. True, there were admissions of disagreements, but in only two families did these result in lasting antipathies. Since most of the informants were past twenty, it is possible that time has softened some of the lines in these pictures. On the whole, however, our case material here is happy reading and indicates that, whatever else may betide, large family living has its compensations. A few examples will suffice:

We rarely had outside company and did not feel the need of it. We had good imaginations and played many games, which were joined in by two dogs and a cat. This life continued for some years, and, as far as we children were concerned, it was the closest thing to heaven.

Most of our childhood games took place at home, possibly because of the fact that we always had plenty of room. We got along well together, and still do. One of my earliest memories is of a gathering around the piano to sing, and this we still do, although this is considered old-fashioned by many people today. Although all of our music was elementary and amateurish, it provided fun and relaxation.

We played together a great deal. We had a big yard but we could not go out of it without permission. Because we had enough children of our own to play with, we did not often bother with others, although frequently the neighborhood kids would come to play in our yard. Mother and dad played with us a great deal. That also was an incentive for the other kids to join us. Together we played cards on Saturday evenings, ping pong, croquet, and holiday games.

Endlessly, while small. We were never around our parents in the daytime except for work and meals. Evenings they read aloud to us. Because it was fun. Because we lived on a farm and it was too far to the neighbors.

We had lots of fun together as children, and there were play groups within the family, based mostly on close age. However, we all enjoyed doing things together—our family sings, reading aloud together, going on picnics together . . . all kinds of indoor and outdoor games.

A complementary phase of the play life of children in large families consists of their play with other children. Of the seventy-seven families for which there is play information, forty-seven reported playing also with other children, the extent of such playing and the ages at which it occurred varying considerably. In the other thirty cases, play with other children was limited to a marked degree. These cases fall into three main groups. First were those families who lived on farms or in open country, so far removed from neighbors that playing with other children was not possible except on relatively rare occasions. A second group consisted of cases where the parents interfered to prevent or limit play with other children. Third were the families in which the children were self-sufficient in these respects, or for other reasons withdrew into themselves.

The play activities of children in large families are much influenced by the attitudes of the parents. There are the parents who facilitate play by furnishing equipment and/or participating in it with the children. There are families included in the study where both parents participated constantly with the children in their play. There are families—fifteen of the hundred—where the parents sought to have other children come to their homes to play with their children. There are parents—not more than four—who simply forbade their children to play with "outsiders." There are homes where the children play by themselves, without visitors, under the shadow of uneasy adult tempers. These are cases where parents' nerves are raw from alcoholic or other excesses, fatigued with overwork, plagued with illness, or ill-tempered by natural endowment. Finally, there are the parents who sought to supervise the companions of their many children, as the following excerpts will indicate.

Our play with other children was limited because the children about us didn't have the attitudes and rearing that my parents thought they should have had for us to play with them.

Our parents had no objection to us playing with other children as long as they were of good moral character, as they would admonish us.

I played with other children quite extensively. It was always more fun to be involved in group play. My interests in sports developed early, mostly due to my father's introducing me to these activities at an early age, so that it was a natural thing for me to engage in group play.

We played with other children frequently. Dad said he would much rather have our playmates in our yard, and then he could see what we were doing. We could always feel free to have our friends visit in our home.

We all had our other friends at school and home, but we never left home much to play with them because mother liked to keep an eye on us.

WORKING TOGETHER

In his study of families under stress, Hill writes:

It was not the form of the family, but its processes and substance of living that determined its success as a family. . . . we found the ingredients of family success in a wide variety of family organizations. These ingredients appear to be: the recognition of interdependence of all members upon one another, the satisfaction of playing one's roles in the family whatever they are, the sharing of home management duties among all members.[1]

Case after case in this study emphasized this factor of interdependence. More than a quarter of the informants who were interviewed spoke of this, often in almost the same words. This part of the interview ran somewhat as follows. The point would be raised as to how the members of such a household got along with each other in the daily routine of family living. Repeatedly the answer would take the following form: "Well, there was a lot to be done. Each had his or her allotted task to do. We worked together. If we got out of line or did not do our part, we heard from the others." Sometimes "the others" meant the parents, as in the family where "if we didn't do our work and got out of line, my father would beat us into line"; but most often "the others" meant the other children.

The phrases "staying in line" or "getting out of line" were used by a number of the informants. The basic idea implied was that of the group as a unity, the interdependence of its parts, the fact that each one had to do his or her part, and that there was group pressure to enforce this. Critical comments by one sibling of another repeatedly took the form of a reference to getting out of line, not doing their share, expecting to do less than the others. Charges of favoritism most often were couched in terms of being allowed to get out of line. References to a good family life almost always spoke of "sticking together." "We helped each other through school. We got through college by helping each other in turn." The most complete of our case records writes about all this at great length, and concludes with how getting out of line was dealt with. "I think we used the word 'fair' more

[1] Reuben Hill, *Families Under Stress* (New York: Harper & Bros., 1949), p. 322.

often than we used any other in settling our childish squabbles and we were much more down to earth and cold-blooded in our definition of fairness than is possible to achieve in the average parent-child relationship because brother and sister do not favor each other. Often parents have a softer spot in their heart for one child than for another, and while they may pride themselves on being fair, they have not really been so, and both the favored child and the unfavored ones are completely aware of this. The child-versus-child relationship in these respects was much more realistic and satisfactory than the parent-versus-child relationship."

Along with an emphasis upon fairness was also that of the advantages of "keeping in line." "Everyone learns," says another, "that if you work together your tasks are completed more quickly and therefore the sooner you are free to play or follow your own pursuits."

One of the main conclusions deriving from the present study is that the large family emphasizes the group rather than the individual. What one can do, as a large family member, depends upon what others do, and plan to do. Most large families operate on a narrow economic margin, if margin at all, which means that economic necessity makes coöperation a virtue. At every turn, it is not only one's own efforts, but the modifying forces of the behavior of other family members, that determine what one can or cannot do. The condition of the hand-me-down that must be worn, the acquiring of a new dress, the use of the living room for your date, of being able to go to town alone, of getting to sleep early, of taking a night school course—all these are grist in the group mill.

Durkheim, the French sociologist, has written revealingly of this in terms of process. In his analysis of the division of labor, he points out that the larger the number of people living together, the greater the division of labor and specialization of function there are apt to be. The greater this degree of specialization, the greater the degree of interdependence that comes about. This in turn demands *concensus*, a term and idea which Durkheim has contributed to sociology. It is this concensus which gives unity to the group, binds the members together, and "the greater the diversity of relations . . . the more it creates links which attach the individual to the group."[2]

LEARNING TO LIVE TOGETHER

While working together means that the group exerts pressure upon its individual members to keep in line, there are other aspects of sibling interaction less noticeable perhaps but apt to be even more pervasive. One of these involves the learning process. Siblings are constantly teaching each other, learning from each other, and learning with each other. The sibling relationship is like a school, but a school in which the scope and quality of the instruction far exceed that found in most other schools. The case material abounds in references to this teaching and learning process. One kind of reference speaks of the children getting together, counseling with each other, deciding what to do. Another kind is where the older sister tells a younger one how to meet given situations, or where the older brother watches over a younger sister because he "knows about the other boy, who is who and what is what." But most of it comes about unconsciously and informally, as an incident of living together. One simply absorbs such incidents in the experience of continuing detailed and close contacts with one's peers. "There was little discipline," writes one of thirteen children, "unless it was that unconscious discipline of living with and growing up with people, and learning to respect the property and privileges of one's brothers and sisters."

An understanding of many of the realities of life comes early to children reared in large families. Many of the in-

[2] George Simpson, *Emile Durkheim on the Division of Labor in Society* (New York: The Macmillan Co., 1933), p. 109.

formants emphasize this. The range of human contacts is enormous and their nature is both naked and incisive. Children in large families tend to live at close range with each other, day in and day out. Often they are a "closed corporation," with relatively few contacts on the outside. Thus there comes a reality of living, a sense of facing actualities, that the child in the small family may lack completely. The occasional child in the large family who is not realistic is soon spotted, as was the biblical Joseph, son of Jacob. The bitter indictment of him by his brethren was expressed in the classic phrase: "Behold this dreamer."

You learn, writes one informant, to live with and have respect for persons of your own age of the opposite sex, an experience that an only son, for example, misses in his family life. One is reminded here of a well-known Hollywood actor who confessed that he had grown up to middle manhood without the slightest understanding of women. It was only in the last few years, he said, that he had gained any knowledge of the female personality and how it works. Conscious of this earlier deficiency, he was willing entirely to assume responsibility for his several divorces, saying: "I really must have been a terrible husband."

One learns about life. "There always was a baby," says the oldest of ten. "I was living always with a baby, and with growing children, helping to rear them, watching as they passed through those stages of development which you had known so recently. You learn to know people, the differences in them, their needs and changes. I was sixteen when my second youngest sister was born. I could not play with dolls when most girls do. I was too bogged down with family responsibilities. I played with younger children instead of dolls. When this sister came along, she was like a doll to me. I bathed her, I made her clothes. I dressed and undressed her." It was this learning about life by seeing it come and develop; this learning about life by living with it; this learning about people by having them constantly about, that one

Interaction Among the Siblings

informant after another emphasized, often in almost the same language.

One of the most important aspects of the educational function of the large family is the insights into life's problems which it accumulates. Every family has its own experience in living and makes its own evaluation of that experience, and all of this accumulates as a family goes on living. In the case of a large family, there are many persons who share and contribute their experience, so that the accumulation becomes larger and more extensive than for the small family, all other things being the same.

There is, for example, the family experience with the school system. Every parent knows that seeing one child through a school teaches one many things—about school, teachers, education, and other parents and children. With two children, these insights are greatly increased; experience with the schooling of a number of children thus builds up a goodly store of insight. Consider, for example, the Carson family, whose ten children went through the same school system, with many of the teachers remaining the same for all ten. Thus, quite naturally, the Carsons built up a tremendous fund of information about "school," which the children shared with each other. This included not only "tips" about subjects but also about teachers and children from other families represented in the school.

But a large family accumulates insights about many more things than the school system. A family with five daughters, for example, acquires considerable wisdom in another area of life. This includes courtship, dating, ways of dealing with boys, what boys to take seriously, who are the triflers, what are "signs of seriousness." Then there is the area of social usages. Take so apparently simple a matter as to how to dress to go where, and with whom. Or there are jobs to be gotten, part-time, summer jobs, permanent employment. How one gets a job, how one keeps it, why Katie was promoted, why Bill got fired, who are "gyp" employers—these are matters of detail but important, too, and the family with fourteen children to launch into occupational careers accumulates a good deal of insight in this as well as in other areas.

No one who has ever gotten the feel of large family living can fail to realize how much siblings contribute to each other in the form of advice. This advice may be solicited or given gratuitously; it may be tendered happily and in friendly fashion or take the form of snarling denunciation or smarting ridicule. The point is that it comes from one's peers, and one's own.

Of course, there is a reverse side to all this. If older children do not have a good record, the younger ones may suffer as a result; if the older ones have developed distorted values and views, they may pass them on to the other siblings. Contrariwise, when older children set high standards of performance, the younger ones may be faced with high standards, invidious comparisons, or the temptation to "cash in" on the older siblings' reputation.

Complementary to the learning process in the large family is the fact that the children receive some training in the art of listening. This art, so completely lost in modern life with its small-family products where everyone talks and no one seems to listen, is a necessary virtue in a family where eight to eighteen sit down at the dinner table together. Seventeen of our informants refer to this, in one way or other. One excerpt is typical. "No fooling or loud talk was allowed," writes one of twelve, "although we were allowed the privilege if we could talk and attend to the business of eating at the same time. We were not allowed to interrupt if our parents were talking, partly because they were adults and partly because children were to be seen and not heard when in the presence of adults, and partly because of the self-evident fact that unrestrained talk would have resulted in bedlam. We did interrupt each other at times, but would be stopped if matters went too far. If there were guests, we were not allowed to speak to them except in answer to questions put to us, and we were required to maintain our silence for the duration of the guests' stay." It might be added that the informant who contributed this never once, in the course of some twelve hours of interviewing, ever interrupted the interviewer.

SIBLING RIVALRY AND CONFLICT

It must not be assumed that all is sweetness and light in the large family. Just as there are conflicts and tensions between parents, and between parents and children, so there are difficulties between the children. This is not a pleasant section to write, yet our own Civil War is a reminder that fraternal strife can be very bitter and tragic. Family intimacy makes for stark reality in personal relationships, and these can lead to conflicts that vary all the way from snide subtleties to physical violence.

Nor is this a satisfactory section to write, for this is one of the areas in which our information is neither complete nor entirely reliable. Various persons who contributed case studies seemed to become defensive and mellow on this point. Apparently they remembered conflicts between siblings during the years they lived together, but years had passed, tempers cool, and jealousies are forgotten often as quickly as they arise. The tendency among informants, then, seemed to be to gloss over this area with benign forgetfulness. It was evident that the relatively few informants who were still living at home stressed these conflicts more than the older ones.

For purposes of analysis, fifty case records that were relatively complete in the information they furnished on sibling relationships were selected. Table 23 presents the extent of sibling conflicts and tensions among the children in fifty families during the time they lived at home, divided into four main categories.

TABLE 23
Sibling Conflicts and Tensions, Fifty Families

	Number of Families
Serious in amount and/or kind	6
Medium in amount and/or kind	16
Relatively little in amount of seriousness	12
Virtually none	16
Total	50

In assessing this summary, it will be remembered that this is based on the report of one informant in each family, and that a complete report from each child in the fifty families might yield different results. There is some evidence to suppose, too, that oldest and inbetween children were more alert to sibling feuding than the youngest one, so that the order of birth among the fifty informants may have been of some significance.

Turning first to the sixteen cases where no conflicts and rivalries of any consequence were reported, these fall into several distinct groups. There were those families, six in number, where the family faced serious problems, chiefly economic in nature, which called forth the coöperation of the sibling members. Father died, father drank excessively, economic pressure due to the depression—these compelled a closing of the ranks and a sticking together to meet difficult problems. Situations were such as not to permit the luxury of bickering. Second, there were six families where the good influence and leadership of one or both parents were reported to be such as to keep the "sibling waters" serene. Two informants attributed the lack of conflict in their cases to the age and sex distribution of the siblings, a fact which was mentioned by a number of others as responsible for the small amount of friction. Finally, there were two families where temperamental placidity might be identified as making for good relationships within the family.

Interaction Among the Siblings

Over what do siblings fight? What are the sources of conflict and rivalry mentioned in the thirty-four case records in which relations of this kind were admitted? The answers cover a wide range of specific issues, and vary in number from one family to another, but they may be summarized under a relatively few headings.

Competition of some kind between siblings is mentioned more frequently than any other factor. This may be competition in school, in "dates" with the opposite sex, for the inside track with a parent or older sibling, or for the control over the younger children. It is easy to understand this competitive aspect. Large family living makes for pressure upon its members, and pressure makes for competition. The specific items involved in the competition are incidental to the life of the group.

Next to competition of this kind are the tensions that grow out of the remarriage of a parent. The step-parent may come with children of his or her own, and may favor that group of children over those of the other parent. Charges of favoritism appear in many of these cases. Consider some of the complications in these homes. A widow, with children of her own, marries a widower with children. The widow owns the home in which they live. Some of the children of the widower, who move in, are older than the other children, and they assume control over the living facilities. There were three families among the fifty that were analyzed where the "money" in the family came from the parent who died, but the lion's share of the income seems subsequently to have been enjoyed by the children of the step-parent. This is a difficult situation for children of the first parent. A second kind of step-parent situation is where the economic resources of the family are quite limited, where some of the children are given new shoes and clothing, which the others must wear subsequently, and where it is the step-parent's children who customarily get the new things. Finally, there are the cases where "my children, your children, and our children" must adjust within the same household, which it may be quite difficult or impossible to do.

Wearing each other's clothes often is troublesome. Complications in sibling relations over this problem are the third most frequently mentioned source of conflict. Doing so without permission or a trade is particularly resented. Lack of care of clothing that is scheduled to be passed on is mentioned, as is the necessity of wearing clothing of an older stepchild. One clothing problem that proved peculiarly troublesome arose in a family with twins, where the two girls fought with each other for the privilege of being distinct persons—in appearance. "We were dressed alike until college days," said one of the twins, "and never liked the same kind of attire. In addition, with limited funds and two of a kind needed, no really attractive clothes ever were available, it seemed to me. We were very close, and yet fought bitterly to win and maintain recognition of our distinctness. The one term that made me see red was 'the Blank twins,' with no recognition that we were separate people, each with her own feelings, thoughts, and possessions."

Most of our immigrant families report dissensions among the children, but it is interesting to note that the informants in these cases attribute their conflicts, not to the fact that many children lived together in the same household, but as "growing pains" in the process of their Americanization. The conflicts between parents and children in these homes are of the kind usually referred to by sociological writers, with the parents holding on to the Old World culture and the children accepting that of the New. Among the siblings, the conflicts seem to stem from the unequal rate of their acceptance of American ways, and the fierce rivalry at times for each to outdo the other. This business of making the transfer to the American pattern becomes in some of these large families a matter of each man for himself, and thus comes to have a disorganizing effect upon the family.

Differences between siblings in regard to life opportunities and other aspects of family treatment are noted in our records. The opportunity to continue going to school, a chance at college, requests to contribute to the family exchequer—all of these tend to vary, and often considerably so, from one sibling to another, and the knowledge of it is not wasted on those involved. Many circumstances are responsible for such variations. Siblings differ in aptitudes and interests. Younger children often can have greater opportunities than older ones. General economic conditions vary. The nineteen-twenties were a period of prosperity, the thirties were a depression decade, the forties included the lush war and postwar years. Broad changes of this kind and their meaning for an individual child at a particular time in a family's history are not always understood by those affected.

Other differences in treatment, particularly between older and younger siblings, are mentioned. One has to do with medical and dental attention. An older child presents problems in these areas that require professional attention, but under the pressure of mounting responsibilities of an increasing number of dependents, the parents are not able to provide such care. A later child, with a similar problem, receives the necessary attention because the family's economic circumstances have improved, now that the father is established and the older children are working. Other differences appear in regard to clothing, allowances, and the like. Then, too, there are frequent references in our material to a decline or softening of discipline with the younger siblings. To the outsider, changes of this kind are easy to understand and accept, but children in large families are no more inclined to impersonal philosophizing about themselves than is the rest of the population.

Favoritism toward one child by the parents, jealousy of an older brother or sister of the one that follows in the order of birth, and behavior-problem siblings—these are other factors that create tensions between siblings. The last mentioned is stressed particularly in our material. Large families tend to be very family-conscious, they develop family pride, group pressure upon conformity to accepted patterns of behavior is pronounced. When, then, one sibling, and especially an older one, does not keep his conduct in line, and behaves so as to injure the reputation of the family, feeling against such a one on the part of the other siblings may become very strong. References are frequent in our case material, not only to resentment against an erring sibling, but, in well-integrated families, to the effort of each one so to conduct himself as not to cast reflections upon any of the others. "We never had any serious quarrels," writes one of these, "nor did we create any problems that might embarrass the others. We were a closely knit group." Keeping in line, in social behavior as well as with the chores, is important in large family living.

Many points of irritation that arise between children in the same family are trivial. This is emphasized over and over in our comments. "We fought with each other many times, but I cannot remember what about." "My sister and I were at sword's point for years, but I cannot now tell over what." "There were many points of irritation, but they were all petty things." Along with these references to the triviality of these quarrels are an equal number who emphasize their brevity. "We fought but we quickly closed ranks." "We quarreled to the point of pulling hair, but never held grudges." "Mother would never let the sun set on our anger." Obviously, then, many of the tensions and quarrels in a large family are the pin pricks incidental to human contacts, as quickly forgotten as they are trivial in character. When, as was the case in several of the families, these quarrels took a serious form, the participants "quickly closed ranks" in the case of attack from the outside. The informant who of the entire number spoke longest of the sibling quarrels added a moment later, "but everyone knew better than to start anything with any one of us, for we quickly came to each other's defense." Or one can look at these "youthful bickerings as a part of the process of growing up," which the "child in the large family gets over with earlier and more easily than the child in the small family."

SIBLING RELATIONS IN LATER LIFE

One test of sibling relations would be the extent to which contacts have been maintained in later years, that is, after the children have left home, embarked on their separate careers, and formed their own families and later life attachments. A question soliciting information on this point was utilized in the study, and data on eighty-eight families were obtained. The twelve families not included are those where all or most of the children were still living at home or where no information was secured. Table 24 presents these data in tabular form.

TABLE 24

Sibling Contacts in Later Life

	Number of Families	Per Cent
Close	60	68.2
Some	16	18.2
None or very few	12	13.6
Total	88	100.0

The sixty families in the first category use such words as "close," "very close," "strongly knit," and "continuing." These are further explained as meaning "getting together often," "seeing each other as often as we can," "helping each other," "writing regularly to each other," and "calling each other by phone." It will be noted that approximately seven out of ten families fall into this group, according to the reports of the informants.

In sixteen cases, the terms used are more restrained. The words "some," "fair amount," and "occasionally" appear to indicate sibling relations. Relations may be cordial but not overly friendly; the siblings may be separated by long distances; they may have just grown apart. The death of one or both parents may lead to a loosening of the family bond. Good relations may exist with some but not all the siblings. These cases were included in this second category, which accounts roughly for one out of every five families.

The twelve families where the reports speak of "no contacts" or "very seldom" or "hardly at all" present a variety of situations. Four of them are cases of vertical social mobility, where the siblings have grown apart culturally and socially, so that a terse "very little in common" tells the story rather well. Two are families in which mixed marriages (religiously mixed) occurred, with its disorganizing effects upon family unity. Two were families where the remarriage of parents and the mixture of several sets of children destroyed an earlier unity, not restored in later life. In two other cases, long distances have separated the siblings, and there has been no will apparently to overcome this handicap. Finally, there were two families where the siblings never played together as children, primarily because of their age and sex distribution, and have maintained little or no contact in later life. One other thread runs through these later life relations, and that again emphasizes a castigation of those siblings who got out of line in their behavior and thus cast reflection upon the other siblings. These continue to be singled out for critical comment in later life, and may be excluded from contacts which the others maintain.

One final question remains: Is there any relation between playing together as children and "sticking together" in later life? Taking the families as a whole, the answer is a limited yes. The reasons for this equivocal answer are as follows. First, taking the five families where the siblings did not play together when young, or hardly at all, it is found that they have had few or no contacts in later years. Again, considering the families where the children played together all or most of the time, and in happy fashion, when young, it is found that they have clung together after leaving home. It is in the inbetween group that the correlation is less clear. In some families, medium playing together is followed by medium contacts later on, but in other cases relations between siblings improved after they left home. There are at least eight families where limited playing together, with considerable conflict and rivalry, was followed by close and happy relations in later life. On the whole, it seems reasonable to conclude that the nature of family play between siblings is an important indicator of their later life relationships, but that other factors operate, too, and must be taken into account.

AGE AND SEX OF THE SIBLINGS

The age and sex of the siblings are of basic importance in their relations with each other, and in a number of ways. They may be viewed from the standpoint of the family as a whole, or of the interactive process between the siblings, or in relation to the personality development and the specialized role of an individual sibling. We are concerned here with the second of these, that is, their effect upon sibling interaction, and only in certain general terms, leaving their more detailed analysis to a subsequent chapter.

The siblings in a family have a unity of their own, a unity which grows out of the number, nature, and relationship of its individual members. As these vary, so does the group, conceived as a unit. So far as the age and sex of the siblings are concerned, there are at least four sets of facts about them that are significant.

1. *The sex of the older children.* The importance of the older children as leaders, disciplinarians, and caretakers has already been emphasized. What is now added is that the sex of these older children is significant, too, for whether these older siblings are boys or girls will determine within limits

whether the dominance accorded by priority of birth will be masculine or feminine in character. The facts of the sex of the older children in our hundred families constitute an interesting study. In fifty-one of the cases, the first-born child was a girl; in forty-nine, a boy. But this is only part of the story. In sixteen of the fifty-one families where the oldest was a girl, the two oldest children were girls; in six, the first three were girls; and in five, the first four, five, or six children were girls. Thus, in twenty-seven of the fifty-one families, two or more girls headed the list. Similarly, of the forty-nine families where the oldest child was a boy, in twenty-one of these the first two (ten cases), or the first three (four cases), or the first four (three cases), or the first five, six, or seven (four cases) were boys.

2. *Imbalance between the sexes.* This matter of the dominance of one sex over against another is also influenced by the sex ratio among the siblings. While one hundred nine males were born for every one hundred females among our families, individual families show wide variations in this respect. In forty-three of the hundred families, for example, one sex outnumbered the other among the siblings in a ratio of two, or more than two, to one. In nineteen families, the girls so outnumber the boys; in twenty-four, the boys thus numerically outnumber the girls. In selected families, the disproportion is quite marked. There is a family with seven boys and one girl, another with six boys and one girl, and a third with seven boys and two girls. On the other hand, there is one with six girls and no boys, one with seven girls and two boys, and another with eight girls and three boys. Imbalance in this respect, and to such a degree, obviously determines dominance by one sex or the other.

3. *The time differential between births.* The time differential between births, involving the respective ages of the children, can be approached in several different ways. There is, for example, the time span between the first and last child. Disregarding for the moment the number of interven-

ing births, the time spans between the first and last in our hundred families, classified by five-year intervals, are presented in Table 25.

TABLE 25

Time Interval Between First and Last Child, by Five-Year Periods

Number of Families	Time Differential (years)
10	10 or less
28	11–15
47	16–20
13	21–25
1	26–30
1	31–35

Detailed study of the data shows that in twenty-five families, the interval is either nineteen or twenty years; in forty families, the difference falls into the seventeen-to-twenty-year brackets.

This birth span for the entire sibling group takes much of its meaning from the number of births intervening between the first and last, that is, from the total number of children. This is an individual situation, varying from one family to another. A few illustrations will suffice. Of the twenty-two families with six children surviving infancy, the time interval between the first and last child in six families was twenty years or over; and in seven more, it was between fifteen and nineteen years. On the other hand, our study includes a family with fifteen children in sixteen years, another with fourteen in seventeen years, and another with twelve in thirteen years.

The time interval between births, and its possible significance in sibling relationships, is modified in turn by the sex order of the siblings. One striking illustration of this was a family of six children, in which each child was born three years after the preceding one, and with the sexes alternating throughout. Thus, while the time interval between the six births was three years in each case, that between the same sex was six years in each case. Combining age and sex of siblings in large families, many different combinations appear, each of apparent significance for sibling interaction.

4. *Sets of children.* One aspect of the time span between the birth of children in the large family calls for special comment. This concerns the grouping of the children into several sets, with the children in each set born close together but with a longer time interval between the sets. Thus, in one of our families, nine children, including two sets of twins, were born in seven years, then followed a seven-year interval before the second set began to be born. In another family, four children appeared in four years, then after an interval of six years two more appeared in rapid succession. In some cases, these groupings or sets are also of the same sex. Thus, in one family, five girls were born in about as many years, then there was an interval of seven years after which three boys appeared in three years. In another family, there were three sets: the first consisting of three girls, then one of three boys, then a third with three girls. In each set, the time interval was between one and two years, but that between the sets was considerably longer. It is significant that in each case where such sets appeared on the basis of fact, they were mentioned by the informants, who in turn reported that their parents and the other siblings often spoke of "our two families" or "mother's three sets of children," or made similar references which indicated an awareness of the facts and their significance.

INTRASIBLING COMBINES

In any group of more than two, pairings, cliques, factions, and/or combinations of various kinds are apt to arise, whereby some of the members of the group have closer and different relations with each other than with the rest of the group. Three of the questions utilized in this study attempted to obtain information on this point. These questions were: (3) To what extent did cliques and divisions develop within the large family? (22) Which of your brothers and/or sisters is closest to you? Is the attachment very pronounced? (23) How many such factions or pairings were there in your family? Other questions concerned with intrafamily relationships also involved information bearing on these questions.

Because of certain changes in these questions, made after the first twenty-five case records were obtained, the analysis of the material bearing on the foregoing questions is confined to seventy-five families. Table 26 presents certain items of this information in tabular form.

TABLE 26

Intrasibling Combines, Seventy-five Families, as Reported by Informants

Existing Combines	Families NUMBER	PER CENT
None reported	8	10.7
Very little	7	9.3
Only one, informant a member	8	10.7
At least two intragroups	14	18.6
Three intragroups	24	32.0
Four "	8	10.7
Five "	3	4.0
Six "	3	4.0
	75	100.0

These combinations among the siblings are of many degrees and kinds. In some instances, they were persistent and pronounced. Thus one informant writes: "There were three groups in our family (nine children). They were almost like three separate families. This persists until the present time. The brothers had their group in which father played an active part. The older girls are married, with families of their own, and have little or no time to bother with their younger brothers and sisters."

By contrast are the combinations—and there are many of these—which are casual and transitory, resulting from changing circumstances, and tending to form and reform through the years. A few excerpts will suffice to indicate this. "At different ages, we paired off differently." "Some of the factions and cliques within our family were tenuous and shifting, changing with circumstances." "The pairings with us have never been constant or inflexible." "Cliques and divisions have changed with the years."

A number of bases appear to govern these combines among the siblings. Of these, the first in frequency undoubtedly is closeness in age. This point is well stated by one of our informants, who writes: "In our family, the relations of the children to each other will best be understood in the context of age differences. These differences had the effect of pairing us off into groups of two, with my older brother and sister forming one pair, my middle sister and I a second pair, and the youngest sister and brother a third pair. In each pair there exists a sphere of interests which effectively limited interaction with the other siblings to areas outside these interests. My middle sister and I were and still are the closest pair because of the nearness of our ages and the similarity of our contacts and experiences." Another writes: "We cliqued by two's right down the line. The attachment was very close and has always been so." This closeness in age involves often the same general stage of development, the same friends, interests, and problems.

Twins presented a particular variant of the closeness-in-age factor. Eight sets of twins are reported in the hundred families. In four cases, they were male twins; in three cases, female; and in one, mixed. (One of our informants was a twin, but before her report was concluded, both participated and agreed on the information contributed.) Comments from all families in which there were twins agree on the closeness of their relations, establishing them as a separate pair in sibling interaction.

Sex ranks with or close in importance to age as a factor in determining intrasibling groupings. Members of the same sex naturally have many friends, interests, and problems in common. Frequently, too, the birth order accentuates the role of sex. For example, when the first two or three children are of the same sex, it is quite likely that they will combine to share the leadership of and responsibility for the younger siblings. Similarly, in the event that several consecutive births are of the same sex, and are sandwiched in between older and younger siblings of the opposite sex, they will hang together. Also, much "pairing off" is by sex, as well as by age. The case material abounds with statements like those that follow. "The two oldest boys were together most of the time until they left home to go to work." "The third and fourth brothers worked together on the farm." "My sisters have always been closer to me than my brothers." "The three girls were in one clique, and the three youngest boys were very close." "As to the relations between the children, there was the usual sex allegiance."

Common interests might be mentioned as the third factor. These grew largely out of age and sex similarities. Many of the informants stress this role of common interests. Those generally mentioned were school activities, dating with the opposite sex, recreational pursuits, and church activities. "There was in our family," writes one, "a selective women vs. men lineup, chiefly on differences which grew out of different interests." "My brother and I never miss an opportunity," says another, "to go fishing together or work with our bees, a project we started years ago." Or, in another family, "pairings and groupings changed with age and interests." "The only clique," states another, "was the two oldest girls because they had so many interests in common."

The remarriage of widowed parents involving the coming in of stepchildren, and perhaps the subsequent addition of half-brothers and sisters, leads to cliques and divisions in families. This has long been recognized in public lore and is commented upon by the informants in all of our families where such circumstances occur. Various references to these cases have been made in the preceding pages, and only the operation of these situations in the creation of factions need be noted here.

Political considerations, the restless search and urge for power, these are found everywhere, and this includes the area of sibling relations. There are an amazing number and variety of references in our material to the "freezing out" of a sibling, or to a combination between two siblings to "rule the roost." In one family, the oldest child, a daughter, combines with the third child, a daughter, to "take the ball away" from the second child, a son, and does so with apparent complete success. Another informant writes: "There was a great deal of cliquing, chiefly in terms of pairs. The first two sisters had a clique, went to school together, went away to school together. The older sister of the pair was physically weak, but a martinet. The younger sister of the pair was physically strong and aggressive, but always subordinate to the older sister. The next two daughters had the same combination, so far as dominance and submission were concerned. They cliqued together a great deal. The third couplet were very much the same. One interesting interclique feature was that the dominant members of the first two pairs combined in order to exploit the younger members of the couplets. In other words, dominance and dominance speak the same language."

Of course, there are the personal factors, as a result of which one sibling is attracted to another. In some cases, they may be separated by a number of years, and be of the opposite sex; in others, these differences are lacking. It might be a sister who admired an older sister's looks or an older brother's school progress; it might be a grown son who took a much younger son under his sheltering wing; or it might be because of a similarity of personality traits. "My second and third brothers," writes one, "were close social companions. I suspect they got along so well because they have similar personality traits, very different from my older brother's and mine." "I was closest to my oldest sister," says another. "It was she who put me through college and medical school." Another informant presents still another aspect. "When I was an adolescent my third brother and I were inseparable. He was born the day before my tenth birthday. It was about that time that I learned where babies came from and I was very much excited about getting a baby for a birthday present. After he was born I assumed complete responsibility for him, claiming him as my own. This close relationship lasted until I went into the Navy. When I returned, I hardly knew the youngster. It seemed to me he had changed a great deal. He found me an old fogie and I found him a fresh upstart. We couldn't seem to agree on anything."

In reviewing the references to intrasibling groupings, it is quite evident that most of them were dyads or pairs. Occasionally a triad is identified, or even cliques of four, such as one sex or one set of children line up against another, but mostly, in the manner of the disciples of old, our siblings "went forth" two by two. Several informants spoke of the "natural pairing" of the children, and perhaps the pair is nature's arrangement within larger groups. "Pairings arose out of needs," writes one, "and these changed with the needs." On the whole, the informant who wrote "we cliqued by two's right down the line" came nearest to identifying the process most commonly found in these hundred families.

Since subgroupings are so common in our families, and seem so natural, a word should be said about the families for which none such was reported. Possibly the questions bearing on this were not properly understood, although this may be doubted, or the facts escaped the awareness of the informants. Whatever the case, the eight families in which no cliques or other combines were reported present the following facts. Three of them were families of a minority group in the population, and reported that they went everywhere "as a gang." Another informant insisted that such combinations should not exist, and so said they did not in his family. In another family, affection between the siblings seems to have been at a minimum. In two other families, the siblings were born so close together that "they played and did everything together." In the remaining family, the existence of any and all combinations was denied, but with various backhanded references to their existence.

LARGE FAMILY LIVING AND THE SOCIALIZATION PROCESS

To what extent does large family living socialize the child? This general question was asked of everyone contacted in the course of the study, and the purpose was mainly to see the specific ways in which the question would be answered. It was anticipated that most every product of large family living would agree that it tended to socialize the child, and ninety-seven of the hundred informants so indicated. The three who disagreed had all been reared under family conditions which fostered patterns of rebellion, and one aspect of the rebellion was to depreciate the type of family in which they had been reared.

Chief interest attaches to the reasons given for the conclusion that the large family was a good socializing medium, or the specific ways in which this was accomplished. Those aspects most frequently mentioned follow herewith.

> Teaches fair play
> You learn to share
> Getting along with people
> Coöperating with others
> Tolerance of other people
> Learn to listen as well as to talk
> Learn to like people

Interaction Among the Siblings

Self-control and self-discipline
Respect for the property and rights of others
Responsibility for other people
Learn to participate in group activities
Life is not a bed of roses
Learn how to keep from annoying other people
Frees children from parental smothering
Less tendency to become selfish
Learn to take stresses and strains of life in stride
Rubs rough edges off
Wears you smooth
Learn to live with both sexes and assorted ages
Accustoms one to having people around
Enriches one's experience
Gives feeling of courage and security
Gives a proper perspective of one's place in life

While these excerpts enumerate the high spots, the more complete statement of attitude as revealed in several longer quotations seems desirable.

We need to care for people, and for people to care for us. We need to talk a lot (too much) and we can all listen well, too. We are not exactly leaders, nor are we blind followers. People are important to all of us, but particularly to someone of a large family. I have, for so long, thought of many, rather than one, and adjusted my wishes and desires to eight other people's wishes and desires. I have experienced great happiness and contentment out of being one of many, each of us important in our own place, shouldering each other's responsibilities, and forgiving one another's mistakes.

I think that large family life teaches self-control and self-discipline. When you have three or four or more brothers and sisters who aggravate you in various ways at various times, you soon learn that it is not considered good conduct to grab, shake, or strike your brothers and sisters. You learn to control those nasty little impulses. . . . How much effect this has in teaching people to curb adult anti-social acts, or to carry their problems to the impartial courts of the law, I don't know. You learn to discipline yourself in many ways, and to govern your conduct along acceptable social ways. . . . I think that being part of a large family establishes the desire to belong or to be needed. It makes you like to love and be loved; a large family does not tend to produce cold, aloof, withdrawn people. It teaches respect for private property, and consideration for each other. It produces the desire to help each other or to guide each other.

Living in a large family socializes a child to an appreciable extent. . . . In general, living and being reared in a large family teaches one that life is not a "bed of roses" and that there are other people in the world all with "equal rights" to the pursuit of happiness in life. . . . a child in a large family has brothers and sisters of contemporary age who understand him as a child and in the "give and take" of their everyday life each learns to control emotions, think in terms of "we" and not "me," "to live and let live," to look out for oneself and yet to consider the rights of others, and a host of similar terms all meaning to live as a real human being should and not as an animal.

It is my conviction that living in a large family has a great socializing influence on a child. . . . In the large family a child has to become adjusted to other people for there is no retreating from their presence. These continual and reinforced relationships by necessity have to assume a character of workability in order for the family to operate as an integrated group. The things that a large family impart to a child better prepare him for living in a large group. The multiplicity of the relationships in a large family form the potential for an easy transition of the child into other group situations. The child of a large family usually learns responsibility toward his fellows by growing up in an environment where such considerations are the rule . . . also tends to give a child a more certain basis on which to meet and interact with other people. . . . In summary, by virtue of the large number of individuals living in close and intimate contact, as in a large family, a child is more easily and less consciously equipped to take his place in adult society.

Living together in a large family compels you to be adaptable. You have to accommodate yourself to the wishes of others around you or you can't survive. A large family is a group situation. A child, particularly a later child, is exposed to both sexes, various age groups, numerous interest groups. There are always people around so that visitors do not excite the youngster. There is always someone to play with him, talk with him, teach him—to walk, to tie his shoe string, to bat, to talk, e.g., I taught my oldest brother how to speak, making the initial sounds and compelling him to observe my facial expressions. There are numerous persons he must please, from whom he can win recognition and affection. If one person displeases him there is always another one to choose. There are older children to copy. There is someone else close to one's own age to go to for advice, comfort, reassurance. Mother and Dad seem so far removed from a 12-year-old's problems. There is the opportunity for sex exploration and conversation. There is better preparation for the acceptance of everyday happenings in life.

Yes, I do honestly believe that living in a large family does have its effect on socialization because consideration must be given to each other during the course of living together. A form of unity develops and with it a sense of attachment for each other. Though privacy is at a minimum or rather impossible one does gain somewhat of a group spirit which implies a thinking through things together and arriving at decisions that are reasonably acceptable to all. I am convinced that a much more charitable consideration for "the other person" is engendered by a person who derives from a large family than one who is a product of a small family.

One somewhat qualifying note to all this must be added. Six of the informants pointed out that, while operating in various ways to socialize its child members, the large family also created counteracting influences. It is significant that the six, all of them of unusual intelligence, agreed upon the nature of the danger involved. Stated briefly, it was that children may live too much within their large families, may find such life so satisfying that they may not wish or be able to transfer their activities and interests to the outside. This may manifest itself at an early age, as the following excerpts will reveal.

We lived within our group, and did not become as well prepared to cope with the outside world as does the only child whose parents seek contacts for it with the outside world. We were not shy within the group, but were mute and unsure as soon as we left the family group. One child attended church with her mother when she was seven years old, and for the first three Sundays she attended she was terrified of the strange people and wept hysterically whenever anyone spoke to her. If she had had the familiar presence of one of her brothers to gather comfort from, this outside contact doubtless would not have been so painful. After three Sundays of tears she gathered up her courage to look around and to discover the people weren't nearly as alarming as she had fancied. But she still felt unsure and alone, away from the safety and comfort of the group. . . . Some of us, even as adults, have not outgrown this sense of fear and insecurity we felt on being exposed to outside contacts, and in one or two cases has developed to such an extent that the feeling has become a sort of inferiority complex.

On the negative side, children in large families tend to lose contacts on the outside. The family life becomes a complete social world. There is no reaching out into other homes. This is particularly true of an isolated farm family.

There is a danger that a large family will provide a sheltered adjustment that will monopolize a child's life and keep it from facing the more difficult adjustments that must be made outside of the home. I may not have retreated into the sheltered life of my own home, but neither did I gain sufficient experience in socializing myself for life outside.

I think living in a large family may be a distinct hindrance to the socialization of a child. He does not have to depend on those outside the family for his friends. Often because of financial pressure, a large family does very little entertaining. The child does not meet strangers and learn how to act with them. He is familiar with social ways and customs only within his own home. I deeply felt that I had been cheated in this respect when I found entirely different ways of life among the friends I made in high school.

Interaction Among the Siblings

Probably the most representative of all the statements on the topic under discussion that was obtained in the course of the study was that given by the oldest of ten children. Writing at an age of maturity and out of a background of thoughtful study of the processes of child development, this woman, herself a mother, summarized this area of our study in the following words:

The larger the family, whether they belong to a large or small income group, the greater the possibility that responsible, stable citizens will emerge because

1. There is no room for selfishness. If parents miss budding tendencies the rest of the group will take care of them in short order.
2. There is no time for oversolicitousness. Each child learns to do things for himself much earlier than in the smaller groups. If he doesn't stand on his own feet he may soon find one of his contemporaries standing on them.
3. Because they are family, as well as contemporaries, there is a sense of well being, a comfortable, secure feeling, a feeling of pride that this is my mother, my father, my brothers and sisters. These feelings, often not consciously thought of until the child is grown, promote contentment and contentment is not a proper garden for unstable seedlings to be planted in.
4. There is a complete social life within the group, and again I believe this to be true whether the group belongs to a large or small income class. In the groups with larger incomes the siblings should become exposed to outside advantages somewhat earlier but I have never seen a large family of children who developed individual frustrations as long as they were children (a bit dogmatic, I suppose) and who could not in the majority get along with people because they had learned to get along with each other. They have to learn that we live happily by obeying the rules. They really have to become inoculated with a certain sense of good sportsmanship which often is not thought of and does not "take" if it *is* thought of in the smaller family.

5. Usually the older children are more self-reliant than the younger children of the group as they all grow up. The older ones have learned all their lessons except the one so many parents of only children never learn—and they try to do too much for the younger members, feeling they want the "babies" to be spared many of the duties and responsibilities they have experienced. Actually this tends to make the younger members demanding and thankless for favors received. This is an unfavorable comment and one aspect which produces a great deal of instability in any size family, i.e., any and all sizes.

SUMMARY

1. Children in large families customarily play together, especially when younger, and to a considerable extent.

2. Working together also is the rule in large families, and this is emphasized as a factor in promoting interdependence among the siblings.

3. Playing and working together makes for learning to live together. Large families make for richness in the learning process.

4. Conflicts and rivalries develop among the siblings, but these more often are trivial and shortlived rather than serious. Most of them are incidental to group contacts and the growing-up process.

5. The overwhelming proportion of siblings in large families maintain close contacts in later life.

6. The age and sex make-up of the siblings is the key to many aspects of the interactive process among them.

7. All kinds of combinations into pairs, cliques, factions, and sets are formed among the siblings. Pairs are most prevalent, and most of these combinations are temporary.

8. Children that grow up in large families are practically unanimous in stating that large family living socializes the child to a marked degree.

· 10 ·

Personality Patterns Among the Siblings

MUCH of what has been said in the preceding chapters is related to the personality development of the siblings in our families, and it seems pertinent at this point to summarize the remaining data in the case records that deal with this process. This chapter, after a general discussion of specialization of role in group life, will include a summary of sibling attitudes toward order of birth, a note on differentiation of sex roles, and the specialized personality roles of siblings as seen through the eyes of the informants.

SPECIALIZATION OF ROLE IN THE FAMILY

Whenever a number of people are in continuing association with each other, differences in the part that each plays in the common life manifest themselves. These may be differences in the tasks that each performs, or differences in other contributions which each makes to the group. Sociologists tend to use the word "role" to designate the specialized function of the individual member of a group. Perhaps the simplest way to define role is to say that it involves the exercise of a person's relative group position, attributed to him by his fellows in their reciprocal relationships.

That such specialization of role occurs in group life can be noted by any observer of a clique or gang or college fraternity. Thrasher, for example, gives an excellent description of this process in his study of the gang.[1] He shows how in the

[1] Frederic M. Thrasher, *The Gang* (Chicago: University of Chicago Press, rev. ed., 1936), chap. XVII.

gang, so like the sibling group of a large family in many respects, every member comes to acquire a place or status with reference to the other members, how this results from a selective process in which each searches for his niche, and how these roles result in action and thought patterns which come to fix his personality.

Such specialization of role obviously occurs within the family. Emile Durkheim, whose brilliant work on the division of labor in society is so well known, wrote:

> The history of the family, from its very origins, is only an uninterrupted movement of dissociation in the course of which diverse functions, at first undivided and confounded one with another, have been little by little separated, constituted apart, apportioned among the relatives according to sex, age, relations of dependence, in a way to make each of them a special functionary of domestic society. Far from being only an accessory and secondary phenomenon, this division of familial labor, on the contrary, dominates the entire development of the family.[2]

This process is, then, a natural and inevitable one in the life of the family, beginning very early in the lives of siblings on the basis of age, sex, order of birth, and age differential, as well as of innate characteristics. While most obvious on the side of functional specialization, it is not so confined but comes to include the whole range of behavior. This means that very early in his life a child acquires a special personality role in the group life of the family, which comes in time to be recognized by the child himself as well as by his brothers and sisters.

The assignment of a particular role has a great deal to do with the personality pattern of the child. The role is in part an unconscious expression of what the person is at a particular stage of development, but also it involves *his* conception of himself and his role. Highly important, now, is his adjustment to the role assigned to him. He may accept it,

[2] George Simpson, *Emile Durkheim on the Division of Labor in Society* (New York: The Macmillan Co., 1933), p. 123.

with varying degrees of satisfaction shading into smugness on the one hand or sullen resignation on the other. Or he may reject it, again with all kinds of resultant behavior ranging from bitter resentment to determined effort to modify or reconstruct the role.

It seems evident that the larger the group the greater the degree and diversity of specialization of role. Durkheim notes this in regard to division of labor, and it is entirely likely that the generalization holds in other respects. Specialization of role is therefore particularly pronounced and important in the large family, and for a variety of reasons. In the small family, specialization of task and of role among peers may not be defined at all, or less so than in the large family. Intersibling experience is more limited in the small family, as is sibling competition, so that it is not necessary to assign or select roles so early in the child's life. This uncertainty of role may have much to do with the feelings of insecurity, frustration, and inadequacy that are prevalent among children in small families. Early assignment to specialized role, and adjustment to it, as tend to prevail in large families, may make for the relative lack of such feelings among large family children.

It is possible too that the assignment and adjustment of specialized role in one's first and most intimate group (the family) are in many ways the key to one's adjustment in later life. Certainly early adjustment to group living in one's family experience does much to determine the nature and degree of adjustment to later groups in school, church, and at work. These are matters that await and merit empirical verification.

Another point of difference between small and large families in regard to specialization of roles is the source of the assignment. In the small family, first selections and assignments are made by adults, chiefly the parents, whereas in large families they tend to be made by the other siblings. Early in life, the children seize upon little differences in traits, aptitudes, interests, and/or idiosyncrasies as a way of distinguishing one from another; they are made much of as a part of the family banter and competition. Calling attention to these differences tends to fix them early in the particular child's mind, and having become aware of himself in these respects he may tend to magnify them into an even greater difference because they make him stand out as a separate person in a group whose members in many other respects may be largely alike. An example will suffice. In the Davis family, with its eleven children, Russell early displays an interest in mathematics and Evelyn in cooking. The other children note this, and soon Russell is referred to as the "math sharp" of the family and Evelyn as its cook. There is bantering, teasing, praising, and the like, about these two and their skills. They are mentioned to relatives and guests. Russell and Evelyn accept these assignments and identify themselves with these respective roles.

A pertinent question presents itself at this point. How can this emphasis upon specialization of role and personality pattern be reconciled with all that has been said about the group pressures in the large family that seek to keep its members in line and to conform to type? The answer to this may best be clarified by a simple comparison. The process of personality development in the large family is like that of a woman shopping for a new dress. Her quest is a dual one. She wants a dress that is in style; in other words, one that conforms to "what women are wearing this fall." But she does not want a dress like all the other dresses that women are wearing. She wants one that is unique and distinctive and different from all the others. It is so with personality formation in the large family. There is the general family type and the pressure to conform to it, on the one hand, but there is also a restless and insistent search to be different.

SIBLING ATTITUDES TOWARD ORDER OF BIRTH

One of the most obvious forms of specialization of role among the siblings in a large family is that which results from order of birth. Considerable emphasis has been given to this factor by students of personality and child development, and its importance would naturally be relatively great in families of larger size.[3] Most studies in this area concern themselves with changes in attitudes of parents and practices in child rearing, as affected by order of birth, and what such changes may mean to the personality development of the child. There is little information, on the other hand, on how the children themselves regard this rank order, particularly in large families. It is interesting and significant therefore to see the nature and variety of the answers given to question Number 10 in the present study: "On the basis of your experience, what do you wish your order of birth had been?" Reasonably complete answers to this question were obtained from eighty-three informants, and these answers are summarized herewith. It is believed that the number is large enough to be of suggestive value.

First, by way of background, it is necessary to note the birth order of the informants. Of the eighty-three, thirteen are first born, sixteen are last born, and fifty-four are in-between children. Of the inbetween children, the most frequently represented are fourth born, a total of fifteen falling into this category. If third-born children (seven in number) and fifth-born (seven) are added, the total for these three is twenty-nine.

How do these eighty-three feel about their birth orders?

---

[3] Cf. Robert R. Sears, "Ordinal Position in the Family as a Psychological Variable," *American Sociological Review*, June, 1950, pp. 397-401; Dora E. Damrin, "Family Size and Sibling Age, Sex, and Position as Related to Certain Aspects of Adjustment," *Journal of Social Psychology*, February, 1949, pp. 93-102. See also James H. S. Bossard, *The Sociology of Child Development* (New York: Harper & Bros., rev. ed., 1954), pp. 108-17.

The answers were relatively decisive: sixty-one said they were satisfied. This is 73.5 per cent of the total, or roughly three out of four. In most cases, there was no equivocation; the answers were clear and direct, often beginning with such statements as those that follow. "I am satisfied with my birth order." "I like my inbetween position." "Exactly where I was born." "I don't believe I would have been any happier if I had been born earlier or later." "I'm just as glad that I was born where I was."

What is the birth order of these satisfied siblings? Table 27 presents this information, as well as the birth order by groups of the eighty-three informants and the percentages of each birth-order group that were satisfied.

TABLE 27

Birth Order, Eighty-three Siblings, by Groups and by Numbers and Percentages Satisfied

	Number	Per Cent of Total
Informants, first born	13	15.6
First born, satisfied with birth order	5	8.2
Percentage of first-born who were satisfied		38.4
Informants, born inbetween	54	65.1
Inbetween, satisfied with birth order	42	68.8
Percentage of inbetween who were satisfied		77.7
Informants, last-born	16	19.3
Last born, satisfied with birth order	14	23.0
Percentage of last born who were satisfied		87.5

From this table, it is evident that first-born children were the least inclined to be satisfied with their birth order, only five of the thirteen first born thus reporting. The last born were the most satisfied, fourteen out of sixteen, or 87.5 per cent, falling into this category. The inbetween siblings constitute the largest group, and approximately four out of five (forty-two out of fifty-four) report satisfaction with their birth order. Of these inbetween children, the fourth and fifth born seem particularly content with their birth order, not one in either group expressing any dissatisfaction. Selected excerpts from the case records will indicate the attitudes of those who were satisfied with their respective birth orders.

First born. When I was younger I often wished I was the third child or the youngest one because they seemed the favored ones. Now that I am older I have been very much satisfied with my birth position. I have as many and possibly more skills than any brother or sister. I am self-reliant, independent, capable of organizing and managing, mature, unselfish because of the many demands to sacrifice, able to cope with crises, and well adjusted. If I had not been the eldest I might never have been so close to my mother nor held such a place of high honor in my father's eyes. Today I have a certain amount of authority over all the family members. I feel a strong responsibility for them and am duty-bound to them. I am frequently asked for advice. I am the only sibling that has lent another money. Today I am very well contented with being the eldest.

Inbetween child. I am quite satisfied with my position in the birth order of my family. I am . . . as close to the center of the birth order as is possible to be. Middle children are in a rather unique position. They are not subject to the same mistakes of the older children and at the same time are not subject to the relaxed discipline and concentrated affection that is often the lot of the younger members of a large family. I was in such a middle position. I was given a reasonable amount of family responsibility, not as little as my younger siblings and not as much as my older siblings. As a part of the older half of the children I was a functioning member of family councils and had a voice in family discussions. My position bred a certain personal independence which differed from the authoritarian attitude of my older siblings and also differed from the more irresponsible attitude of my younger siblings. Thus I think my place in my family's birth order was a source of benefit to me.

Youngest child. As the youngest of seven, I concur heartily in the opinion that the younger children have the most opportunities. As the youngest member of my family, I would not, if I had been able, have exchanged my position in the order of birth.

I am the youngest of nine and am happy with my position. The youngest profits a lot from the experience of older brothers and sisters. They go through things first and see how they work. As a result, they tip you off and you learn a great deal that way without having to learn it yourself. I think I would always like to be the youngest one.

The attitudes of the twenty-two informants who were not satisfied with their birth order are equally revealing. Of these, eight were oldest children who tired of the responsibilities of their prior position and indicated a preference usually for the middle position. Another nine were inbetween children in the earlier or higher birth order, and they too expressed a preference to be at or below the middle position. Three inbetween children wanted to be first born, and two youngest children said they preferred a higher birth order. Thus, seventeen out of twenty-two dissatisfied informants would rather have been born later, most often at or near the middle of the birth order. The following excerpts are typical of the above attitudes.

First born. I do not like being the oldest member of a family of six children. All of my life I have been set up as an example for them to follow, and knowing this has made me overly conscious of all I fail to accomplish. . . . As the oldest child I have had to pave the way for my other brothers and sisters, and of course this means my parents were much stricter with me in childhood than they are on the other children, now. It seems that automatically a certain responsibility falls upon you and I am ashamed to admit that at times I bitterly resented this responsibility. . . . One thing I am certain I am not, is spoiled. That is why I would not like to be the youngest child in a family, because I have seen how spoiled my sister became before the baby was born, and even now she expects to be pampered as she was then.

Inbetween child. I would like to have been born later in the birth order, so that my opportunities would have been greater, especially the educational opportunities. I was the third born and would have preferred a place somewhere after the middle.

I sometimes think that if I had been born later, I would have had more advantages, and would have seen the value of finishing college and would not have married so soon after I finished high school.

I was the eighth child in a family of nine and was forced to take the position of a Cinderella. If I had my way, I would be born either first or last. My primary choice would be to be born first. My oldest sister had a very happy childhood, I'm told. She was given everything she wanted and never had to take hand-me-downs as I have had to do. When the family got overcrowded she was able to marry and get away from it all. My baby sister didn't have things too badly. She was treated with kid gloves and didn't have to do the work that my next oldest sister and I had to do.

Youngest child. I think I would prefer to be somewhere closer to the middle, with fewer hand-me-downs to wear. Also, if I had been born sooner, I could have left an unhappy home situation sooner.

It was hard at times to be the youngest. I wanted to go everywhere and see everything the others did, and when I was told "When you are that old, you can too," my stock answer was, "Suppose I die before I get that old." I suppose this plaint is common to youngest children.

One leaves the whole body of this material with one overwhelming impression: that the middle place in the birth order is the most coveted position among the children reared in large families. Older children carry too much responsibility, they are too often the practice child, they tend too often to be exploited. All children, regardless of birth order, recognize these facts. Youngest children most often like their position, but other children know why and do not envy their place nor their treatment and resultant characteristics. It is the middle position that avoids both extremes. Such children profit from having others precede them but avoid their responsibilities; they are followed by younger children and have the advantages that accrue therefrom but avoid the disadvantages and overadvantages of those who are at the lower end of the birth order.

How the birth order affects the personality patterns of various siblings will appear in a succeeding section of this chapter. In the meantime, reference must be made to another factor in the specialization of roles among the siblings.

SEX DIFFERENTIALS IN ROLES

Sex, like age, is a simple and universally used reference point in the specialization of roles within a group. Sex differences are apparent from birth and remain fixed for life. The sex typing of behavior and privileges begins early in life and is both rigid and lasting. Also, like other forms of specialization, it is more pronounced in the large than in the small family.[4]

Our case material is filled with references to differences in duties and responsibilities on a sex basis. There are various statements of exceptions to such differentiation, but these are made always as if to underscore the fact that they were exceptions rather than the rule. Division of function on a sex basis is clearly defined in most large families.

"The girls did the housework; the boys, the marketing and the ash cans."

"I did the housecleaning, my brother looked after the lawn."

"Even the boys had to wash their overalls."

It is significant that a number of informants, in characterizing their brothers and sisters, did so in terms of the specialized tasks allotted to them, and the extent to which they

[4] For a more complete analysis of sex as a factor in the assignment of roles, see Bossard, *op. cit.*, chap. XVI.

met their obligations. Here is another illustration of the emphasis upon "keeping in line" or "playing fair" that has been noted in a preceding chapter.

SPECIALIZED ROLES AS SEEN BY INFORMANTS

One of the questions included in the study concerned the specialization of sibling roles as seen through the eyes of the informants. It was stressed that the study was particularly interested in securing information on this point, and they were asked to describe brothers and sisters as fully as possible in this regard.

It seemed important to obtain this information and it was hoped that it might be made so complete as to permit a statistical summary and analysis. Unfortunately, this part of the research proved unduly difficult and illusive. Some informants seemed to have difficulty in understanding what was wanted; others insisted that the siblings "were alike and acted as a group." A number wrote out their characterizations in terms of the division of labor that obtained in the family, as has been noted. Still others described themselves and perhaps two or three siblings to whom they felt attached or the reverse as types. There were, however, sixty-four informants who furnished definite characterizations of their brothers and sisters, and this information is the basis of the analysis which follows.

Before proceeding to the analysis, a few samples of the nature of the material on which it is based seem to be in order. Parts of several case records are cited verbatim.

Daughter. First born. Bossy by own admission, aggressive, calculating, a trifle hard.

Son. Third born. Antisocial, compared with the rest of the family. Did not speak much to others. Was interested in sports. Took no responsibility for anything at home. Contributed nothing to home life.

Daughter. Second born. She is the student of the family. Responsible, and yet something lacking. Seems the sweet type, yet really is not. She has the least social graces of all the children. She never gives out anything.

Son. Seventh born. A good mixer. Gets along well with people. Is likable but extremely irresponsible. Tends to be the secretive type. Hard to get to know. Never says what he really thinks.

Daughter. Fourth born. Social interests at expense of all other things. Could always dig up a date. Always the life of the party. Never left out of anything. Could turn her hand to many things and do them well.

Son. Third born. The scholarly one. Intellectual interests. Learned quickly. Did home work for the others. First of the family to graduate from college.

In searching for the most effective way of organizing and presenting the characterizations furnished by the informants, the concept of a composite picture has been utilized. That is, the sixty-four groups of siblings have been imposed upon each other, with the result that eight general types appear. These eight types are not found in each family. Some families do not have eight siblings. Other families have two or more of the same general types. These eight types must be considered as representative of the study as a whole.

1. Every family identifies at least one of its siblings as the responsible type, the one that is looked up to, the one that assumes direction or supervision of the other siblings, or renders service to them. The word "responsible" is the one used most frequently in referring to these siblings, but in some cases such words as dutiful, bossy, drudge, leader, helpful, martinet, and policeman are also used. These seem to identify chiefly the way in which this position of responsibility was exercised.

Male siblings who were thus described usually were older sons, who aided the parents and acted as father surrogate in the father's absence. The same applies to female siblings of this type. Most often these responsible ones were the oldest children of their sex, but to this there were numerous exceptions. The oldest son might not be able or inclined to measure up to such a position of responsibility, he might be mother's favorite and be excused from such cares, or he might be in constant conflict with his father and from earliest days solve this problem by being away from home as much as possible. Similarly the oldest daughter might be irresponsible, or be papa's pet, or be in continual conflict with the mother. In these and other cases the post of responsibility falls to those lower in the birth order.

The most clearly and frequently identified of all these responsible siblings is the oldest or older daughters who become in varying degrees a second mother to the younger children. The oldest child has already been described in Chapter 7 as a type of early responsibility, of dutiful help to the parents, of service to the younger children and of sacrifice of self in many cases, so that no further comment is needed here. Suffice it to say, and the fact should be emphasized, the children in most large families grow up by grace of the sacrifices of one or two of the older siblings. Large families place a heavy responsibility on the shoulders of the older children.

2. The second most frequently identified is the popular, sociable, well-liked sibling. This quite often is the second born, or the one that follows in order of birth the responsible sibling. It seems in many cases as if, finding the post of responsibility pre-empted, he or she (and most often it is a he) proceeds to gain recognition and self-esteem through personal charm rather than personal power. Some excerpts will help to identify this type.

Second son. He is a good mixer. Gets along well with people. Is very likable. Is sweet to the rest of us to the point of being henpecked.

Second son. He has developed the most normal personality of all of us. He is best liked by our parents and by the other children.

Second daughter. The attractive one. Most popular one among all of us. Interested in the personal appearance of all of us. She would wash your hair and fix you up to go out if mother was busy.

Second son. He was the one with *the* personality. He was much admired by all of us.

Second son. Everybody likes him. He is very sociable. He gets along well with everyone. He is good-looking, and always knows the right thing to say and do and wear.

3. The third is the socially ambitious type. The term "social butterfly" is often used by the informants in describing this type. The picture is quite clear. Whereas the preceding type was described chiefly in terms of appeal to the other siblings, this third group directed its social interests mostly to persons outside of the family. Most of these siblings were women, mostly third, fourth, or fifth in the order of birth. A few brief descriptions follow.

Daughter. Fifth born. Social interests at the expense of all other things. Could always dig up a date. Was the life of the party. Was never left out of anything. Could turn her hand to many things and do them well.

Daughter. Third born. She was the social butterfly of the family. The only one of the girls who had a debut. Instead of staying at home in the summer she must be off to summer camps. Had a wedding that knocked a hole in all of her brothers' pockets.

Daughter. Fifth born. She wanted to be the social butterfly in the family. All she ever wanted to do was to primp and go out. But mama wouldn't stand for it. We all have to work, even the older boys washed their overalls when we were growing up.

4. Fourth of the types by order of frequency were the studious ones. These apparently sought and found recognition within the family and outside by doing well in school,

or withdrew from sibling activities to find surcease in books. Male and female siblings appear in about equal proportions, and are usually described as quiet, hard-working, and, in some cases, as methodical. Some excerpts of descriptions follow.

Daughter. Sixth born. She was the smart one. She had a high I.Q., and an excellent academic record. She was preoccupied with her books.

Son. Third born. He was always very quiet and studious. A lover of books, with intellectual interests.

Son. Third born. He was the scholarly one. He learned quickly. His interests were altogether intellectual. He was the first of the family to graduate from college.

Daughter. Second born. She is the student of the family. Responsible, but yet lacking something, or what is not lacking manifesting itself in a curious way. She seems the sweet type but really is not. She has the least social grace of all the children.

5. The self-centered isolate appears as the fifth of the types identified by our informants—this in spite of all that has been said about the socializing effects of large family living. Descriptions of this type vary from references to their secretiveness to stubborn antisocial attitudes toward the other siblings and/or life. In some instances the chief fact noted is an unwillingness to participate in family activities; in others, a withdrawal from the family and an organization of life on an away-from-home basis. Brief descriptions of other types follow.

Son. Sixth born. He always was uncoöperative. He would not eat nor would he work. He was bright enough, but was at war with the world. He never worked out his adjustments until he got out of college, and he avoided his family until we got a car.

Son. Fourth born. He was stubborn, bull-headed, dogmatic, with very set ideas. I was never quite sure that he believed what he said, or whether he just wanted to be ornery.

Son. Seventh born. He always had to have his own way. He was stubborn and antisocial. He did not like school. He spent much time by himself. He seemed always to be in rebellion against his family and withdrew from it. He is a policeman now.

Son. Fifth born. Always a lone wolf. Very independent. Feels less responsibility for the family than any other. He takes life very seriously.

These family isolates constitute a challenging group that merits further study. Enough has been revealed in the present study to show that most of them are quite understandable when viewed in terms of specific family situations which confronted them. Three basic types of such situations appear with frequency. One is order of birth, with special reference to age and sex differentials. Examples are cases where the other siblings pair off on the basis of age or sex or both, leaving an odd one to shift alone. Or there may be a boy born after two girls and succeeded by three more. Or there may be a considerable time span separating the isolate from the others. Second are the cases where the isolate sibling is interested in some activity, like sports, in which the others are not. Finally, there are the cases where conflict between parent and child develops early, so that the child's rebellion against the father develops in time into a larger pattern of rebellion.

6. Many large families report at least one member who is largely or wholly irresponsible. These siblings seem to withdraw from the family life but in ways that differ from the family isolates. They do not withdraw their physical presence or their participation in group activities; they simply sit back, as it were, and withdraw from the responsibilities which the others accept. A few illustrations will suffice.

Daughter. First born. Extremely irresponsible. She is our gadabout. The most immature of the whole family. Neither is her husband mature. She is definitely the flighty type. It is fortunate that her sister, a year younger, was a responsible person, for she left everything to this younger sister.

Son. Third born. He is irresponsible and always was. A drifter. He was bright but it was a job to get him through school. He finally got to the university but was so irresponsible that father withdrew him after a year.

Daughter. Fourth born. She was cowed and timid and irresponsible. It was all father's fault. He had a high temper, completely dominated the family. The older boys who might have given him a battle left home early to go to war.

7. There were the siblings who were not well. Some of these had physical defects, sufficient to set them apart and to create special problems; some had to carry the burden of chronic or long-drawn-out illness; and still others seemed hypochondriacal, and/or learned to utilize their illness to gain them special favors or to justify their failures.

Daughter. Third born. She was seriously ill for a time when she was a child, and received a great amount of attention which was soothing to her and which she has continued to demand ever since. She sulks frequently, and complains and feels sorry for herself.

Son. Fourth born. We had very little that we were made to do. We didn't even make our own beds. My younger brother was sick a good deal of the time, and was always being protected, and urged to eat this and that.

Daughter. Fourth born. She never liked to do housework. She was considered frail, so she never did as much as the rest of us. Mother treated her and one of the boys who once sprained his back very leniently.

Daughter. Second born. She was a premature baby. As she grew older, she was nervous because of a thyroid condition. Her eyes were not good either. She never took an outside job, but stayed at home and helped mother.

8. Not many large families escape having a "spoiled" sibling. Most often this is the last-born child, although there are

cases, like that of Joseph of Old Testament fame, where it is the second youngest. What apparently happens in this latter type of case is that the parents, and particularly the mother, conceive of the second-last one as the last one, and proceed to "spoil" that one. Then, perhaps several years later, perchance as an accident, another child is born. Possibly the mother resents the coming of this last child, and having started to spoil the second-last one, continues to do so. This was pointed out as particularly true in two of our families where it was common knowledge among all the other siblings that the mothers resented the coming of the last born and doted unduly (in one case, the rest of her life) upon the second youngest.

There are several "angles" to the problem of the position of the terminal or last-born child. The older children tend to emphasize the fact that the youngest ones are "spoiled," that discipline is less rigorous for them, that they have fewer responsibilities thrust upon them, and that they enjoy more opportunities. Our older-born informants clearly reveal these attitudes.

Girl. Last born. She was protected and babied and never expected to participate fully until most of the others left home.

Boy. Last born. All the older children had to submit to his demands. He was known as the baby, and mother referred to him as the baby until her dying day.

Girl. Last born. She was lazier than the rest of us and shirked all kinds of work. She loved to play and daydream, and because of her age was always petted and pampered and allowed to have her own way.

Girl. Last born. She was the baby. Very much spoiled but with a pleasing personality. She got more than any of the others. Everybody babied and spoiled her. Mother gave in to her more than to the other children. She was cute, everybody recognized it, and she worked at it. She was the teacher's pet all through high school.

Son. Last born. "The baby." The older siblings resented the parents' protectiveness toward him and consequently tried to control him more. The older children thought he was "spoiled," and it caused considerable conflict in the family. He continued to confide in me, but had no time for the others. He is sensitive but covers up by a carefree "I don't care" attitude.

When the last born are enabled to speak for themselves they present other aspects of the problem. One complains, for example, that he never had a new toy, but inherited an accumulation of used, repaired, rebuilt, and just plain unrepaired toys. A second one points out that he wore hand-me-down clothes until he was fully grown. A third says that he was always at the end of the line along which each passed the buck to the one younger. "Always you are the kid," says still another, "you are the younger one. The older ones boss you, but you have no one to pass it on to. It is a frustrating experience." Finally, there is the youngest, a son, with a succession of older sisters, who writes: "Always I was the boy, to be made over; yet all the sisters determined that I should not be spoiled. I was subjected to a great deal of criticism and dominance and bossing. Sisters were not only older, but stronger and wiser and smarter. Thus I accepted early in childhood a role of submission, which has continued down to the present time. I think I accepted this role, and do so now, because of my experience in early childhood."

There are isolated references to other kinds of siblings—the scapegoat, the tomboy, the weak one, the perfectionist, the silent one, the black sheep, the handy one—but such references are few in number, and the eight types set forth in the preceding pages cover the range of the generally identified personality patterns.

These eight types fall into an intriguing sequence, suggesting a theory of specialized personality roles and behavior patterns in the large family that is breath-taking in the challenging leads which it opens up. Keeping in mind always the constancy of the individual child's drive for recognition and status, let us consider the eight types in the order of their presentation, which is essentially the order of frequency of identification. The first ones to appear develop patterns of responsibility because they are first and are followed by younger and more helpless siblings. The next ones, finding this role pre-empted, seek recognition by making themselves agreeable. They do not seek to wrest control from the older children; they compete with it or supplement it with their personal charms. The next children, finding these two roles pre-empted, turn from the family to the community. They become social-minded and socially ambitious. Those that follow in turn have to turn to a new avenue of achievement. These turn to the schools. They become the scholars, the studious ones, the sophisticates, the intellectuals. Finding all of these avenues under active cultivation, the next child withdraws from competition. This is the family isolate. Or he may not withdraw his presence, only his sense of responsibility—these are the irresponsible ones, who participate but let others hold the bag. Both the isolate and the irresponsible are patterns of withdrawal and often of failure to find a satisfactory avenue of achievement. The physically defective, the sickly, and those who pretend to be—they have their excuse for relative failure to find their roles, if they wish to use it. Finally, at the end of the line is the terminal child, either pampered into relative ineffectiveness or wearing the "magic boots" to overtake the older ones.

This, to be sure, is a theoretical sequence suggested by the composite of all the characterizations. Actually the order may begin with any type in any particular family, and it frequently does. The more fundamental point involved is that in a large family each child's drive for recognition is expressed in a specialized role related to the roles already pre-empted, and that only a limited number of choices are open in the average family. Putting the matter another way, each sibling in a large family develops his specialized role on the basis of, and in relation to, the roles which have already been established. No sibling wishes to be the exact counterpart of another, so that choices and possibilities are limited with each succeeding birth.

There is, too, the pressure of expectations. The first born faces only the expectation of his parents; the second born, that of the parents and the first born; the third born, that of the parents and the first two siblings; and so on with each succeeding birth. As time goes on, the expectations of the siblings, based on their own roles and experiences, accumulate and become increasingly effective and may outweigh completely those of the parents.

SUMMARY

1. Specialization of role occurs whenever a number of people are in continuing association with each other. The family is such a group.

2. The larger the group, the greater the degree and diversity of specialization of role. The large family therefore is a particularly important form of family in this connection.

3. One of the most obvious forms of specialization of role in a large family is that which results from order of birth.

4. A study of sibling informants in eighty-three families shows that three out of every four are satisfied with their birth order, and one out of four is not.

5. Middle and younger children are more satisfied than is the oldest one. The number four and five place are the most coveted positions.

6. Sex is another basic differential in the specialization of role.

7. A composite of specialized roles in sixty-four families reveals eight main types. They are the responsible one, the popular one, the socially ambitious one, the studious one, the family isolate, the irresponsible one, the sickly one, and the spoiled one.

· 11 ·

Selected By-products of Large Family Living*

MUCH OF what large family living does to and for its members has been touched upon in the preceding chapters. Certain additional facts, solicited in the course of the study and contributed by a considerable number of informants, remain to be summarized. These include: (1) feelings of security or insecurity of siblings; (2) their sense of possession; and (3) their adjustment in life, as rated by the one sibling informant in each family. The present chapter is devoted to these three subjects, with special reference to their relation to large family living.

I. FEELINGS OF SECURITY

The concept of security has been a much discussed and emphasized one in our recent literature, particularly in that dealing with the life and development of the individual. Much recent thought has tended to consider security as one of the inherent rights of the individual. Thus one hears of the child's right to security in his family setting and the adult's right to security in his economic life. A child, in other words, has the right to be wanted and to be loved; the worker has the right to a job and to be guaranteed the minima of existence.[1]

An opposing point of view is that expressed by the famous

* This chapter, both in its written form and analysis of the data, is the work in large measure of Dr. Eleanor S. Boll.
[1] For a criticism of this tendency, see A. H. Hobbs, *Social Problems and Scientism* (Harrisburg: The Stackpole Co., 1953), chap. V.

historian, Arnold J. Toynbee, who insists, on the basis of his lifelong studies of history, that insecurity is one of the normal conditions of human life. "But for short periods of abnormal conditions of relative security for small groups of people within limited geographic areas, this life of insecurity has been the normal human lot as far back in history as our records go."[2] Economic and political security weaken our capacity and drive for action, and especially for creative action.

Mindful of the emphasis upon security for the child in the family-life literature, the present study included the following questions: "Do you think a large family makes for a sense of security among its members: (a) economic security; (b) emotional security?" Informants were encouraged to write out their thoughts on this, and the question was discussed with those who were interviewed personally. Relatively adequate responses were obtained from ninety out of the hundred families.

What do ninety large family siblings say about large family living and feelings of security? Their answer is overwhelming. Seventy-three of the ninety agree that large family living produces feelings of security; seventeen appear to disagree. The ratio is more than four to one: 81.1 per cent to 18.9 per cent.

Is one kind of security emphasized more than the other? The answer is decisively yes. Only four informants stressed economic security alone. Another forty-three mentioned both economic and emotional security, but in most instances emphasized the emotional aspect as the more apparent and important. The remaining twenty-six spoke or wrote only of emotional security.

These informants, then, clearly presented a majority feel-

[2] Arnold J. Toynbee, in Commencement address, Bryn Mawr College, June 3, 1953. For a more complete development of this point of view, see the abridgment of his large work by D. C. Somervell, *A Study of History* (New York: Oxford University Press, 1947).

ing that emotional security is not necessarily related to economic security; that the former is of greater importance; and that there is something in the atmosphere of the large family which tends to promote emotional security even in the face of economic, and other, difficulties. Their specific attitudes as to the relation between large family living and security feelings can be summarized as follows.

1. *Attitudes Toward Emotional Security.* Sixty-nine (76.6 per cent) of the informants felt that the large family provided emotional security for them, and some of these informants gave more than one reason as to why this was so.

Eighteen cases felt, with Dr. Toynbee, that the challenge of a difficult situation created a positive stimulus. Or, as one informant put it: "In a large family a child learns early that life is a difficult proposition and that many occasions arise when negative action only makes things worse. A positive viewpoint is developed." According to others, this "positive viewpoint" was that, in a group in which material things have to be spread thin, and in which personal relationships are intricate and involved, an appreciation of the value of the dependable and coöperative person is developed. Since all of them share the exigencies of the group, the member who contributes, either in work or in warmth of relationship, adds to the wealth of the whole group. The informants felt that, since there was this special need in the large family, the members usually tended to grow in that direction. Thus, it was the numbers of dependable and loyal people that spelled security for every member. Some of the informants remarked:

> We did feel a sense of security that must be lacking in small families, because we were required to work together and to the well being of all of us. This feeling remains—even in our adult years.

> We have the philosophy that if we stick together we can get through any crisis. If we stand alone, it makes a hardship on the

family. . . . Fear with us was unknown, probably because we never stood completely alone.

Emotionally there was strength in being a member of a large family. A crisis was met by everyone and to back up an individual there was a whole clan.

Another twenty-six of the informants felt that mere numbers of family members created a sense of security, no matter what were their individual personalities. There were, however, two different attitudes about the relationship between numbers and security. The first was voiced by those who found emotional comfort in identifying intimately with a large number of people. There were always "lots of your own around." Illustrations of such feelings usually concerned some sort of contact with the outside world, some fright or problem from which you could come back "home" to the family or which some members helped to ease for you. Second, there were eighteen cases who explained that the strength of numbers lay in the fact that although you might not be able to get along well with the whole group, there was always sure to be someone with whom you could pair up and find adequate help and companionship. As one writer put it:

We always had at least one other family member to play with. In smaller families, if you are feuding with your only brother or sister, you would be quite lonely. One very seldom feuds with seven or eight other people though, so in a large family there is always someone left to turn to for consolation and love.

There were thirty-seven informants who very clearly indicated that their sense of emotional security had derived not just from mere numbers of family members but from the number of siblings with whom they had lived. This comprised 52.2 per cent of the cases who reported positively on emotional security, and was the most common response. In view of current psychiatric and child development literature on the subjects of security and sibling relationships, this material was thought-provoking—and for three reasons. First, a child's security has been considered almost exclusively as based on adequacy of the parent-child (and usually just mother-child) relationship; while the role of siblings has been considered chiefly in the light of "displacement" and "rivalry." It is rarely that one finds any but the negative aspects of sibling relationships, and warnings as to how to deal with them.[3] Second, although the number of close-kin relationships has been dealt with by anthropologists who stress the security value of the consanguine family, discussions have been largely in terms of adult protectors and providers. James Plant, as psychiatrist, had gone a bit farther than this in describing the effects of number of family members. In his clinical experience, "extra members," such as aunts, uncles, and grandparents, provide more sources of security or insecurity, but arouse such feelings only against certain people in certain situations and not as a generalized personality trait. Dr. Plant felt that "there are few more exciting trends than those in the numbers of relatives living in the household. Apparently, the decrease in the family is rapidly intensifying the emotional load on a very few people. The issues are clearer, the successes richer, the failures not to be escaped from."[4] He suggested that "all trends as to the number of persons in the household should be broken down into the relationships of these persons to the child."[5] Sibling relationships, however, he did not discuss. Third, the significance of the peer group in providing a sense of security is well recognized; but having come into prominence in an era of the small family system, the peer group has meant, exclusively, nonfamily peers. Children are said to find security in the situation of being age-culture mates in an adult-

---

[3] For the positive aspects of sibling relationships, see James H. S. Bossard, *The Sociology of Child Development* (New York: Harper & Bros., 1948), chap. V.
[4] James S. Plant, *The Envelope* (New York: The Commonwealth Fund, 1950), chap. 1 and pp. 16-17.
[5] *Ibid.*

dominated world. They discover that they are crew members in the same problem-ridden vessel. Apparently, from our case records, siblings from large families found such crew members among peers within the family group. A possibly significant comparison between the small family and the large family in this respect may be pointed up by the remark of a woman with only one sibling. "Not until long after we were both married did my sister and I discover that we had had the same kinds of problems with our parents. Each one of us had thought our own troubles were unique and that the other one had a better relationship. Our parents had made their own neurotic demands upon both of us, but had managed to keep us far enough apart so that we did not know we were sharing the results similarly." In the large family the weight of the numbers of children makes it difficult for parents to keep children so apart. In the cases under consideration, there was only one that reported such a situation, describing a mother as "managing to keep all the children at variance with each other." The child-group numerical superiority seemed so significant in all other cases that they were analyzed individually. Five distinct contributions of numbers of siblings to emotional security were noted.

(a) Siblings turned to each other when they did not get enough attention or understanding from a harried or indifferent parent. When a parent was cruel or thoughtless, the children stuck together to protect each other. One informant mentioned, for instance, the horrors of having an alcoholic father, but said that the children had presented a solid front against him. Another wrote:

We children at times felt that we had been wronged by the adults—so got together, talked it over, and if we decided that we had a good case, we would take it to our parents.

Another, fully aware of the "rivalry" aspects of sibling relationships, said:

What can be lost in this area from competition to get parents' attention is gained from the fact that children find their security in one another.

(b) Other informants felt that their own siblings had a better understanding of the problems and new situations that younger children faced than did their parents—because the siblings were still children together. They realized how frequently, and under what circumstances, youngsters do feel insecure; and the older siblings did something about it. What was done, specifically, in some families was reported.

My oldest brother took my youngest brother to his first Scout meeting. I took him to his first day at school. When a child is faced with a new experience it must be a great comfort to know that someone is there who has been through it all before.

Mother spanked my third brother. Sister cried as hard as if she had been spanked and as soon as Mother left the room, she ran to his side, put her arm around him, and said through her tears, "You'll be all right, don't cry."

Three of us had mumps at the same time. We could console one another as we lay sick in bed.

The boys down the street and my second brother would get into a fight. The minute my eldest brother and I discovered it we were also in it, beating the other kid up or helping our little brother to hold his own. Surely it is a good feeling for a child to know there are others to help fight his battles, whether he be right or wrong.

There may very well be a great difference in security feeling, depending upon whether it is siblings who help a child to fight or encourage him; whether it is Mother who rushes out to protect or chide him; or whether he has to fight it out all alone.

(c) Three of the informants thought that security feelings were related to the adequacy of an individual's performance

Selected By-products of Large Family Living

and the range of his skills. They felt that siblings were better teachers than parents. Although security and adequacy have been rather strictly separated in psychiatric literature [6] and there is some logic in the separation, there is also some logic in the reports of our informants. Siblings, they said, were able to understand how hard it is to learn something new. They had so recently been through such learning processes. They were therefore patient, and got right down to their students' level. They did not push and, so, frighten and frustrate, as adults frequently do. Siblings had no vested interests in teaching younger siblings which would result in unrealistic expectation. They shared skills for the fun and companionship of it. Also, with many children in the family, there were many and varied skills to teach one another. One informant listed all the skills of the children in a family of seven. She was fourth in order of birth. The first four had all had different skills. Each had taught the others a bit about his own personal interests, and they had passed all of these down to the siblings who had arrived later. Another aspect of the adequacy of performance was related to the fact that in a large family there are usually a few siblings who are going through a certain age period in close succession. They not only share the age period, but some of them are just slightly ahead of the others, with a little bit more experience. As one informant explained: "We could talk over adolescent problems—dating, dancing, necking, drinking, smoking." The inference was that this gave them more security in knowing how to perform than they would have found in talking these things over with a "passé" generation.

(d) In one case it was stated that emotional security came from numbers of siblings because there was little opportunity for the emotional coddling of any except the youngest. The writer compared the small family system unfavorably in this respect.

[6] Plant, *op. cit.*, pp. 18-19.

(e) Finally, two cases spoke of the large family as giving security within the group but suggested overdependency upon it for emotional satisfaction to such an extent as meant a lack of security away from it. One of them wrote, somewhat confusedly:

> The feeling of security I have at home, which means wherever the family is, is something I cannot find away from them. But I am secure away from them in that I know they will always be there if I turn back. I can depend on all my brothers and sisters, and both my parents, even if the rest of the whole world rejected me. A tremendous interdependence, even if we don't all live together any more. . . . We have lived much and through much together.

Twenty-one of the informants were just as decided in their views that the large family did not create a sense of emotional security. With the exception of one case, all those who analyzed the reasons for this described them in terms of a too arduous struggle for life. Whereas, for other families, it had been a stimulating challenge, in these it was said to have been sufficiently weighty to tip the scales in the direction of insecurity. Dr. Toynbee has cited a few historical examples where challenges were too severe to provoke a positive response. There were some large families in this study whose informants felt this to be true of their own families. A sibling from one of them wrote:

> In the church I learned what it meant to be needed and experienced deep satisfaction when I received thanks for a task well done. It seemed there was never time for any such expression in our house. Food, a clean house, and clean clothes always seemed of prime importance. . . . The numbers of children in the family decide the volume of work that must be done to meet their needs, and when one becomes so busy providing food, clothing, and shelter that there is no time to really live, a large family is a disadvantage. We did have happy times together, but there were so many gaps that were not filled we could not appreciate these joyful days fully.

In another case, an alcoholic father was abusive and cruel and "for some reason or other, we never developed much of a tradition of mutual aid among each other." Again, a mother and father separated and "family inconvenience, intensity of family struggle for financial support, and unfair emotional upheaval were the consequences of such a marital disaster." One more informant felt that his insecurity resulted from his being the last child in a family with six older girls. He explained that he had gotten no support from his sisters of the kind a person usually gets from siblings. What seems significant in the examination of all these twenty-one cases is that it was not just the severity of the family problem that created insecurity but that its nature had prevented the family from using the best resource—the unity of numbers. Parental relationships had been inadequate, and children had not been able to compensate for this by forming close sibling ties.

2. *Attitudes Toward Economic Security.* Forty-seven (52.2 per cent) of the informants felt that the large family developed a sense of economic security in its members. Forty-three (47.8 per cent) did not. Three informants explained that money and material things had been abundant, and they had felt secure economically. The other eighty-seven made it clear that large family living had meant a continuous consciousness of the pressure of many needs. The responses on economic security and insecurity, therefore, came almost wholly out of situations of acute economic awareness.

The major difference between those who felt economically secure and those who did not seemed to lie in whether or not the whole family worked as a team. When they did, the informants stated with positiveness that a large family makes much more for economic security than does a small family. "Each individual is more aware of economic problems and contributes more himself." "We all worked together and could always depend on each other if we needed something."

In many of these cases a sort of family mutual-aid society was existing to the present time, when siblings were grown and separated. A typical example was this:

> My eldest brother wanted to get married. He could not find an apartment, but he could buy a trailer. My folks agreed to let him put it in their back yard. My brothers agreed to help fix up the inside. However, he lacked about $1,000 toward the purchase price. . . . If he could not get the money he could not get married because they had no place to live. He . . . asked me to lend him the money and I answered "Yes." It never occurred to me not to grant his request. Another example, the second brother married, moved to Florida, had two children and with his wife six months pregnant lost his job. My father by good fortune found him a job in his line. He wrote giving all the necessary details, beseeching him to come, and assuring him that the family was back of him financially. He agreed to come and the family members contributed each as he could towards moving the family north.

In contrast were those families without such *esprit de corps* whose sibling informants had felt economically insecure. They spoke of lack of funds creating competition among the members of the family; of older children having always resented the "sacrifices" they had to make for the younger ones; of children not being able to work in proportion to the work they make; and "when size makes the struggle for life paramount, the responsibilities are too much."

A second difference between the two groups of informants lay in the extent to which their families stressed nonmaterial values and found satisfactions in them. In families where highest values were nonmaterial ones, the informants, again, felt that a large family is much more conducive to economic security than is a small one for the simple reason that in a large family one learns early that the best things in life are free. They wrote:

> If parents "think poor" then the children will be discontented about their lot and worried about the future.

I think that a large family could make for the maximum of economic security, with skillful handling on the part of the parents. With very little money, it is possible to live a kind of life which, while frugal, is not niggardly and is rich in imagination and things of the spirit.

One informant expressed great satisfaction over not having been able to spend money frivolously for family entertainment, because they had, together, discovered the wealth of free "cultural opportunities" which the community provided.

In the material on economic security and insecurity, the role of the parent assumed much greater significance than it had in connection with emotional security. Parents were applauded for instilling "higher values"; for being good managers; for fostering sibling coöperation without exploiting certain of the siblings. Or, they were accused of being the reason for the economic insecurity of the whole family since they had none of these virtues. It is interesting to note that the informants in these particular large families expressed a greater need of economic leadership than of emotional leadership from parents.

Finally, four cases felt that the large family produced economic security and emotional insecurity. They were among the informants who had come to believe that life is an individual battle. One had to "stand on one's own feet and depend upon no one" and "make one's own way." The four had been successful in so doing, quite early, and now felt economically secure in themselves. They expressed resentment against any siblings who happened to ask them for help and a great reluctance to, and humiliation about, having ever to ask for help for themselves.

3. *Insecurity in the Large Family.* Although seventeen (18.9 per cent) of the informants felt that the large family resulted in both emotional and economic insecurity, they were very cryptic as to why this should be so. An examination of such case materials as they gave showed no significant differences

between their families and others so far as stated emotional and economic problems were concerned. Certain "possibly influencing factors" in these cases were then examined. These were: sex of informant; size of family; birth order of informant; area in which family lived; religion; and occupation of father. Statistical analysis of the ninety cases was intended only as a search for pertinent questions, and some questions did arise.

(1) Are economic and emotional insecurity more closely related in the male than in the female? Is the male more oriented to the responsibilities of providing, economically; and does insufficiency in this area of his early family life disturb his emotional security more than it does his sister's? Or does a large family group offer greater emotional satisfactions for a girl, even in the face of economic hardship? Table 28 indicates that although almost the same percentage of male and female informants felt economically secure, the females showed a lower percentage of emotional security and of negative responses toward both emotional and economic insecurity.

TABLE 28

Security and Insecurity, by Sex

Sex	Emotional Security	Economic Security	Emotional and Economic Insecurity	Number of Cases
Male	72.0	52.0	28.0	25
Female	78.5	52.3	15.4	65

(2) Is the degree of largeness of a family related to security feelings in its members? If there is security in numbers in a primary group, as our informants suggest, is there more security in larger numbers? In order to inspect this, with a reasonable number of cases, the families were divided into two groups by the median size of family in the sample reporting. Exactly half the cases had seven or fewer children;

the other half, eight or more. Table 29 shows a higher percentage of the larger family informants feeling a sense of security.

TABLE 29

Security and Insecurity, by Family Size

Size	Emotional Security	Economic Security	Emotional and Economic Insecurity	Number of Cases
7 members, or under	73.3	42.2	24.4	45
8 members, or over	80.0	62.2	13.3	45

In an attempt to discover whether there was some point in family size which produced diminishing returns in security, a tabulation was made of individual family sizes. This, of course, made samples of very small numbers. Nevertheless, there was an increasing percentage of security responses with increasing family size, and a diminishing percentage of negative responses toward security. The one difference that appeared was that economic security was highest in the six-member families, and lowest in those with fourteen, fifteen, and sixteen members.

(3) Does one position in birth order cause more insecurity than another? In Table 30 the older children show the lowest rate of insecurity. Although both older and younger children, as informants, had pointed to the preferability of a middle position in the family (Chapter 10) the middle siblings ex-

TABLE 30

Security and Insecurity, by Birth Order

Birth Order	Emotional Security	Economic Security	Emotional and Economic Insecurity	Number of Cases
Older	86.2	58.6	3.5	29
Middle	75.0	41.7	20.8	24
Younger	70.3	54.1	29.7	37

pressed more economic insecurity than any of the others and more emotional insecurity than did their elders. Yet these elders were the siblings characterized as the "exploited." Though their security records were more positive in all respects, they were the ones who had most frequently been through the repeated experience of displacement through subsequent births, and who had served most time with the vulnerabilities of the large family—the economic ups and downs, the illnesses, deaths, separations, and increasing complexities of relationship. Did they feel secure through these experiences because they had been the first members of a, then, small family? Had they, in their earliest years, gotten the benefits of undivided attention and economic resources so that the pattern of security was indelibly printed upon them? An inspection of their case records makes this seem hardly likely. Some of these "elder children" (according to definition) were in families so large that being an older child meant being a third or fourth one in a family where siblings had come close together before the informant's birth and after it. With these, there had been a high degree of emotional and economic sharing from the moment they entered the family. There had also been a high degree of emotional and economic responsibility. Was it the latter, then, that created security—self-reliance and the ability to provide for one's dependents? Those younger children, who were so frequently designated as "pampered" by their siblings, expressed themselves as feeling the least emotionally secure, although they felt more economically secure than the middle siblings. These younger children had the advantage of economic help from elder and middle siblings; but they did not express feelings of economic security in as high a percentage as did the older siblings.

(4) Does the area of residence of the large family influence the security feelings of its members? Do some areas provide opportunities for maximum economic support of a large group? Do some areas have subjective values about

family size that penetrate into the large family's attitudes about itself? Many of the informants stated their convictions that cities and suburbs were not the healthiest locales for rearing a large family and that "the country" was its natural habitat. Table 31 serves to reinforce their opinions.

TABLE 31
Security and Insecurity, by Living Area

Area	Emotional Security	Economic Security	Emotional and Economic Insecurity	Number of Cases
Towns, Villages, Farm Villages, and Farms	83.7	55.1	12.2	49
Cities and Suburbs	67.5	50.0	27.5	40

(5) A number of the informants mentioned their religion as being more closely related to their security feelings than was the size of their family. This raised the question: Given a large family, does its religion influence the security of the children? Unfortunately, the cases of Jewish families, and of families with mixed religious parentage, were too few to tabulate in even this limited study. The bulk of the cases were Protestant and Catholic. Table 32 shows a higher percentage of security in the Catholic families. Again, this may have to do with family inner values, and with community attitudes on family size in relation to children's security. Other interpretations, also, are possible.

TABLE 32
Security and Insecurity, by Religion

Religion	Emotional Security	Economic Security	Emotional and Economic Insecurity	Number of Cases
Protestant	75.4	38.6	21.1	57
Catholic	87.5	75.0	8.3	24

(6) Occupation of the father, in terms both of status and income, seemed an important factor to analyze in relation to security. Occupations, in this sample, were so diversified as to provide very small numbers of cases. Only the four largest were tabulated. Table 33 shows the results.

TABLE 33

Security and Insecurity, by Father's Occupation

Occupation	Emotional Security	Economic Security	Emotional and Economic Insecurity	Number of Cases
Proprietor and Manager	91.7	75.0	8.3	12
Farmer	82.4	29.4	17.6	17
Skilled	77.3	72.7	9.1	22
Professional	76.5	35.3	23.5	17

Children of a professional parent fared least well in terms of security. These informants were children at a time when the birth rate of college graduates was not only the lowest of all educational groups, but had not yet started the increase that has occurred since the 1940 Census. Was the large family, then, unpopular and unwanted in the professional class, and did this reflect upon the security of the children? Were professional standards of living at a professional income level a great strain upon a large family? The children of farmers had high emotional security, lowest economic security, and low negative responses. Does this add to the evidence on the divorcement of large family security from economic hardships and add to that on the importance of the intra- and extra-group relationships? What is it about the large families of proprietors and managers that makes them experience the highest rate of security? Are these the people, who in an earlier era were economic individualists, who made their own way and welcomed children to further it? And were the children of skilled workmen, who struck a consistent pattern of medium security, in a position of having much financial confidence and comparatively little value judgment against family size?

Finally, the suggestions of several informants that the spacing of the children was related to insecurity led to an investigation of the cases in which this material was available. Two interesting situations came to light. First, insecurity was felt in families where children were greatly separated in age and could find no playmate but only "overseers" and "little nuisances." Second, it was felt in cases where one or two children were members of a small family for many years and then became increasingly depended upon by parents who had produced large families fairly late in life.

SUMMARY

The foregoing materials suggest that there are group factors which influence the security of children, over and above the more generally recognized individual parent-child relationships. The materials suggest, further, that a large family is a distinctive kind of group and that to study security in the small family system is not necessarily to understand it in a large family. Specifically, the following very tentative hypotheses are offered:

1. The large family system, because of its numbers, creates its own peculiar challenge to security, economically and emotionally. It also carries within it certain unique resources. The adjustment between the two seems to be related to the security feelings in the members of these families.

2. Within the separate large families there are individualized factors, such as sex, birth order, and spacing of children, which seem important in terms of security. The exact significance of them, however, relates only to the large family situation. Sex, birth order, and spacing of children may have quite different meanings in the small family.

3. The position of the large family in respect to other

societal groups seems to have some effect upon security, particularly as concerns the values, and the attitudes toward family size, of the neighborhood, religious, and occupational groups.

II. SENSE OF POSSESSION

It has long been a conviction of the authors that the way in which one regards money, real property, and other material possessions is an important part of the personality structure. At least two observations have resulted from a curiosity about human beings and their sense of possession. First, the common man—and even the academic man in his common moments—classifies individuals as "misers" or "spendthrifts," as "speculators" or "safe investors," as "spongers" or "too proud to accept help." Second, case records of marital conflicts usually reveal some "economic problems." Upon close analysis of these cases, many appear to have no economic problem at all. What troubles is the differing attitudes of the marital partners about material possessions. Difficulties arise over what belongs to whom; how much is to be shared; to what extent the present is expendable for future security; what is the emotional and traditional value of certain possessions; and what is the relative importance of material and nonmaterial values.

Theoretically, and logically, it would seem that a sense of possession is a part of the personality structure of every living human being. None can survive without having certain things to use when one has to have them. Whether these things are supplied by one's own efforts, by coöperative labor, or by the state, is beside the point—they are still essentials to survival. Because of this, the sense of possession, as a deeply ingrained part of the personality, may be likened to the sex instinct which is essential to the survival of the species. Important differences between them are, however, that the latter is inborn and the former is "learned"; and that the latter has been studied, ad infinitum, while the former has received relatively scant attention from social scientists.

Orthodox psychiatrists have related the sense of "possessiveness" to the struggle between basic urges and experiences encountered in specific personal relationships in very early years. At oral and anal stages of life, a child's personality may be set as "retentive." He may be the person who wants to "keep" and "hold," rather than to "give" and "let go." Furthermore, if frustrations become too deeply identified with other human beings, he may withdraw as much as possible from association with them and crave the possession of material objects.

Anthropologists have considered the sense of possession from the point of view of cultural conditioning of personality. A classic example is Dr. Benedict's comparison of three Indian tribes.[7] In one, the religio-ceremonial is the prime value of the society, and possessions are worked for only as they can be expended to fulfill ceremonial duties and acquire ceremonial roles. In a second, the living is very hard. Everyone wants material possessions, but anyone who has them and does not share them is suspect and the subject of attack. Therefore, everyone tries to accumulate possessions and to hide the fact of success. In the third, there is opportunity for acquiring a great deal of "wealth." These people have a strict sense of ownership to the point of obsession. One gains prestige by the amounts of material goods one can lend, at one hundred per cent interest. Anyone of any importance enters into this competition as a small child.

In child-management literature there is some stress on helping the child learn to share, and care for, his belongings. He has possessive and destructive tendencies that will out. The wise parent will not be shocked by them but will "use" them so that they can be expressed in ways that are least inconvenient to families and the society. Occasionally one meets a parent who has read a great deal of the literature and

[7] Ruth Benedict, *Patterns of Culture* (Boston: Houghton Mifflin Co., 1934).

who still asks, "Yes, but just how *do* I teach my child to share, and yet not have his playmates break, or steal, all his toys?" Such parents are realists, of necessity. They see that they are rearing children in a culture that knows all too little about the significance of a sense of possession and is ambivalent about what it thinks it does know.

Erich Fromm has commented upon this ambivalence in discussing American attitudes toward selfishness and self-interest. He writes:

> The doctrine that selfishness is the arch-evil and that to love oneself excludes loving others is by no means restricted to theology and philosophy, but it became one of the stock ideas promulgated in home, school, motion pictures, books; indeed all instruments of social suggestion as well. "Don't be selfish" is a sentence which has been impressed upon millions of children. . . . This picture . . . is in a certain sense one-sided. For besides the doctrine that one should not be selfish, the opposite is also propagandized in modern society: keep your own advantage in mind, act according to what is best for you; by so doing you will also be acting for the greatest advantage of all others. As a matter of fact, the idea that egotism is the basis of the general welfare is the principle on which competitive society has been built. It is puzzling that two such seemingly contradictory principles could be taught side by side in one culture; of the fact, however, there is no doubt. One result of this contradiction is confusion in the individual. Torn between the two doctrines, he is seriously blocked in the process of integrating his personality. This confusion is one of the most significant sources of the bewilderment and helplessness of modern man.[8]

This bewilderment about a sense of possession is apparent not only in learning children and worried parents. It is at the heart of many a citizen's wavering back and forth between the seemingly conflicting ideals inherent in capitalism and communism, in nationalism and "One World." For these

---

[8] Erich Fromm, *Man for Himself* (New York: Rinehart and Co., 1947), pp. 126-27.

reasons, and others, any additional information about the human's sense of possession would appear to be valuable.

In the present study there was an attempt to secure information about a sense of possession in a specific situation—the large family. Informants were asked: "Do you have a strong sense of possession? Do you think family size affects this?" As with other questions, they were encouraged to write out or talk out their feelings and ideas on this subject. The attempt was purely exploratory. It was hoped that even little material might create greater interest in the sociological aspects of attitudes and behavior around possessions.

Eighty-three informants gave material on the sense of possession in a large family. Forty-six felt they had a strong sense of possession, thirty-seven did not. The percentages were 55.4 and 44.6, respectively. There was some confusion in the informants' minds as to the meaning of "sense of possession." In spite of explanations, the more popular concept of "possessiveness" in respect to other human beings entered into the records. Three informants discussed only possessiveness toward other people; forty-five gave information on attitudes toward material possessions and money; and thirty-five included statements about both. Thus there were eighty informants who provided the data for the following analysis of (1) a sense of possession in the large family setting; (2) attitudes and how they were learned; (3) related personality types; and (4) the influence of sex, birth order, and family size upon sense of possession in the large family.

1. *The Setting.* Homes in which the children in these large families developed their sense of possession had certain features common to almost all of them. They contained many people, all with the normal human need, and wish, for personal belongings, for some things they could count on as being available for their own use when they wanted to use them. It was impossible for the parents to provide separate sets of everything for all the children, even in respect to

clothing and toys. Young children, then, if not discouraged or trained, would simply take and use and spoil as they wished. This is, of course, characteristic of children before they learn the difference between "mine" and "thine." In the large family, however, there was a continuing and growing pressure of demands against material possession, with increasing size of family and age of siblings. A student from a large family recently commented:

> My three sisters and I are all just one year apart in age. Two of us are in college and the other two are seniors in high school. We are all dating, and often we all go together. Dad can't buy four of everything we need to make us feel and look right. When we go to a dance together, this becomes a crisis. It is just as bad when we don't go together, for then the last ones to plan are the ones who get what is left. It is the same with my two younger brothers who are in junior high school. They need two sets of football equipment and two musical instruments in order to play in the school orchestra. In a few years, it will be two tuxedos. Now, we have one car. Mother, Dad and us four girls all drive. All too soon, both my brothers will be driving and wanting the car for dates, too. Our friends have started to make a joke about which one of us girls has gotten the "favorite" dress on any particular night. They don't see that it is not so funny, because they don't have to bother with that kind of thing.

In all of these homes sharing was inescapable, and was a problem consciously recognized. How, and whether, this problem was dealt with in the separate families seemed to determine what the children learned and what were their attitudes toward possession.

2. *The Attitudes and How They Were Learned.* The informants described how, in this setting, interaction with parents and with siblings had influenced their own attitudes and behavior around possession. The story was this. Parental management and sense of fairness were exceedingly important. Children acquired feelings for peaceful communality

or well-regulated, if limited, private ownership under good parental direction. Comments were:

Our parents laid down rules as to ownership—and no interference.

It was necessary for our parents to insist that each child keep his own possessions for his own use and to take care of clothing, books, rooms, etc., due to the fact that these could not be replaced or renewed without causing restrictions to be placed on the whole group.

Dad instilled in us the desire to save to own something.

Mother insisted that we all share and share alike. Everything belonged to all of us and we were not to be selfish.

The role of the parent who was aware of this special family problem and who did something constructive about it figured high in the comments of the informants. More frequent, however, were descriptions of how siblings learned together in sibling interaction. Even the wisest parents were not always at hand when the children began showing signs of acquisitiveness, and some parents simply did not bother with this problem. Then the children "taught" each other. In the majority of cases, very definite things were learned. First, there was much to be gained by sharing possessions. If you didn't let your brother use your baseball, you couldn't ride his bike. One girl wrote: "When you are the same clothes size as your sister, which I am, you are just as willing to let her wear your clothes as you are anxious to wear hers." It was interesting to note how many informants used the word "selfish" as a biting epithet, and how many of them spoke as though selfishness and a sense of possession were synonyms. Second, if all the children do not learn how to take care of things, no one has anything for very long. Thus, discriminations were made, in the sharing process, against members who were careless about belongings and until these members had learned their lessons. Third, sharing was in order, but if it were not regulated no one could ever be sure of the use of any possession at any particular time. This produced a sense of the importance of owning some few things personally and not having them touched without asking. These same possessions were important also, in bargaining for loans from other members.

Among themselves, the siblings set up certain rules and proper modes of behavior. The mother of an only child described her own experience with nine other siblings and contrasted it with her daughter's situation.

These things were very much easier to settle in the large family than they are in small families. If Jim wanted to use or play with something belonging to Bill or Olive he would tentatively ask permission, and have permission granted or denied by the owner of the possession. If the no was too decided, or if he thought there might still be hope if handled properly, he would return again with one of his own possessions and offer it in exchange for the loan of the one he wanted. Occasionally there would be an argument but usually the owner's decision would be accepted without any particular rancor. The teasing to gain one's end which an only child, for instance, indulges in when dealing with its parents was almost entirely absent in our family. The children teased each other as testing and growing pains; were much more expert in deciding what was fair between themselves, and with much less friction than can be worked out when the relationship is with parent and child rather than brother and sister.

One record reveals a pleasant bit of jockeying within the confines of sibling law:

At our house . . . whoever cut a piece of candy or cake, or divided anything . . . was bound to take the smaller piece. Because of this a family friend was once highly amused to hear my sister and me one day in this conversation: "You cut it." "No, you cut it." "No, I don't want to, you cut it." Finally the friend cut the candy in one-half.

A third record shows the firm distinction between "lending" and "giving" in one family:

My bicycle was mine, my skates mine, my books mine, and if my brothers wanted to use any of them they had to ask me. If they could not ask me . . . they did not dare to take them. By the same token I could not use their things without asking their permission. Although I guarded zealously the privilege to grant permission to my brothers to use my things I don't think I ever said "no" unless I were angry with them. Yet when I outgrew the toys, they then became a younger brother's with my having no claim any longer. . . . When my sister came along, there was a shelf full of dolls which I had collected, one a year. Today no doll is whole, so hard did she play with them. I don't regret that she literally destroyed them. I didn't lend them to her; I gave them to her, without a thought of the fact that they were being given. It was as if I had been saving for her what was rightfully her own.

3. *Personality Types.* Experiences with possessions in the large family appeared to be productive of certain attitudes and behavior patterns that became so well incorporated into the personalities of the informants as to identify them with "a personality type."

First, there were those who felt they had little sense of possession. What they meant was that they had developed a thoroughgoing communal attitude and pattern of behavior. They felt it was mean, wrong, or stingy to consider things as one's own; they felt completely free about using whatever they wished at any time, and they gave freely. Most of these informants mentioned this as indicative of strong family feeling. One of them related it to religious principles, saying that nothing belongs to any individual but is merely loaned by God. They decried attitudes toward possessions which they felt were characteristic of small families. Several records in this category were of particular interest. One of them stated very clearly that the sense of sharing and using, communally, was very strong in the family but that it did not extend outside it. The children, here, resented very much having to share anything with even close relatives who were not immediate family members. In another case, a boy told of the troubles waiting for him when he went to college. He discovered that having no sense of possession meant also having no sense of other people's possessions. His college roommates found him very difficult in this respect. He partly appreciated their point of view, but experienced some disillusion about other people's unwillingness to have him use their belongings as he wished. A woman from a small family, who had married a man from a large family, mentioned this same problem. She said, "I have a very strong sense of possession, which I work hard at to control . . . while my husband and children regard possessions lightly."

There were also informants marked by a very precise sense of "mine" and "thine" and a respect for both. They were quite willing to share with people who had the same kind of respect, but not with others. They were also willing to borrow, if necessary, but did so as little as possible because of the grave feelings of responsibility for other people's belongings. Many of these came from families in which the children had earned their own money fairly early and had thus learned the price, and care, of possessions. Others had learned to appreciate what they thought was the high value of such attitudes and behavior because of the well-regulated system at home which had made personal relationships run smoothly. Several of them reported thus:

I would no more think of getting something out of a desk drawer in the home of one of my married brothers than stealing. We never did and never do open letters addressed to one family member, even though these are often read aloud to all the others. From my observation of people, I consider that large families tend to develop respect for one another's property to a greater degree than very small families do.

You learn the value of owning because you have to help earn.

It is safe for me to say that because I grew up in a large household my sense of personal ownership is strong but also a sharing

Selected By-products of Large Family Living

(if only temporary) has its place and needed place on occasions. To get something or hold something at the expense of another is distasteful and was impressed early and continuously. That would never do. On the other hand, charity and the acting for others has its limits and is, in my case, often thought out before it is allowed to take place.

Finally, there were the informants who came out of their large family experience determined to get something for themselves—something they could really call their own and share with no one. They spoke of having been "forced to share" all their lives. They mentioned with great feeling the few things, or the one thing, that had been exclusively their own: "A ball my mother made me by filling an old sock with rags—it was mine and I could play with it whenever I wanted to"; "at least you could claim your own horse or dog personally"; "the memory of a special French doll survives." One informant wrote that the large family fostered early an emphatic identification with one's own possessions. "True, many things are used in common, but this makes a person all the more alert to claiming things, to making them his own, putting his own stamp on them." An interesting record included this:

> I want to have a home equal to none. I buy many things of value to have about my house and take pride in showing it off. I also take great pleasure in owning furs and diamonds, but this, I feel, is just normal in all women. My sister, who is the next oldest after me, really is very desirous of possessions. She will cause herself to go into debt so as to have new things, either for her body or for her house. She just can't keep herself from buying. Her marriage turned out to be unhappy because of this desire. She married a man twenty years older than herself so that she could have money. She was miserable and when her children were old enough she left her husband and got a divorce. I feel this was caused by her not having anything of her own in childhood.

It is not intended to suggest that only the large family

produces such types. This is obviously untrue. The point is that in viewing the whole situational experience of certain individuals around possessions, one can see how firmly the results have become imprinted in the adult personality. It would be very useful to have a comparative study of members of the small family system in order to find what differing experiences produce different, and the same, types and to see whether one kind of family is more prone to develop a certain personality type than is the other.

The weight of evidence from the analyses of personality types in the large family is that it has developed a rather strong sense of possession in the children—to a greater extent than the informants themselves reported when confronted with the bare question. For, among the different types, there were only seven cases which revealed a continuing pattern of communality about possessions. All others fell into the last two types. Those who felt they had a strong sense of "mine" and "thine" seemed happy and contented about it. The others showed great bitterness, or tried, unsuccessfully, to conceal bitterness.

4. *Sense of Possession in Relation to Selected Factors.* Male informants reported a strong sense of possession less frequently than did the females (43.5 per cent and 56.1 per cent). Perhaps this is a mere sex-determined difference. But the case records suggested a social one. For girls, articles of personal adornment are among the most important of possessions, and clothing and accessories, or the lack of them, were mentioned by almost every female informant. They were not mentioned at all by the males. It was to a large extent the lack of such female weapons to fight a successful social battle that rankled, or that made the girls guard very carefully what they had. It may well be that imposed social expectations for the female make for their stronger sense of possession in the large family.

By order of birth, the percentage reporting a strong sense

of possession ran as follows: older children, 61.5 per cent; middle children, 34.8 per cent; younger children, 58.1 per cent. Again, as in so many other analyses, the middle children seem to stand in a special situational position. Perhaps, here, they do not have to "expend" as the older ones do, nor yet receive the last leftovers as the younger ones often do.

According to size of family, 48.9 per cent of the informants with seven or fewer siblings reported a strong sense of possession. The percentage for those with eight or more siblings was 57.1. This serves to reinforce the former impression that there is something within the large group which fosters this strong sense. It might be pointed out also that while the sense of possessiveness was strongest in the larger groups, so were both emotional and economic security (see p. 224). This appears a contradiction to the usual assumption that possessive feelings grow from insecurity.

SUMMARY

Although the materials on a sense of possession are too scant to permit any statement of "findings," consistencies within the records point in the direction of certain "possibilities."

1. The majority of informants felt that the large family tended to produce a strong sense of possession. The percentage of such reports from the largest families was higher than that from the smaller ones.

2. The reasons the informants gave for this lay in factors within the life situation which may be considered "sociological." Given a young child, with no sense of possession as initial equipment, he learned in a group where there were many people and relatively few possessions. The importance of ownership and sharing were highlighted, of necessity. In interaction with other family members, certain attitudes toward property and behavior toward property were formed. These varied from one family situation to another, with the

size of the family and the sex and birth order of the children.

3. It seemed possible to delineate three personality types as emerging from the integration of the individual's attitudes and behavior patterns in respect to possession.

III. ADJUSTMENT OF SIBLINGS

Perhaps the final test of what large family living does to children is the extent to which they develop into well-adjusted adults. Accepting for the moment this measure of adjustment, what is the rate of success of large family child rearing? What proportion of its products are well adjusted?

An effort was made to answer this question as specifically as the resources of the present study permitted. To do so, each sibling informant was asked the following question: "Considering your brothers and sisters one by one, do you consider them (a) well adjusted, (b) not well adjusted, (c) medium adjusted?" The informants were invited to rate themselves along with the other siblings. Many did so, but a few abstained, in which case an effort was made to find someone who knew the informant who would do so. In case of last resort, the authors made such a rating if the informant was at all personally known.

The question naturally presents itself: What is the value of such a rating? Manifestly, most of the persons making it had no professional skill nor used any scientific criteria. Moreover, there is the influence of their prejudices to consider. On the other hand, the informants who rated the other siblings had lived, and lived on close and intimate family terms, with the persons whom they rated. And what better test of adjustment than close contact over an extended period of time can there be?

Another question that arises is this: How was adjustment defined? Many informants asked this question before proceeding with the rating of siblings. The explanation that was given to all was as follows. If a person is capable of arranging his relations to other people and social situations with reasonable propriety and success, he is a well-adjusted person. Another word that might be used instead of adjustable is adaptable. Or, stated in still another way, if a person has a perspective of himself and his fellows of a kind and sufficient in amount to get along reasonably well with people, that person may be termed a well-adjusted person. The emphasis is not upon the innate traits of the person as much as upon his attitudes and patterns of response to social situations.

Proceeding on this basis, adjustment ratings from informants in fifty-eight families were obtained for a total of 457 siblings, of whom 235 were males and 222 were females. This was the total number of siblings in these families over twelve years of age. Ratings for one or more, but not for all, siblings were obtained in the other forty-two families, but since the record was not complete for all siblings these families and ratings were not included in the summary that follows.

MAIN FINDINGS DERIVED FROM ADJUSTMENT DATA

1. Approximately two out of three siblings were reported as well adjusted, one out of four was medium in his adjustment, and one out of nine was poorly adjusted (see Table 34).

Is this a good or a poor record? What percentages of persons in the general population are well, medium, and poorly adjusted? It would be very helpful if one knew. Restricted studies of selected groups of persons are available giving information pertaining to adjustment, but these scarcely serve for comparable purposes here. As a matter of interest, the reader might recall the experience of the armed forces in World War II. Out of 15,000,000 men called to service, 1,825,000 were rejected for military service because of psychiatric disorders, and another 600,000 were discharged foi neuropsychiatric reasons. These two groups constitute 16.2 per cent of the total number of men called to service. To these, Dr. Eugene Meyer, Chairman of the National Committee on Mental Hygiene, adds another 500,000 who attempted to evade the draft and all war responsibility. The inclusion of this group would raise the total of psychiatric failures to almost one out of five.[9]

This comparison is made merely for suggestive purposes. Obviously, the two sets of data are based on quite different types of observation. Moreover, our sample lacks completely the representative character of the millions of men in the armed services. The comparison, however, does serve to raise the question whether boys reared in large families tend to show higher rates of adjustment in later life than those reared in smaller families.

2. A larger percentage of male siblings than of women in our study are well adjusted and of medium adjustment. The percentage of poorly adjusted siblings was higher among women than among men (see Table 34). The differences do not appear to be significant.

TABLE 34

Adjustment Totals and Percentages, by Totals, Sex, and Percentages

Adjustment Status	Total	Per Cent	Males	Per Cent	Females	Per Cent
Well adjusted	287	62.8	151	64.2	136	61.2
Medium adjusted	119	26.0	64	27.2	55	24.8
Poorly adjusted	51	11.2	20	8.6	31	14.0
	457	100.0	235	100.0	222	100.0

3. Inbetween children show higher rates of good and medium adjustment than do first-born and last-born children.

[9] Eugene Meyer in Edward A. Strecker, *Their Mothers' Sons* (Philadelphia: J. B. Lippincott Co., 1946), p. 6.

Of the latter two groups, the last born have the better record. First-born siblings have the highest percentage of poor adjustment, and by a wide margin. First-born daughters in particular have a poor record of adjustment (see Table 35).

TABLE 35

Adjustment, First Born, Inbetween, and Last Born, by Totals, Sex, and Percentages

Adjustment Status	Total	Per Cent	Males	Per Cent	Females	Per Cent
First born:						
Well adjusted	33	56.9	17	58.6	16	55.2
Medium adjusted	15	25.8	8	27.6	7	24.1
Poorly adjusted	10	17.3	4	13.8	6	20.7
Inbetween children:						
Well adjusted	222	65.1	115	67.2	107	62.9
Medium adjusted	83	24.3	43	25.1	40	23.5
Poorly adjusted	36	10.6	13	7.7	23	13.6
Last born:						
Well adjusted	32	55.2	19	54.3	13	56.5
Medium adjusted	21	36.2	13	37.1	8	34.8
Poorly adjusted	5	8.6	3	8.6	2	8.7

4. Adjustment ratings classified by specific order of birth show that first-born children have the poorest record, with the second born as a close second. Fourth-born children have by far the best record, with nine out of ten identified as well adjusted. It will be recalled from the preceding chapter that fourth in the order of birth was the coveted position, as indicated in the preferences expressed by siblings who were dissatisfied with their order of birth. Table 36 shows the percentages of adjustment by rank order of birth for totals and for male and female siblings separately. It will be noted that higher rates of adjustment for males prevail at all birth orders except at fourth, sixth, and tenth place.

TABLE 36
Adjustment Ratings, by Rank Order of Birth, by Sex, and by Percentages

Adjustment Status	Total	Per Cent	Males	Per Cent	Females	Per Cent
First born:						
Well adjusted	33	56.9	17	58.6	16	55.2
Medium adjusted	15	25.8	8	27.6	7	24.1
Poorly adjusted	10	17.3	4	13.8	6	20.7
Second born:						
Well adjusted	39	67.2	18	78.3	21	60.0
Medium adjusted	9	15.5	3	13.0	6	17.1
Poorly adjusted	10	17.3	2	8.7	8	22.9
Third born:						
Well adjusted	34	58.6	22	62.9	12	52.2
Medium adjusted	16	27.6	9	25.7	7	30.4
Poorly adjusted	8	13.8	4	11.4	4	17.4
Fourth born:						
Well adjusted	51	87.9	24	85.7	27	90.0
Medium adjusted	4	6.9	2	7.15	2	6.6
Poorly adjusted	3	5.2	2	7.15	1	3.4
Fifth born:						
Well adjusted	39	67.2	18	72.0	21	63.7
Medium adjusted	13	22.4	5	20.0	8	24.2
Poorly adjusted	6	10.4	2	8.0	4	12.1
Sixth born:						
Well adjusted	28	48.3	16	43.2	12	57.1
Medium adjusted	24	41.3	19	51.4	5	23.8
Poorly adjusted	6	10.4	2	5.4	4	19.1
Seventh born:						
Well adjusted	23	65.7	18	69.2	5	55.5
Medium adjusted	9	25.7	6	23.1	3	33.3
Poorly adjusted	3	8.6	2	7.7	1	22.2
Eighth born:						
Well adjusted	14	51.8	7	58.3	7	46.7
Medium adjusted	11	40.8	4	33.3	7	46.7
Poorly adjusted	2	7.4	1	8.4	1	6.6
Ninth born:						
Well adjusted	11	68.7	5	71.4	6	66.7
Medium adjusted	4	25.0	2	28.6	2	22.2
Poorly adjusted	1	6.3	0	0.0	1	11.1
Tenth and over:						
Well adjusted	15	48.4	6	46.1	9	50.0
Medium adjusted	14	45.2	6	46.1	8	44.5
Poorly adjusted	2	6.4	1	7.8	1	5.5

THE POORLY ADJUSTED

Fifty-one siblings, it will be remembered, were identified by brothers or sisters as poorly adjusted. Twenty of these were males and thirty-one were females. As already noted, this is 8.6 per cent of the total number of males in the fifty-eight families and 14 per cent of the females. Approximately one out of every nine siblings was rated as poorly adjusted.

Classified by families, it was found that there were five families with three siblings each who were poorly adjusted; eight, with two each; and twenty, with one each. In other words, thirty-one of the poorly adjusted siblings were found in thirteen families; the total number was confined to thirty-three families. Twenty-five of the fifty-one families had no poorly adjusted sibling members.

The case records of the thirty-three families with poorly adjusted sibling members were read carefully with reference to any information that might bear on the lack of adjustment of a child member. From this analysis, the following facts emerge.

1. Thirteen of these families contained positive, and for the most part critical, references to an autocratic, domineering father or mother or both. These thirteen families contained twenty-four poorly adjusted siblings. Most of these siblings were in the older birth orders, and it seems reasonable to suggest that, as the older children, they had to bear the brunt of the parental domination.

2. Supplementary to these were five additional families where the comments were not directed so much at the domineering behavior of the father as upon the exploitation of the children. In these five families, the siblings who were poorly adjusted were oldest daughters who were made to carry much of the burden and responsibility for rearing the

younger children. In two of these cases, the sibling who rated them as poorly adjusted referred to the fact that they were suffering from persecution complexes.

3. Oversolicitous or irresponsible mothers were stressed in six of these families, and there were ten poorly adjusted children in them. In addition, there were four more families where as many siblings were reported as being spoiled to the point of poor adjustment, not by a parent, but by older brothers and sisters. All of these poorly adjusted children in these ten families were in the middle or lower birth orders. Criticism of the parents on the foregoing scores included, in a majority of cases, charges of favoritism toward some sibling or siblings.

4. There were three families in which four sibling members were identified as poorly adjusted, due to physical defects or long-continued illness.

5. In the remaining six families, with eight poorly adjusted siblings, no pertinent information could be found in the case records.

In presenting the foregoing summary, it seems important to add that there was not one family in which more than three children were poorly adjusted. It seems obvious, therefore, that the factors involved in lack of personal adjustment are at least individual, so that the factors that have been mentioned must be thought of as general and predisposing rather than specific and personal in their operation. Special features in a few cases can best be indicated by brief case summaries.

The first family is one with ten children, two of whom were rated as poorly adjusted and four as medium. The father is described as a strong man, who spoke very little, accepted the financial responsibility for his children, but showed very little interest otherwise. His temper was such as to interfere seriously with the happiness of the family. No one could assume any responsibility around the house so long as he lived. He completely dominated the family life and would brook no interference of any kind. The mother was easy-going, hard-working, and completely cowed by her much older husband. The two oldest boys left home at sixteen, went into the armed forces, and never returned to live at home. The two oldest sisters early became interested in church work. All of the children but one were described as timid and shy, and showed other signs of having been cowed by their father. The one thing that has helped the children has been the fact that they have stuck together closely, "helping each other over the tough spots."

The next family is one with thirteen children. The informant identified only one as poorly adjusted but ten as being of medium adjustment. The author was inclined to think that the term "medium" in several of these cases was questionable. The whole life of this family was dominated by the father's sternness. He ruled his family with a rod of iron, utilizing corporal punishment with frequency and severity. Apparently the entire family lived under the shadow of fear. The informant repeatedly spoke of not daring to do this or that; about being punished, and punishment invariably was physical. Temptations to rebel seemed to be constant among the siblings, but the informant said: "If we would have gotten out of line, we would have been beat to death." Even during the interview, the informant, who was middle-aged and no longer living at home, would look behind her before speaking of her father. Most of the children left home as early as possible, going their own way, and having almost no contact with each other in the years since.

The third family was one of six children, two of whom were reported as poorly adjusted and three as medium so. Both parents seemed to be immature, and were said to be always at cross purposes. "As I approached adolescence," said the informant, "I resented my father's strict control and harsh methods of punishment. To this day, I do not feel at ease with my father. During the early years of my life, my mother's temper caused me to bear the brunt of much harsh treatment, such as knocking me on the floor and kicking me. I may have deserved some punishment, but not of this kind or in such bitter anger. I used to go upstairs and try to hang myself, but never quite had the nerve or the power. For a time I turned to my mother for comfort from my father, but after I left home to work elsewhere, I rebelled against my mother's domination, and now, years later, I still wake up shuddering from dreams in which I have bitter conflicts with my mother, although we now get along well together the very few times we do see each other."

The final case is that of a family with more than a dozen children, three of whom are not well adjusted and seven only medium so. Concerning this family, the informant writes in part: "One thing which has been the plague of our family has been my mother's devotion to Child Psychology. She considers herself an authority on this subject. She devotes her time to reading all the latest books in this field and arguing theories with anyone who will listen. She spends much time with groups of people interested in child problems, and has served as leader in some of them. Rather than spend time with her own children, she spends it in reading about children in general. Most of us resent this, particularly since she does not practice anything of which she preaches except on her one pet daughter. My mother enjoys posing before people as being the mother of 'so many children' rather than in living with those that are her own."

SUMMARY

The personal adjustment of 457 large family siblings, as made by the informants in fifty-eight families, shows the following results.

1. Approximately two out of three siblings are reported as

well adjusted, one out of four was medium in his adjustment, and one out of nine was poorly adjusted.

2. A larger proportion of male siblings than of women were well adjusted, and of medium adjustment.

3. Inbetween children show higher rates of good and medium adjustment than do the first and last born. Of the latter two groups, the last born have the better record.

4. First-born children have the poorest record and fourth-born by far the best record.

5. Poorly adjusted children, considered as a whole, tend to be grouped in homes in which the father is domineering, or the mother is ineffective and irresponsible, in which the children are exploited, and where health problems abound.

· 12 ·

Family Formation in the Next Generation

ONE TEST of a social system is the extent to which it perpetuates itself. Translating this general observation into terms of the present study, it suggests the question: To what extent does the large family tend to reproduce itself? What is the family behavior of children who grow up in large families? Are they given to marrying more or less than other persons? Do they in turn have large families, thus continuing the family tradition; do they have smaller families than commonly prevail, as if in resentment against their family experiences; or do they conform to the general social pattern of family size prevailing at the time of their own child-bearing span? What differences in family size appear on the basis of age, sex, and order of birth? These are questions that inevitably suggest themselves, and it is to a consideration of them that this chapter is devoted.

MARITAL STATUS OF LARGE FAMILY SIBLINGS

In keeping with the practice of the United States Bureau of the Census and various scientific studies, marital status is reckoned customarily in terms of percentages of the population fourteen years of age and over. This practice, accordingly, is followed here. In the present study, there were 764 persons who had grown up in the hundred families who were fourteen years of age and over and whose marital status had been reported. Table 37 summarizes these data by number, sex, marital status, and per cent, for these siblings, and the comparable percentages for the population of the United States for the years 1920, 1930, 1940, and 1950.

TABLE 37

Marital Status, 764 Large Family Siblings, Fourteen Years of Age and Over, by Number, Sex, Per Cent, and Comparable Percentages, U.S. Population, Fourteen Years of Age and Over, 1920, 1930, 1940, 1950[1]

Sex	Marital Status	Large Family Siblings NUMBER	PER CENT	Comparable Percentages, U.S. Population 1950	1940	1930	1920
Male	Ever married	278	72.0	73.7	65.2	64.1	62.9
Male	Single	108	28.0	26.2	34.8	35.8	36.9
Female	Ever married	251	66.4	79.9	72.4	71.6	70.5
Female	Single	127	33.6	20.1	27.6	28.4	29.4
Both	Ever married	529	69.2	76.9	68.8	67.8	66.8
Both	Single	235	30.8	23.1	31.1	32.1	33.2

Several facts stand out from this tabular summary. First, more males than females proportionately, reared in large families, have ever been married. The difference, 5.6 per cent, is a considerable one, and all the more striking when compared with the percentages for the general population, where those for women ever married are consistently higher, and by as much as 7.5 points. Combining these two differentials, the percentage of women fourteen years of age and over and reared in large families who were reported as having ever married is approximately 13 per cent lower than for the corresponding female population in the country as a whole.

Possible reasons for this appeared in the comments made by women informants during the course of the study. The social activities of girls in large families, they pointed out,

[1] U.S. Bureau of the Census, *U.S. Census of Population: 1950*, Vol. II, "Characteristics of the Population," Pt. 1, chap. B (Washington, D.C.: U.S. Government Printing Office, 1952), pp. 1-97.

were interfered with and limited by the family chores imposed upon them. During the "courtship years," when other girls are out socializing with boys, large family girls are at home doing housework, taking care of the younger children, and in various ways sharing the responsibilities of a large household. Boys in these families tend to escape these and are more free to step out during the "courtship years." Of particular significance in this connection is the practice, seemingly followed in many large families, of "sacrificing" one of the girls to the care of the family. This is the dutiful daughter, the good girl, who stays at home with mother, who looks after father, who works to send a brother through college, and in various other ways devotes herself to her family to the exclusion of her own marriage and family development.

Another comment frequently made by female informants concerned the fact that they had to wear hand-me-downs and/or did not have the kind and variety of clothes that other girls had. Limitations of this kind may have an effect upon matrimonial chances. The female of the species, while more deadly than the male, needs the appropriate plumage to achieve her ends. Clothes, let it be remembered, serve many functions other than protection against the weather, and a lack of proper adornment affects attitudes, conceptions of one's role, feelings of self-confidence, as well as bodily warmth. One of our informants, the oldest of a large family, spoke with great emotion of the fact that, thirty years ago, she had to wear an old dress at her high school commencement exercises, and of the psychological trauma and social withdrawal that followed that experience.

Finally, one wonders if the very familism of the large family may not at times predispose some of the girls in such families to develop a luke-warm attitude toward forming families of their own. This may work in two ways. One would be to see it as resulting from the very happiness of some large families, where the members have such a good life and develop such strong ingroup feelings that they are reluctant to leave it. We have encountered cases among our families where this seemed quite evident. On the other hand, there were families where the daughters seemed to be fed up with family life and were not inclined to jump hastily from one frying pan into another. As one woman informant put it: "By the time I was eighteen, I had changed so many diapers and blown so many noses that I wanted to do other things than marry and keep on doing more of the same." The large number of childless marriages among large family siblings, pointed out later in this chapter, may be of significance in this connection.

A second fact to be noted in Table 37 concerns the percentage of large family sons who have married. This percentage is relatively high, especially when compared with the percentages of the general population for the Census years 1920 and 1930. Such comparison is more proper than with the year 1950, for our sample is made up largely of older men whose marrying years were found largely in those earlier decades and the conditions and practices which then prevailed. In fact, the Census figures for 1950 on marital status are so far out of line with those of previous Census enumerations that one cannot but wonder whether factors other than an increase in the proportion of those married, and conceivably of a methodological kind, have not been operative. Large family sons, then, seem more prone to marry than males in general, just as large family girls do so to a lesser extent. Concerning the reasons for this higher percentage among the sons, one can only speculate. Is it because they are more inclined by cultural conditioning to be the marrying kind, or are they stimulated to marry by a desire to escape from the hecticness of their own parental home situations? Unfortunately, our case material contains no objective data bearing on this.

MARRIAGES OF OLDER SIBLINGS: A SPECIAL KIND?

Reference has been made repeatedly in the preceding pages to the fact that the oldest or an older one of the children in a large family develops marked habits of accountability, aiding the parents in their family duties, sharing responsibilities, and taking over much of the rearing of the younger siblings. Many a younger child in the large family finds an older brother or sister to be more of a parent than the biological one has the opportunity to be. Most often this is the oldest child; often, however, it may be one or several of the older children.

One wholly unexpected hypothesis formulated in the course of the present study concerned the kind of marriage that these responsible, often prematurely responsible, older children made. Over and over, in gathering the family data, it was mentioned that this particular sibling, if a girl, had married a man younger than herself, or a widower with children, or a man markedly dependent upon her. Similarly, if the responsible sibling was a son, he would be likely to have married a widow with children, or some clinging, dependent, or irresponsible woman. It is as though, having grown up to "mother" younger brothers and sisters, and having carried the responsibility for the care of others, this pattern became so habitual that a marital partner was selected that involved its continuance. You have been *the* responsible one in the family in which you grow up. You continue to be so in the family you form.

The case of Jane Hartel is an excellent illustration. Jane is the oldest of a large family. From early age on, she was the responsible child, acting as the parental surrogate in many ways. After graduation from high school she soon found exacting but relatively remunerative employment. Yet for several years she continued to carry many of her home household burdens, as well as spending some of her salary to buy things for her younger brothers and sisters. At the age of twenty-five she married a college graduate three years her junior. It was she who obtained a scholarship and supplied the money for him to continue his studies. She supported him while he floundered about in a series of occupational ventures. Now that he has found his niche, it is the wife who, despite her ill health, handles all finances, makes all decisions, sees to it that he gets to work on time, takes his clothes to the tailor although he passes his shop several times a day, and in many other ways "mothers" him as she did her younger brothers and sisters.

How typical are marriages of older, responsible siblings of this kind? Our statistics here are not as complete as one could wish, mainly because the hypothesis was not formulated until the study was considerably under way. Information, however, was obtained for thirty-eight older siblings who were characterized as the, or one of the, responsible older children, and twenty-nine of them were found to have made marriages of this kind. This study was supplemented by data from twelve large families not included in the one hundred cases, and seven of the responsible siblings in them made marriages of this kind, so that, of the total number of fifty, thirty-six, or about three out of four, substantiated the hypothesis that older, responsible siblings in large families make marriages in which they continue their responsibility role.

CHILDREN BORN TO LARGE FAMILY SIBLINGS

A second and more crucial test of the perpetuating power of the large family system is to be found in the size of the families of married persons who have been reared in large families. Do large family children have large families in turn, thus maintaining a type of family life they have known; do they conform to the prevailing type as to size; or do they tend to have families that are smaller than those in the population as a whole? Complete data on the number of children ever born to 529 married siblings reared in the hundred large families are recorded in our case material. Of these, 251 are women and 278 are men. In regard to the married women reared in large families, the information notes the number of children ever born to them; in the case of the men, it is the number of children that their wives have had born to them. Adopted children and children from a previous marriage of the wives of large family reared males are not included.

TABLE 38

251 Married Women Reared in Large Families, Fourteen Years of Age and Over, and Number of Children Ever Born, by Per Cent, and Corresponding Percentages for the United States in 1940 [2]

Number of Children Ever Born	Number of Married Women, Reared in Large Families, 14 Years and Over	Per Cent	Per Cent, Total Female Population, U.S., 14-74 Years Old, 1940
None	48	19.1	20.2
One	55	21.9	21.6
Two	70	27.9	19.5
Three	44	17.5	12.9
Four	24	9.5	8.4
Five	6	2.3	5.6
Six and over	4	1.5	11.7
Total	251	99.7	99.9

Table 38 reveals certain very significant facts:

1. Approximately one out of five of these married women reared in large families was childless. This is in line with the percentage for the population at large.

2. Almost half (49.8 per cent) had given birth to one or two children. This exceeds to a considerable extent the percentage (41.1) for women in the population at large.

[2] U.S. Bureau of the Census, *Differential Fertility for States and Large Cities* (Washington, D.C.: U.S. Government Printing Office, 1943), p. 2.

3. Combining those with one, two, or three children, which constitutes the small family system of contemporary society, the total for large family reared women is 67.3, as against 54.0 in the general population.

4. Most striking are the differences in the larger family brackets. Only 1.5 per cent of our sample, all of whom came from families with six or more children, have borne as many as six children, whereas in the population at large the percentage is 11.7. If five or more children are considered, the percentages are 3.8 and 17.3, respectively.

5. The outstanding conclusion to be derived from this table is that the 251 married women reared in large families show a considerably higher percentage of small families and a smaller one of large families than are found in the corresponding female population in the entire United States.

Table 39 shows the number of children born to the wives of 278 men reared in our large families. As has been noted, this is the number of children born to these women with these husbands. The table shows no marked changes from that of the daughters reared in large families. The percentage

TABLE 39

Wives of Husbands Who Were Reared in Large Families, by Number and Per Cent of Children Born to Both

Number of Children Ever Born	Number	Per Cent
None	55	19.8
One	58	20.8
Two	87	31.3
Three	48	17.3
Four	12	4.3
Five	7	2.4
Six and over	11	3.9
Total	278	99.8

of one-, two-, or three-children families is 69.4, as against 67.3 for the large family daughters, and there is a slight increase in the percentage of cases with six or more children, both at the expense of a decline in the percentage of four- and five-children families.

It will be pointed out at once that these cases include married women of various ages when child bearing has not been completed, and that age of wife and duration of marriage are important factors in determining the number of children ever born. Accordingly, the number of children ever born to the female siblings of our large families who were married and forty years of age and over was tabulated. Age forty, rather than the forty-five customarily taken, is utilized here to increase the size of our sample. There were 126 such cases in our records for whom the necessary data were available. Table 40 presents this in summary form, together with a Census Bureau study of the total number of children ever

TABLE 40

Children Ever Born to 126 Married Women Reared in Large Families, by Number and Per Cent, and Per Cent of the United States Cohort of 1920, and for White Women Forty Years of Age and Over Reporting in 1940[3]

Number of Children Ever Born	Number of Women, 40 Years and Over	Per Cent	U.S. Cohort of 1920	White Women, 40 and Over, in U.S., 1940
None	24	19.0	14.8	15.7
One	23	18.3	16.7	16.7
Two	37	29.4	20.0	19.1
Three	21	16.6	15.3	14.5
Four	14	11.1	10.6	10.3
Five	4	3.1	7.2	23.6
Six and over	3	2.4	15.3	

[3] Data on the cohort of 1920 and for white married women in the U.S. in 1940 are taken from a special report of the 1940 Census, *Differential Fertility, op. cit.*

born to 2,945,980 white women ever married and who were forty-five to forty-nine years old in 1940, and hence were in the midst of the bearing years in 1920. These are spoken of as the cohort of 1920. Included also are the percentages for 11,792,560 white women, forty years of age and over, in the United States in 1940.

Another question that may be asked is this: How does the reproductive record of the older married siblings reared in large families compare with those in the lower age groups? To answer this question, Table 41 is presented, showing the number of children ever born for 126 women forty years of age and over, and for 125 who are under forty.

TABLE 41

Number of Children Ever Born to 126 Married Women Reared in Large Families and Forty or More Years of Age, and for 125 Women Similarly Reared but Under Forty Years of Age

Number of Children Ever Born	Women 40 and Over		Women Under 40	
	NUMBER	PER CENT	NUMBER	PER CENT
None	24	19.0	24	19.2
One	23	18.3	32	25.6
Two	37	29.4	33	26.4
Three	21	16.6	23	18.4
Four	14	11.1	10	8.0
Five	4	3.1	2	1.6
Six and over	3	2.4	1	.8
Total	126	99.9	125	100.0

While this is an unusual procedure, and open to obvious criticism, the number of children born to the wives of the male siblings of the hundred families, forty years of age and over, and with these male siblings as the fathers, was also tabulated. Table 42 presents this information in tabular form. It will be noted that this pattern conforms to that of the women reared in large families.

272 The Large Family System

TABLE 42

Number of Children Born to Women Married to Large Family Male Siblings, Forty Years of Age and Over

Number of Children	Number of Fathers 40 and Over	Per Cent
None	30	18.0
One	34	20.3
Two	50	30.0
Three	28	16.7
Four	10	6.0
Five	7	4.1
Six and over	8	4.8
Total	167	99.9

SOME POSSIBLE DIFFERENTIALS

Before proceeding to an overall summary of the foregoing data, it seems advisable to consider certain possible differentials in the number and percentages of children born to married persons reared in large families. These possibilities may be stated in the form of questions. Are there significant variations on the basis of racial and religious groupings? Is there any relationship between the number of children and the size of the family in which one is reared? Is order of birth of any significance? Are other differentials of any importance? Each of these will be considered on the basis of the available data.

1. Are there significant variations in the number of children ever born on the basis of racial and religious groupings? Three tables are presented by way of answer to this question. Table 43 summarizes the data for 251 married women, fourteen years of age and over, reared in the hundred large families; Table 44 shows it for 126 of them who are forty years of age and over; and Table 45 for 167 wives of men reared in the large families, the men all being over forty years of age.

While one hesitates to draw conclusions from so limited a number of cases, these tables reveal no overall difference be-

TABLE 43

Children Ever Born to 251 Married Women Reared in Large Families, Fourteen Years of Age and Over, by Number, Per Cent, and Racial and Religious Grouping

Number of Children Ever Born	Number of Married Women	PER CENT	Protestant NUMBER	Protestant PER CENT	Roman Catholic NUMBER	Roman Catholic PER CENT	Jew NUMBER	Jew PER CENT	Negro NUMBER	Negro PER CENT	Protestant-Catholic NUMBER	Protestant-Catholic PER CENT
None	48	19.1	32	22.1	9	15.2	3	12.0	3	15.0	1	50.0
One	55	21.9	25	17.2	16	27.1	4	16.0	10	50.0		
Two	70	27.9	41	28.3	17	28.8	8	32.0	4	20.0		
Three	44	17.5	26	17.9	10	16.9	6	24.0	1	5.0	1	50.0
Four	24	9.5	13	9.0	5	8.4	4	16.0	2	10.0		
Five	6	2.3	5	3.4	1	1.7						
Six and over	4	1.5	3	2.1	1	1.7						
Total	251	99.7	145	100.0	59	99.8	25	100.0	20	100.0	2	100.0

TABLE 44

Children Ever Born to 126 Women Reared in Large Families, Forty Years of Age and Over, by Number, Per Cent, and Racial and Religious Grouping

Number of Children Ever Born	Number of Married Women	PER CENT	Protestant NUMBER	Protestant PER CENT	Roman Catholic NUMBER	Roman Catholic PER CENT	Jew NUMBER	Jew PER CENT	Negro NUMBER	Negro PER CENT	Protestant-Catholic NUMBER	Protestant-Catholic PER CENT
None	24	19.0	19	23.1	2	22.2	2	9.5	4	36.3	1	33.3
One	23	18.3	14	17.1	2	22.2	3	14.3	3	27.2		
Two	37	29.4	21	25.6	2	22.2	9	42.9	1	9.1	2	66.7
Three	21	16.6	14	17.1	2	22.2	4	19.0	3	27.2		
Four	14	11.1	8	9.8	0		3	14.3				
Five	4	3.1	4	4.9								
Six and over	3	2.4	2	2.4	1	11.1						
Total	126	99.9	82	100.0	9	99.9	21	100.0	11	99.8	3	100.0

TABLE 45

Children Ever Born to Wives of 167 Men Reared in Large Families, Forty Years of Age and Over, by Number, Per Cent, and Racial and Religious Grouping

Number of Children Ever Born	Number of Wives	PER CENT	Protestant NUMBER	PER CENT	Roman Catholic NUMBER	PER CENT	Jew NUMBER	PER CENT	Negro NUMBER	PER CENT	Protestant-Catholic NUMBER	PER CENT
None	30	18.0	16	15.7	3	20.0	1	4.3	9	42.8	1	16.6
One	34	20.3	22	21.5	0		9	39.1	1	4.8	2	33.4
Two	50	30.0	30	29.4	6	40.0	8	34.8	6	28.6		
Three	28	16.7	20	19.6	3	20.0	4	17.4	1	4.8		
Four	10	6.0	5	4.9	1	6.7	0		3	14.3	1	16.6
Five	7	4.2	6	5.8	0		0		0		1	16.6
Six and over	8	4.8	3	2.9	2	13.3	1	4.3	1	4.8	1	16.6
Total	167	100.0	102	99.8	15	100.0	23	99.9	21	100.1	6	99.8

tween the five groups in their adherence to the small family system. Variations within this general observance do occur from one category to another, but these can be attributed quite properly to statistical vagaries such as one finds in small samples.

To meet the possible criticism of the limited statistical base in the preceding three tables, and to include the largest possible number of cases, one additional tabulation is presented. Table 46 combines the 529 married persons who grew up in our families and for whom is known the number of children ever born to the women and to the wives of the men reared in these families. The data are classified for the five racial and religious groups involved, and clearly warrant the conclusion in the preceding paragraph, namely, that all racial and religious groups show a consistent acceptance of the small family system.

2. Is there any relationship between the number of children ever born and the size of the family of the parents?

Students of population have given only scant consideration to the study of the relationship between the fertility of successive generations, but those studies which have been made have tended to emphasize some positive association between family sizes of two generations. The work of Karl Pearson and his associates in 1899 is still regarded as a classic on the subject, although confined to families extracted from the British peerage.[4] In this country, Huestis and Maxwell found the correlation coefficient of +.124 among 638 families sending children to the University of Oregon.[5] More recently, Berent, working with the data of the British Royal Commission, concludes that family size tends to run through generations. "The associations between the number of children born

[4] Karl Pearson and Alice Lee, "On the Inheritance of Fertility in Mankind," *Royal Society of London Philosophical Transactions*, Series A., Vol. 192, 1899.
[5] R. R. Huestis and A. Maxwell, "Does Family Size Run in Families?" *Journal of Heredity*, Vol. 23, 1932, pp. 77-79.

TABLE 46

Total Number of Children Born to 529 Married Persons Reared in One Hundred Large Families

Number of Children Ever Born	Total Number of Cases	PER CENT	Protestant NUMBER	PER CENT	Roman Catholic NUMBER	PER CENT	Jew NUMBER	PER CENT	Negro NUMBER	PER CENT	Protestant-Catholic NUMBER	PER CENT
None	103	19.4	58	19.3	20	17.9	5	9.1	16	32.6	4	30.8
One	113	21.3	60	20.0	24	21.4	14	25.4	12	24.5	3	23.0
Two	157	29.9	91	30.3	33	29.4	20	36.3	11	22.4	2	15.4
Three	92	17.4	56	18.7	20	17.9	12	21.9	3	6.1	1	7.7
Four	36	6.8	18	6.0	8	7.1	3	5.4	6	12.2	1	7.7
Five	13	2.5	11	3.7	1	.9	0		0		1	7.7
Six	5	.9	3	1.0	1	.9	0		0		1	7.7
Seven	4	.7	1	.3	2	1.8	1	1.8	1	2.0	0	
Eight and over	6	1.1	2	.6	3	2.7	0		0		0	
Total	529	100.0	300	99.9	112	100.0	55	99.9	49	99.8	13	100.0

and the size of the family from which the parents themselves come has been found to exist both with respect to the husband's and to the wife's family size, but the effect of the latter seems to be stronger." [6]

The data presented here are somewhat more specific, and are concerned with the exact size of the family of one parent, the mother, and the number of children ever born to her. All women are forty years of age and over. Table 47 presents the facts from this study in tabular form.

TABLE 47

Average Number of Children Ever Born to 126 Married Women, Forty Years of Age and Over, and the Number of Children in the Families in Which They Were Reared

Number of Children in Mother's Family	Number of Cases	Average Number of Children Ever Born to Mother
6	23	2.3
7	16	1.4
8	15	1.4
9	20	2.4
10	13	1.8
11	17	2.2
12	8	2.5
13	4	1.5
14	6	2.7
15	0	0.0
16	4	3.5

Obviously, this table shows no consistent pattern of relationship between specific variations in the size of the mothers' families and the number of children ever born. One particular combination of the data yields a noticeable result. If all the cases where the mothers' families consisted of six to ten children are combined, the average number of children ever born to the mothers is 2.0; when those coming from families

[6] Jerzy Berent, "Relationship Between Family Sizes of Two Successive Generations," *Milbank Memorial Fund Quarterly*, January, 1953, p. 49.

with eleven or more are combined, the average number of children is 2.4.

3. Is order of birth of the mother a factor in the number of children she bears in marriage? Table 48 presents the answer for 126 married women reared in large families, tabulated by order of their birth in their large families.

TABLE 48

Number of Children Ever Born to 126 Married Women, Forty Years of Age and Over, Who Were Reared in Large Families

Order of Birth	Number of Cases	Average Number of Children Ever Born
First	23	2.5
Second	21	2.3
Third	12	1.9
Fourth	16	1.8
Fifth	11	1.4
Sixth	6	1.6
Seventh	7	2.1
Eighth	10	2.2
Ninth	6	3.2
Tenth	6	2.0
Eleventh and over	8	1.7

This table shows some consistency of pattern. Starting on a relatively high plateau with the first born, the decline in the average number of children is regular until the fifth order of birth, after which there is a gradual rise. Inbetween women as a group have fewer children than their older and younger sisters. Returning to our concept of the interacting size of the family, it is clear that fourth-, fifth-, and sixth-born children tend to grow up when the family is at its maximum interacting size. The older children often leave home before the youngest ones are born or are much in evidence, and those at the lower end of the scale grow up after many of the older ones have left. The fourth-, fifth-, and sixth-born bear the brunt of family pressures, and there is a hint here of the impact of mere numbers of a group upon the attitudes of its members toward size of the group. One cannot escape the impression that the sociopsychological factors in family limitation have been explored much less adequately than the socioeconomic ones.

4. Other possible differentials have been explored. Since many of the children who grew up in our hundred families married and/or were in the active child-bearing stage during the depression decade, their family sizes have been compared with those who passed through this stage at an earlier or a later time. Similarly, the number of children born to those raised on farms and in rural areas has been compared with the city-bred siblings. Occupational differences have been considered. In each of these cases, the tests of statistical procedure have been applied, with negative results. The reproductive behavior of children reared in large families is consistent, regardless of many commonly emphasized differentials. This consistent behavior will next be summarized.

CONCLUSIONS AND INTERPRETATIONS

A. Conclusions. Four main conclusions bearing upon the reproductive behavior of children reared in large families emerge from the present study.

1. Persons reared in large families tend to marry to a lesser extent than comparable segments in the general population. This is more true of women than of men reared in large families. The proportion of women, fourteen years of age and over, reared in large families, is less by approximately one-seventh than the proportion in the country as a whole.

2. Children reared in the large families included in this study do not in turn produce large families. Of 529 married siblings, only fifteen had six or more children. Of 126 married

women, forty years of age and over, only three had six or more children; of the total number of 251 married female siblings, only four had six or more children. The percentages which these numbers represent are strikingly lower than those found in the same category in the population at large.

3. The proportion of large family siblings in this study who are childless is larger in all of the more refined comparisons with the general population. The percentage of childless marriages for all groups among the large family siblings approximates 19; for the United States cohort of 1920, it is 14.8; and for white married women in general, forty years of age and over in 1940, it was 15.7.

4. Large family siblings in our sample who marry go in almost exclusively for the small family system. More than two out of every three have two or fewer children; of the women, forty and over, only one out of six has four or more; only one out of forty has as many as six. The record is consistent and decisive.

B. Interpretations. How are these findings·to be interpreted? A number of questions immediately present themselves, which need clarification in other studies based on a larger and more representative body of data. The questions are stated, then, for suggestive purposes.

1. Do the data mean that large family siblings, not unlike other persons, respond to the practices and values of the place and time in which they live? In recent years, American families have tended to follow the practice, long since honored by the French, of standardizing the size of the family. This standardized family is a small one, including from one to three children as a rule. This contemporary family not only has its characteristic size but also its commonly accepted procedures and values.[7] Do the foregoing conclusions mean

[7] James H. S. Bossard, *Parent and Child: Studies in Family Behavior* (Philadelphia: University of Pennsylvania Press, 1953), chap. IV.

that large family children, rejecting the example, experience, and traditions of their own families, accept the prevailing norms of the small family system? The obvious answer is yes, at least in part. Both the quantitative data and a wealth of comments heard from large family persons during the course of the study support this conclusion. But there is more to the story than this. Large family children do not simply conform to the prevailing family norms: they go beyond them. This suggests the next question.

2. Do the findings mean that persons reared in large families, on the basis of their experiences while growing up and with an awareness of the pressures which large family living is prone to involve, react, and perhaps overreact, by having relatively smaller families than the population at large? The reader will recall here the data from Chapter 4 which showed that 72 per cent of the informants were critical or obviously restrained in their attitudes toward the size of their families, and that additional ones had passed through such a stage. Particularly strong was the sentiment concerning the economic problems which the large family presents. That many of these informants, as well as other large family members, emphasized the salutary effects of large family living does not mean that they want to impose them upon their children. The same kind of contrast is found in many families where the father, for example, after triumphing over innumerable hardships in his youth and glorifying them as the circumstances which "made" him, proceeds then with the utmost unction to shield his own children from similar hardships. It is so with many large family children. It was nice, it was fun, it was wonderful, it was good for us, they say, and then proceed to keep their children from having similar experiences.

The theory of alternating attitudes toward family size. The present study, complemented and supported by much other information gathered by the author, suggests a theory of alternating attitudes, generation-wise, toward family size, which implies that a more extreme size of family tends to breed a reaction against it. That is to say, life in relatively large families impresses many of its members with the difficulties it presents, so that the next generation reacts by having relatively small families. Similarly, the small family system, particularly that which includes only one or two children, impresses them with the disadvantages of such a size, so that they react in the direction of having larger families. It is further implied that such generational changes operate against the background of the larger trends in reproductive behavior, and are influenced also by them.

A suggestion of this theory and support for it can be found in the 1949 report of the British Royal Commission on Population. The report says:

There is some evidence that not only during the war but during the last two decades a change of attitude to size of family has been taking place. The extremely small family is no longer as "fashionable" as it was in the early 1920's. Much has been written in recent years of the disadvantages of the one-child family both for child and parent, and this discussion may both record and encourage a fall in the popularity of families of this kind. The motives at work may include something more fundamental than adherence to a new fashion; a change in convention may be taking place under the stress of experience. Among the generations of people who became parents before, say, 1925, the great majority had been, as children, members of large families and knew their disadvantages. They were anxious to avert those disadvantages from themselves and their children. In recent years, for the first time, the married couples who were engaged in building up their families included a large proportion of people who knew from personal experience that very small families also have their disadvantages. In this sense, it is possible, and even probable, that there has been a reaction against the very small family.[8]

[8] *Royal Commission on Population Report* (London: His Majesty's Stationery Office, 1949), pp. 56-57.

This theory of alternating attitudes needs further verification. Such verification involves the study of families over a period of a number of generations, noting not only the number of children born in each but also with reference to prevailing sizes of families in the population at large. This study of family continuity over a period of several generations is one of the great needs of family sociology not only for size but also for many other aspects of family life. There is a great need for historical perspective in the study of family life. Such perspective now is largely lacking.

SUMMARY

1. Persons reared in our large families marry to a lesser extent than comparable segments of the population at large.
2. Women reared in our large families marry to a less extent than men so reared.
3. Such women may be socially handicapped during the marrying years, and conceivably may react unfavorably to family life.
4. Older, responsible siblings often make a special kind of marriage, to dependent mates.
5. Persons reared in our large families do not in turn produce large families. Rather they show relatively many childless marriages and small families.
6. Racial, religious, occupational, and other factors are of little or no effect in the reproductive behavior of large family siblings.
7. A theory of alternating attitudes toward family size is suggested as a possible key to the reproductive behavior of large as well as small family children.

· 13 ·

Marital Happiness of Persons Reared in Large Families

ANOTHER TEST of a family system is how well it prepares its sibling members for life in the families which they will form in turn. A number of questions in this connection suggest themselves. Does large family living produce persons who will make happy husbands and wives? How do the happiness ratings of such persons compare with those of other groups? How do racial and religious groups vary in this respect? Is there any relationship between the happiness of such persons and the happiness or unhappiness of the large families in which they were reared? Does the presence or number of children affect their happiness ratings? Does marital success or failure change with age? Does it vary by sex? Is the birth order of the large family member of any importance? Is there any relation between the happiness and personal adjustment ratings of large family members? The present chapter presents the available data from the present study in answer to these questions.

1. Do persons reared in large families become happy husbands and wives when they marry?

Of the 529 persons reared in the hundred large families who married, ratings of the marital happiness of 440 are available. This information was obtained in the following manner. The informant in each family was asked to rate the happiness of his married brothers and sisters on a threefold scale: happy, medium happy, or unhappy. This method differs from that employed in some other studies where the married persons are asked to rate themselves. Still other studies have utilized the ratings by acquaintances. In this case, the rating is by a brother or sister. Where the person rated has been married more than once, only the rating of the first marriage is tabulated in the following summaries, although information concerning the subequent marriages was obtained.

The data thus gathered indicate that persons reared in large families show a high percentage of marital happiness. Of the 440 cases, 314, or 71.4 per cent, were rated as happy; 66, or 15.0 per cent, as of medium happiness; and 60, or 13.6 per cent, as unhappy.

Of the 60 unhappy ones, 28 had been divorced and there was one legal separation. These 29 cases represent 6.4 per cent of the total.

Of the 28 that had been divorced, eight had remarried, and of these, seven were reported as happy and one as medium happy.

2. *How does this record compare with other studies of marital happiness?*

Reference has been made in Chapter 5 to the studies of marital happiness that have been made in recent years, and it is important to recall them here and compare our data with the more representative of these. The study by Dr. R. O. Lang, published in 1932, it will be recalled, reported that for 8,263 couples married from one to sixteen years and rated by close acquaintances, 64.9 per cent were identified as happy, 19.2 per cent as of average happiness, and 15.9 per cent as unhappy.[1]

Burgess and Cottrell, in their study of 526 couples, and based on ratings by husband or wife, found 63.1 per cent were happy or very happy, 14.4 per cent reported average

[1] R. O. Lang, *A Study of the Degree of Happiness or Unhappiness in Marriage as Rated by Acquaintances of the Married Couples,* unpublished M.A. thesis (Chicago: University of Chicago, 1932), p. 35.

happiness, 21.5 per cent were unhappy, and 1.0 per cent made no reply.[2]

Terman, in his random sample of 902 husbands, found that 68.0 per cent rated themselves as happy above average, 18.2 per cent as average, and 13.8 per cent as unhappy. A random sample of 644 wives showed corresponding percentages of 65.3, 16.3, and 18.4 respectively.[3]

Assuming that the happy, medium, and unhappy categories employed in this study are similar to the happy, average, and unhappy ones of the studies that have been cited, it is clear that persons reared in large families have a relatively good record for marital happiness. The percentage of happiness is higher in our sample than in any of the other studies cited and the percentage of unhappiness is lower. Large family products are good matrimonial risks.

3. How do racial and religious groups compare in these ratings of marital happiness of persons reared in large families?

Table 49 presents the facts for the 440 married persons,

TABLE 49

Ratings of Marital Happiness for 440 Persons Reared in Large Families, by Race and Religion

Group	Total NUMBER	Total PER CENT	Happy NUMBER	Happy PER CENT	Medium NUMBER	Medium PER CENT	Unhappy NUMBER	Unhappy PER CENT
Protestant	239	100.0	170	71.1	35	14.7	34	14.1
Catholic	85	100.0	59	69.4	17	20.0	9	10.6
Jew	50	100.0	34	68.0	9	18.0	7	14.0
Negro	52	100.0	41	78.9	5	9.6	6	11.5
Protestant-Catholic	14	100.0	10	71.4	0	0.0	4	28.6

[2] Ernest W. Burgess and Leonard S. Cottrell, Jr., *Predicting Success or Failure in Marriage* (New York: Prentice-Hall, 1939), p. 32.
[3] Lewis M. Terman, et al., *Psychological Factors in Marital Happiness* (New York: McGraw-Hill Book Co., 1938), p. 78.

classified by racial and religious groups. A study of this table warrants the following conclusions:

(1) The percentage of marital happiness is approximately the same for all groups except the Negro, which is somewhat higher.

(2) The percentages for those rated as medium vary considerably, being relatively high for Roman Catholics and low for Negroes.

(3) The percentages of unhappy marriages do not show much variation except for those reared in mixed-marriage homes, but the number here is too small to have much statistical significance.

4. *Is the degree of happiness of the homes in which they were reared of any importance in determining the marital happiness of large family siblings?*

Students of the family are in rather general agreement today that happiness of persons in marriage is significantly related to the happiness of their parents. Children who grow up in happy homes tend to be happy when they marry; children who grow up in unhappy homes tend to be less so. Is this equally true of large family children?

To answer this question in terms of the present study, a special analysis was made of sixty-one family case records which were wholly complete and satisfactory in their information on the points involved. Of the children who had grown up in these sixty-one families, 346 had married and had been rated by a brother or sister for happiness in marriage. These data are presented in summary form in Table 50.

Children who grow up in happy large families are more likely to establish happy homes of their own than those who grow up in medium happy or unhappy homes. The pattern of the accompanying table is consistent throughout, clearly showing that there is some considerable relationship between the kind of a home in which a person is reared and the kind of a home he or she will establish in turn.

TABLE 50

Happiness Ratings of Home Life and of Marital Happiness of 346 Large Family Children

Home Condition	Total NUMBER	Total PER CENT	Happy NUMBER	Happy PER CENT	Medium NUMBER	Medium PER CENT	Unhappy NUMBER	Unhappy PER CENT
Reared in happy homes	202	100.0	150	74.2	29	14.3	23	11.4
Reared in medium happy homes	99	100.0	64	64.6	20	20.2	15	15.1
Reared in unhappy homes	45	100.0	23	51.1	11	24.4	11	24.4

That this should be so seems very natural, but exactly how and why it happens is another story. Is it because a happy home life makes for a more stable personality in the child, which in turn makes for a better adjustment in marriage? Does it mean that certain biological traits of the parents, which make for successful family living, are transmitted to their children, to serve in like manner in turn? Are good relations or quarreling habit responses, like ways of walking or tugging at one's ears when talking, that are learned when young and then continued in later life? Or are there certain ways of living which make for success in family relations which are learned when young and maintained in later life? These are matters that are as yet not fully determined.

5. *Does the presence, absence, or number of children affect these happiness ratings?*

It is commonly supposed that the presence of children makes for happiness in marriage, an idea that has been emphasized by their apparent deterrent effect upon the divorce rate. On the other hand, a number of studies bearing on this question have been made, and these come to quite different conclusions. Burgess and Wallin, in their recent book, after reviewing these studies, conclude that "research on marital success and number of children has produced no evidence of a relationship in some studies and inconsistent results in others."[4] But such studies do emphasize, as Burgess and Wallin point out, and as their own studies show, that there is a relationship between marital success and the attitude of parents toward having children.[5]

Two facts of general import should be noted in this connection. One is that the effect of children upon the success of a marriage is a highly individual one. The available studies, which are statistical in character, deal with the overall relationship and tend to ignore the variations from one family to another.

A second and highly pervasive fact is that the individual case develops against the prevailing cultural background. Every society tends to have, as a part of its family culture pattern, a general and somewhat reasoned attitude toward marriage and children. Some societies emphasize children to such an extent that the woman who cannot bear any is almost an outcast. An occasional society carries this to the point of placing a premium upon the girl who has borne children before marriage. Other societies give great value to male children and especially revere the mother of sons. In our own recent industrial-urban culture, a quite different attitude has developed, due largely to the high cost of rearing children in our urban centers, with their high standards of child care and education. Motives growing out of this complex of factors, reinforced by the contraceptive sophistication of an increasing number of persons, have not only popularized the small family system but have also removed the sting from the childless marriage. One would expect therefore that the present study would yield no positive results of a relationship between marital success and the number of children.

[4] Ernest W. Burgess and Paul Wallin, *Engagement and Marriage* (Chicago: J. B. Lippincott Co., 1953), p. 719.
[5] For additional data on the relationship of marital happiness and number of children, the reader is referred to Norma E. Cutts and Nicholas Moseley, *The Only Child* (New York: G. P. Putnam's Sons, 1954), and Paul Popenoe, *Modern Marriage: A Handbook for Men* (New York: The Macmillan Co., rev. ed., 1946), Appendix VI.

To answer the question posed in this section, we have grouped together the data for all married women thirty years of age and over, their happiness ratings, and the number of children born to them. Table 51 presents this material in tabular form for 175 women.

There is no consistent pattern in Table 51. Certainly nothing about it shows any relationship between marital happiness and the presence of children. The happy women, for example, show the largest percentage of childless marriages, and the medium-happy women have a record of more limited child bearing than the unhappy ones. Obviously, the number of children is a product of many factors in the life of a couple, some of which may relate to marital happiness.

To supplement the data on the married women, a similar table has been prepared for 195 large family reared men, married and thirty years of age and over, with ratings of marital happiness and number of children born to their wives.

Upon the surface, the table for the men shows more of a relationship than that for the women. Careful study of the data, however, reveals that the average number of children for the happily married men is raised by four cases with a total of thirty-five children. If these are eliminated, the average number of children for the husbands is 1.9. Again, fourteen of the twenty-five unhappy men were divorced, which naturally lessens the number of children in these cases. On the whole, the data concerning the men are confusing, with no consistency in the general pattern. From a careful reading of the case material, one gets the impression that children seem to have more significance for marital happiness for the men than for the women, and a comparison of Tables 51 and 52 would seem to justify such a conclusion.

6. *Does marital happiness or unhappiness vary with the age of those married?*

Studies of divorce have shown that the highest percentage of separations of couples who are later divorced occurs in the

TABLE 51

175 Married Women, Thirty Years of Age and Over, Rated for Happiness and Number of Children

			Per Cent					
Happiness Rating	Number of Married Women	Average Number of Children	NO CHILDREN	ONE CHILD	TWO CHILDREN	THREE CHILDREN	FOUR CHILDREN	FIVE CHILDREN	SIX OR MORE CHILDREN
Happy	110	2.1	20.0	15.4	27.3	20.9	10.0	3.6	2.8
Medium	22	2.2	6.2	25.0	28.1	21.8	18.9	0.0	0.0
Unhappy	33	1.9	15.1	24.3	33.3	18.2	6.0	0.0	3.0

TABLE 52

195 Married Men, Thirty Years of Age and Over, Rated for Marital Happiness and Children Born to Wives

Happiness Rating	Number of Men	Average Number of Children	Per Cent						
			NO CHILDREN	ONE CHILD	TWO CHILDREN	THREE CHILDREN	FOUR CHILDREN	FIVE CHILDREN	SIX OR MORE CHILDREN
Happy	144	2.1	16.7	20.1	30.5	18.7	4.9	4.1	4.9
Medium	26	1.9	19.1	3.9	50.0	19.1	3.9	3.9	0.0
Unhappy	25	1.5	28.0	40.0	24.0	8.0	0.0	0.0	0.0

first year of marriage and declines thereafter with each succeeding year. From this, it is often concluded that the earliest years of marriage are the most difficult, and that for those unions which survive this period the rate of happiness is unduly high. Actually, the ratings of marital happiness show a quite different result. Lang's study, which is the most comprehensive of those made on this point, reveals that for 7,393 couples, the longer they are married the lower the rates for good and/or fair marital adjustment, and the higher the rates for poor adjustment. Unfortunately, this study does not go beyond the sixteenth year of marriage. It will be noted that his conclusions are based on duration of marriage rather than the age of those married.[6]

The other studies referred to differ materially in their age structure. The Burgess-Cottrell couples were mostly younger people: 80.6 per cent of the husbands and 87.7 per cent of the wives who reported their age at marriage were under thirty, and all couples were married less than seventy-eight months.[7] In the Terman study, 16.2 per cent of the husbands and 30.3 per cent of the wives were under thirty; and 59.8 per cent of the husbands and 70.6 per cent of the wives were under forty.[8]

In the present study, 15.5 per cent of the husbands and 16.3 per cent of the wives were under thirty; and 39.5 and 49.3 per cent, respectively, were under forty. A comparison with the percentages cited in the preceding paragraph for the other groups studied will show ours to be an older group in terms of chronological age. Our group alone shows a majority of the persons rated to be over forty years of age.

Tables 53 and 54 present the data for 215 married women and 225 married men in our own study. These tables show significant variations by age periods and seem to confirm, with one important modification, the study by Lang. There

---

[6] Lang, *op. cit.*
[7] Burgess and Cottrell, *op. cit.*, pp. 20-21.
[8] Terman, *et al.*, *op. cit.*, p. 44.

TABLE 53

Happiness Ratings, 215 Married Women, Classified by Ten-Year Periods

Age Period	Total NUMBER	Total PER CENT	Happy NUMBER	Happy PER CENT	Medium NUMBER	Medium PER CENT	Unhappy NUMBER	Unhappy PER CENT
20–29	35	100.0	31	88.6	3	8.5	1	2.8
30–39	71	100.0	48	67.6	11	15.5	12	16.9
40–49	43	100.0	26	60.4	7	16.5	10	23.2
50–59	46	100.0	27	58.7	10	21.7	9	19.5
60–69	16	100.0	11	68.8	4	25.0	1	6.2
70 and over	4	100.0	3	75.0	0	0.0	1	25.0

appears, according to our data, a middle-age dip for both men and women. Rates of unhappiness for women increase until the high point is reached during their forties; for men, it is reached during their fifties. After these respective periods, the trends are reversed, and rates for unhappiness decrease.

TABLE 54

Happiness Ratings, 225 Married Men, Classified by Ten-Year Periods

Age Period	Total NUMBER	Total PER CENT	Happy NUMBER	Happy PER CENT	Medium NUMBER	Medium PER CENT	Unhappy NUMBER	Unhappy PER CENT
20–29	35	100.0	26	74.3	7	20.0	2	5.7
30–39	54	100.0	44	81.5	7	13.3	3	5.5
40–49	64	100.0	51	79.8	7	10.9	6	9.3
50-59	47	100.0	26	55.3	8	17.0	13	27.7
60–69	22	100.0	18	81.8	2	9.1	2	9.1
70 and over	3	100.0	3	100.0	0	0.0	0	0.0

STATISTICAL ANALYSIS

With due recognition of certain inadequacies in our data, it seems proper to submit them to statistical tests now in current use. The one most applicable is the Chi-square test of independence, to test the null-hypothesis that variation in proportions of happy and unhappy is independent of variation in age. The results of this test follow.

Because of cell frequencies in the "unhappy" column and the "60-69" and "70 and over" rows, these columns were collapsed. It will be noticed that the test columns contrast "happy" with "medium and unhappy."

Test I relates to happiness rating with age variation in women. If we get the .05 level as the criterion probability point, the null-hypothesis is rejected and we can conclude that there is significant variation in marital happiness among women. If, however, the more rigorous .01 level is established as the criterion, then the null-hypothesis must be accepted and the conclusions of happiness variation with age consequently must be rejected.

Test II poses the same null-hypothesis, but for men. In this case, there need be no concern regarding the criterion probability level. At any reasonable level, the null-hypothesis must be accepted and we must conclude that (for men) happiness does not vary with age.

Tests: x^2 of Independence

♀

$fe = *$

	Age		Happy		Medium and Unhappy	
TEST I	29–29	31	23.77*	4	11.23*	35
	30–39	48	48.21*	23	22.79*	71
	40–49	26	29.20*	17	13.80*	43
	50 †	41	44.82*	25	21.18*	66
		146		69		215

$x^2 = 8.87 \sim .05\,P > .02$
$df = 3$

♂

	Age		Happy		Medium and Unhappy	
TEST II	20–29	26	26.13°	9	8.87°	35
	30–39	44	40.32°	10	13.68°	54
	40–49	51	47.79°	13	16.21°	64
	50 †	47	53.76°	25	18.24°	72
		168	168°	57	57°	225

$x^2 = 5.53 \sim P > .10$
$df = 3$

New Hypothesis: Among ♀'s 30 years †, there is no significant variation in happiness rating by age.

	Age		Happy		Medium and Unhappy	
TEST III	30–39	48	45.36°	23	25.63°	71
	40–49	26	27.47°	17	15.53°	43
	50 †	41	42.17°	25	23.83°	66
		115		65		180

$x^2 = .73 \sim P > .5$
$df = 2$

Returning to the data for married women, examination of the variation of observed frequencies from expected tends to suggest that women fifty and over manifest as much unhappiness as do those in their forties. The data further suggest that any significance for women might be attributable to an excess of "happy" women among the 20-29 age group rather than to any marked loss in this column among older groups. This notion was put to a tentative test in Test III. Here the data were restricted to marital happiness among women thirty and older. This test intimates that there is no significant variation by age among women thirty and older in so far as rated marital happiness is concerned.

SUGGESTIONS FROM THE CASE MATERIAL

In the conduct of the study, considerable time was spent with the informants who rated their brothers and sisters for marital happiness. Many aspects of family life were discussed with them, including the marital experiences of those rated for happiness. While no systematic probing of the marital problems of these was attempted, a good deal of information relating to them was obtained. Some of this information bears particularly upon one aspect of the main problem raised in this study, and it seems pertinent to summarize this along with the negative results of the statistical analysis.

First, there was a great deal of reference to the forties, the late forties and early fifties, as a critical period for the married women who were rated. The information obtained centered around two groups of facts. One relates to the forties as the age period when women have given birth to their children, for the most part, and also, in a majority of cases, reared them to the stage where at least their more complete dependence upon the mother has materially lessened. The statistically average mother, according to the United States Census Bureau, gives birth to her last child now at the age of twenty-seven, from which it follows that the above-mentioned changes have full opportunity to take place by the time the forties are at hand.

It is pertinent to recall that the persons rated in this study, although reared in large families, are parents, for the most part, of small families. Of the women reared in the hundred large families, and married, and rated for happiness, 86.4 per cent had three or fewer children; and of the wives of the men reared in large families, and rated for happiness, 91.2 per cent had three or fewer children. Of a total of 126 of the women reared in large families, married, forty years of age and over, and rated for happiness, 83.3 per cent had three or fewer children.

Marital Happiness of Large Family Children

A second group of facts pertain to the sexual development of women by the time they are in the forties. Our information here is far from adequate; what we have fits in with the Kinsey studies on the human female. These, it will be recalled, show that it is not until later in life, i.e., their forties and fifties, that many women lose their earlier inhibitions and develop more interest in sex relations: this at the very time when interest in coitus and responses of the average male may have declined considerably.[9] Our information suggests that in many cases, as for those in the Kinsey study, a relative lack of marital happiness is related to a lack of sexual satisfaction.

There is the added factor of the menopause, operating customarily during the years under consideration. The disturbances, both in the sexual and emotional life of many women, in this stage of the life cycle are sufficiently well known to students of the family and require no more than mention at this point. The case material, then, suggests the late forties and early fifties as a crisis period for many women: their children no longer retain their earlier dependence, their husbands are inadequate as sexual mates, and the menopause casts its passing shadows.

The material on the marital lives of brothers who were rated contains many references to the decade of the fifties as a similar crisis period in the lives of married men. Here, however, the frustrations and unhappinesses tend to center around occupational rather than sexual matters. Two groups of men are identified by our informants. One consists of men who have attained some degree of prominence and success in their chosen field, only to find that their wives have not kept pace with them in their upward climb. Such men often make a determined effort to remain loyal to their mates. Some of them are reported as succeeding; others fail and are aware

[9] Alfred C. Kinsey, et al., *Sexual Behavior in the Human Female* (Philadelphia: W. B. Saunders Co., 1953), pp. 353 ff.

of it; and still others appear to their brothers or sisters as failing in spite of outward evidences of success.

A second group of men are in their fifties and have failed, absolutely or relatively, in their occupational efforts. Such failures lead them to rationalizations: they never had a chance to succeed, they say. Their wives were of no help to them. If it were not for the handicaps which their wives imposed, they would have succeeded, as did other men. Such wives become scapegoats for the failures of their husbands. The husbands find comfort in the development of feelings of self-pity and animosity toward their wives.

7. Does marital happiness differ in frequency from one sex to another?

It has been shown in the preceding chapter that men reared in large families are more prone to marry than their sisters, and Table 55 reveals that they are more likely to be happy in marriage. The differences in percentage in each of the three categories of happy, medium, and unhappy, while not large, are consistently in favor of the men. Women reared in large families are less likely to marry and somewhat less likely to be happy in marriage than their brothers.

TABLE 55

Ratings for Happiness, by Sex, for 440 Persons Reared in Large Families

Total		Happy		Medium		Unhappy	
NUM-BER	PER CENT	NUM-BER	PER CENT	NUM-BER	PER CENT	NUM-BER	PER CENT
225 men	100.0	168	74.7	31	13.8	26	11.5
215 women	100.0	146	67.9	35	16.3	34	15.8

8. Do rates of happiness and unhappiness in marriage vary by order of birth for large family reared persons?

Because such interesting variations in other aspects of this study have appeared by order of birth of large family siblings, it is pertinent to raise the question of the possible relationship of this factor to marital happiness. Table 56 presents these data for the married men and women in this study.

Two facts which are revealed in this table deserve special comment. One is the lower rates of happiness for first-born men and women. This is at variance with the findings in other studies which give them a slightly superior chance for happiness.[10] Since these studies were based on families unselected for size, the findings suggest that the facts may differ for persons reared in large families.

The other fact is the unique record of the fourth born. The unusual ratings of the fourth born have been noted repeatedly in this study, and Table 56 shows a similarly differ-

TABLE 56

Happiness Ratings of Married Women and Men, Classified by Order of Birth

Order of Birth	Total NUMBER	Total PER CENT	Happy NUMBER	Happy PER CENT	Medium NUMBER	Medium PER CENT	Unhappy NUMBER	Unhappy PER CENT
Women								
First born	36	100.0	20	55.5	8	22.2	8	22.2
Second born	32	100.0	18	56.3	6	18.7	8	25.0
Third born	28	100.0	21	75.0	3	10.7	4	14.3
Fourth born	28	100.0	22	78.6	5	17.8	1	3.6
Fifth born	31	100.0	20	64.5	5	16.1	6	19.4
Sixth born	15	100.0	11	73.3	2	13.3	2	13.3
Seventh born	11	100.0	7	63.6	2	18.2	2	18.2
Eighth and over	34	100.0	27	79.4	4	11.7	3	8.9
Men								
First born	36	100.0	23	63.9	8	22.2	5	13.9
Second born	29	100.0	19	65.5	5	17.2	5	17.2
Third born	35	100.0	26	74.3	6	17.1	3	8.6
Fourth born	26	100.0	22	84.6	2	7.7	2	7.7
Fifth born	22	100.0	16	72.7	2	9.1	4	18.2
Sixth born	30	100.0	24	80.0	2	6.6	4	13.3
Seventh born	23	100.0	19	82.5	3	13.1	1	4.3
Eighth and over	24	100.0	19	79.2	3	12.5	2	8.3

[10] Burgess and Cottrell, *op. cit.*, pp. 107-17.

ent record for marital happiness. Here, again, one sees place No. 4 as the favored position in the family race.

Because reference has been made repeatedly in the preceding pages to the unique position of family responsibility of the oldest daughter in the large family, even if not always the first born, a separate analysis was made of the marital ratings of first-born daughters, regardless of previous birth of sons, and, for the sake of comparison, the happiness record of the last-born daughters in each family. The contrast, revealed in Table 57, is striking.

TABLE 57

Marital Ratings for Happiness, Oldest and Youngest Daughters Reared in Large Families

Order of Birth	Total NUMBER	Total PER CENT	Happy NUMBER	Happy PER CENT	Medium NUMBER	Medium PER CENT	Unhappy NUMBER	Unhappy PER CENT
First born	75	100.0	44	58.6	15	20.0	16	21.4
Last born	47	100.0	35	74.5	7	14.9	5	10.6

9. *What relation is there between the personal adjustment and marital happiness ratings of persons reared in large families?*

It will be recalled that informants were asked to rate their brothers and sisters for personal adjustment as well as for marital happiness. Both ratings are available for 338 persons, and Table 58 presents them in tabular form.

At first glance, the conclusion to be drawn from this table is that personal adjustment is the predominant factor in marital adjustment. More careful consideration of the facts, however, raises the question as to which is horse and which is cart. Are people happy in marriage because they are otherwise well adjusted, or do people tend to be rated as adjusted or maladjusted on the basis of their marital success or failure? A number of informants gave the impression that their rat-

TABLE 58

Personal Adjustment and Marital Happiness Ratings, 338 Persons Reared in Large Families

Adjustment	Total NUMBER	Total PER CENT	Happy NUMBER	Happy PER CENT	Medium NUMBER	Medium PER CENT	Unhappy NUMBER	Unhappy PER CENT
Well adjusted	224	100.0	187	83.5	26	11.6	11	4.9
Medium adjusted	73	100.0	42	57.5	20	27.4	11	15.1
Poorly adjusted	41	100.0	12	29.3	7	17.1	22	53.6
	338	100.0	241	71.3	53	15.7	44	13.0

ings followed such a sequence of thought. "My brother," they seemed to reason, "is not happy in his marriage, he is not a well-adjusted person." On the other hand, it will be noted that 46.4 per cent of the persons rated as poorly adjusted were rated as happy or medium happy in their marriage. Another question that might be raised is whether the continuing experience of being unhappy in one's most intimate life does not find expression in behavior which other people will deem other than normal. One sees remarkable improvements in behavior with the change from unhappiness to happiness in marriage. For the present, we must be content to say that our data tend to give some support to the theory of the importance of psychogenetic factors in marital failure or success.

SUMMARY

1. Of 440 persons reared in large families, who married and were rated for happiness, 71.4 per cent were rated as happy; 15.0 per cent as of medium happiness; and 13.6 per cent as unhappy.

2. Comparisons with other studies indicate that this is a good record, and that large family products are good matrimonial risks.

3. Ratings compared by racial and religious groups reveal no significant differences except for a relatively high percentage of happiness for Negroes.

4. Children reared in happy homes are more likely to be happy in their own marriages than children reared in medium and unhappy homes.

5. Variations in the number of children seem to have little if any importance in the determination of family happiness.

6. The degree of marital adjustment may vary with age. Statistical tests question the apparent variations in the data of this study, but a study of the case material suggests that marital unhappiness reaches a high point for women in the forties and for men in their fifties.

7. Men reared in large families have a better record for marital happiness than their sisters.

8. First-born children, and especially first-born girls, have relatively low rates of happiness.

9. Fourth-born children have unusually good records.

10. Variations in marital happiness show close statistical correlation with personal adjustment ratings of those married. Several interpretations may be placed on this fact.

· 14 ·

The Large Family System

A GREAT MANY PERSONS, including some serious students of the family, seem to think of it largely as a personal, somewhat romanticized relationship between a man and a woman, with children thrown in to boot, half as a reward and half as a punishment, for their life together. It is in keeping with this concept that the judicious selection of complementary personalities is considered a prerequisite to a good marriage, that the problems of married life concern the adjustment of personal relationships, and that the success or failure of marriage is to be measured statistically by a scientifically devised thermometer that records the temper of personal rapport.

Obviously, there is much truth to all this. Marriage entails a peculiarly intimate personal relationship, and a family has aptly been defined as a unit of interacting personalities. The wise selection of mates is important, so important that most societies in human history have delegated the responsibilities to the families of those marrying; and many a marriage which would otherwise have succeeded has failed because of a clash of personalities. Much of what has already been said in this volume bears out this approach, and nothing that follows is meant to depreciate it.

There is, however, another, and perhaps a more inclusive, concept of the family that has been slowly coming to the fore, which considers it in cultural terms, seeing family life as a segment of the larger culture, its problems as those of cultural harmony, and its success or failure in terms of cultural integration. Such a concept makes it easy to see the family as a way of life, as a pattern of attitudes, and as a complex of values. The term "family system" is used to designate this concept, and the final chapter of this volume considers the large family primarily in this light.

THE SMALL FAMILY SYSTEM

Educators have found contrasts to be helpful for purposes of exposition, and what the large family system entails may be the more clearly seen when compared with the small family system, a term which has been utilized for a number of years to identify the type of domestic life that develops when the family includes one, two, or, at the most, three children.

Most of the characteristics of the small family system are matters of general agreement. They have been indicated by the author in an earlier volume, a condensation of which exposition is presented here.[1] First is its overall theme. The term "theme" is used here to mean its dominant attitude-value.[2] In the small family system, the overall theme is planning. Planning is the substance of its procedure and its thinking—planning of size; of the spacing and timing of the birth of the children; of the emphases and programs to be followed in child rearing; of the main objectives in education, with careful attention to its status-achieving and promoting possibilities; and of preparation for subsequent careers.

Second is the fact that parenthood in the small family is intensive rather than extensive. This emphasis begins at the onset of pregnancy, as the mother receives continuing prenatal care. After the child is born, the pediatrician is consulted on matters of diet, immunization, as well as the slightest sickness. Later on, the "child psychologist" may be consulted on the "everyday problems of the everyday child."

[1] James H. S. Bossard, *Parent and Child: Studies in Family Behavior* (Philadelphia: University of Pennsylvania Press, 1953), chap. V.
[2] Morris E. Opler, "Themes as Dynamic Forces in Culture," *American Journal of Sociology*, November, 1945, p. 198.

Should Junior show symptoms of deviant behavior, the psychiatrist is called in. All this marshaling of scientific aids is utilized so that each pregnancy may eventuate in a normal child, that every possible child shall survive and develop to the utmost of his capacities.

Another characteristic has to do with the type of interaction that prevails within the small family. Recent studies have shown that size determinant is an integral part in group interaction.[3] These and other more abstract and generalized studies give full warrant to the idea that the small family tends to make for a coöperative and democratic type of relationship. Each member, and especially the child, can receive a good deal of attention and consideration. Each is given a voice in group discussions, or at least has the opportunity to be heard. It may be more than a coincidence that the democratic and the small family have appeared together in point of time. Furthermore, family planning, motivated so largely by hopes for the future of its child members, naturally emphasizes the importance of coöperative relationships between parent and child. The child is the hope of the family plan. The essence of good parent-child relationships is to have the child coöperate voluntarily rather than be high pressured into the family program. Here is another reason for small family parents to take recourse to books and courses on child psychology, the better to understand children and to promote such coöperation.

[3] Robert F. Bales, *Interaction Process Analysis: A Method for the Study of Small Groups* (Cambridge, Mass.: Addison-Wesley Press, 1950); "A Set of Categories for the Analysis of Small Group Interaction," *American Sociological Review*, April, 1950, pp. 257-63; Robert F. Bales, *et al.*, "Channels of Communication in Small Groups," *ibid.*, August, 1951, pp. 461-68; James H. S. Bossard, *The Sociology of Child Development* (New York: Harper & Bros., 1948), pp. 145-49; John James, "A Preliminary Study of the Size Determinant in Small Group Interaction," *American Sociological Review*, August, 1951, pp. 474-77; Alexander Paul Hare, *A Study of Interaction and Consensus in Different Sized Discussion Groups* (Chicago: University of Chicago dissertation, 1951); and William M. Kephart, "A Quantitative Analysis of Intragroup Relationships," *American Journal of Sociology*, May, 1950, pp. 544-49.

Coupled with this greater freedom and democracy of expression in the small family is the individualizing of the activities and roles of its members. Small family living makes for individual emphasis, in development and in thinking. The family members are noncompeting: father, mother, and child each goes his own respective way.

This lack of competition within the family turns its "green" eyes outward, accounting for what Margaret Mead [4] has called the sidewise look by the parents, meaning that they compare and measure their children primarily with children in other families in the same residential area, the same social class or clique, or the same school. This reinforces the pressure by the parents on the child, already inherent in the planning procedure which underlies small family living.

This sidewise look applies characteristically to kinsfolk and certain other close associates. Relatively little attention is given to kinsfolk unless they fit into, and can contribute to, the planned goals of the small family. A study made of the attitudes toward kinsfolk of sixty-eight university students revealed that much importance was attached by them to the fact that relatives live at different economic and social levels.[5] This attitude on the part of the students obviously is a reflection of that of the parents.

The planning emphasis in the small family; the sidewise view which characterizes its thinking, particularly in regard to its child members; the relative lack of contacts with kinsfolk: all combine to lead the small family to make an appraising selection of home sites and residential areas, on the basis of their contribution to family plans. School facilities, recreational opportunities, social contacts, are three of the important considerations which underlie these selections. To a very large extent the contemporary suburb, with its stand-

---

[4] Margaret Mead, *And Keep Your Powder Dry* (New York: William Morrow and Co., 1943), p. 109.
[5] James H. S. Bossard and Eleanor S. Boll, "The Immediate Family and the Kinship Group," *Social Forces*, May, 1946, p. 383.

ardization of some specialized pattern of living, is the product of these selections. Small families tend to group themselves on the basis of their family plans and ambitions.

The small family system is a quality system. It prevails primarily at the middle- and upper-class levels. Its driving force is one of ambition, in an open-class system, in which a large proportion of the population aims at raising the status or pretends to have a status higher than is actually attained. Small families invariably are under stress, stress to achieve and to get ahead. This stress or pressure falls with particular heaviness upon the children, who are the potentials of the family's status-raising program. Most children in small families grow up under the shadow, so to speak, of the family level of expectation. Because the parents do so much for the children, they expect a great deal from them in turn. Children are pushed to the utmost, often without regard for their capacities, limitations, interests, or needs. Because of the small number of children, the parents allow no margin of error or failure, as tends to be the case in the larger family.

An added factor here is that the parents tend to impose not only their own ambitions, but also their unfulfilled desires, upon their children. The man with a lifelong but unfulfilled wish to be a doctor drives his son toward the medical profession, willy-nilly; the mother who never rated socially when a girl now grooms her daughter for a social career, regardless of the latter's abilities or interests. The drive of these unfulfilled desires of the parents, and how they may complicate the lives of their children, are particularly obvious to educators at the college and university level.

THE LARGE FAMILY SYSTEM— ITS CHARACTERISTICS

The characteristics of the large family system are in many respects the direct opposite of those of the small family. In presenting a summary of these, we are drawing not only on the explicit findings of the present study but are also recording outstanding impressions formed during the years devoted to it.

1. The large family is not as a rule a planned family in the sense that that term is used in the current literature. True, there are large families that are planned for size, but the plan is general rather than specific. There are other families that are large by consent, usually because moral, religious, or other beliefs forbid interference with "the processes of nature." There are families that are large for other reasons, but the large family as a type is not a planned family in the sense that a specific number of children are scheduled, to be born at the time and intervals that the parents desire.

2. Parenthood in the large family tends to be extensive rather than intensive. This does not mean that parents of large families love their children any less or are less concerned with their welfare and development. It simply means that, under sheer weight of numbers, there is often not the concentrated care of the large family child, nor the solicitous anxiety over him, nor the officious oversight, nor the pervasive possessiveness, that are the more common lot of the small family child. Large family children are left on their own, to care for themselves, to meet life's little problems, both earlier and to a greater extent: there just isn't enough parent to reach around and leave as large a piece of parent for each child as is possible in the small family.

3. Large family living makes for an early acceptance of the realities of life. To put it another way, being reared in a large family makes for an early and a continuing adjustment to the changing vicissitudes of a realistic world. Things are always happening in a large family, its members live in an ever-changing milieu, minor crises are constantly arising. Moreover, they are shared in by so many more people. The large family member learns therefore to take minor disturb-

ances in stride: it is almost as if one developed an immunity against them.

Furthermore, the large family is peculiarly vulnerable to major crises, especially when the children are young. Such vulnerability grows not out of the prevalence of divorce or separation, as is the case in the small family system, but out of other developments. One of these is drunkenness, which was prevalent in our families and which, as always, has serious repercussions for the children. Drinking fathers tend to be harsh and cruel parents. Death of one parent or both parents is the most serious hazard: almost a third of the families were thus afflicted during the years when as many as four of the children were under fourteen years of age.

Major crises of this kind are serious for any family; they are particularly so for large families, many of which have previously been under economic pressure. These crises have to be met, through the sacrifices of the older children often, and through the "sticking together" of all of the family. The latter is the most common device in the large family for weathering family crises.

4. Inherent in every fact and impression that one gets from the study of the large family is its emphasis upon the group rather than the individual. This group emphasis expresses itself in a number of ways. First, from childhood on, children in large families play together, and their play is confined as a rule to the family group. Second, and almost from the start, the children work together. There are a great many things that need to be done. Each has his or her allotted task, and one must stay in line. You work as a member of a team or group. Third, problems must be solved and crises have to be met by sticking together, as has been pointed out in the preceding paragraph. Fourth, decisions must be made on a group, i.e., family basis. What one can do, as a large family member, depends upon what others do, and plan to do. Most large families operate on a close eco-

nomic margin, if margin at all, which means that economic necessity makes coöperation a virtue. At every turn, it is not only one's own efforts, but the modifying forces of the behavior of other family members, that determine what one can do or cannot do. The condition of the hand-me-down that must be worn, the acquiring of a new dress, the use of the living room for your date, of being able to go to town alone, of getting to sleep early, of taking a night school course—all these are grist of the group mill.

Another factor that emphasizes the group is the feeling of family awareness that large family members develop. Various circumstances contribute to this. Size calls attention to itself *per se,* and this makes for an awareness of itself. There is the constant reminder of the family because of the deprivations and limitations, as well as of the joys and satisfactions, which it brings. There are the continuing comments of friends and neighbors. This apparently begins early in life for the children reared in large families. Their school mates tease them, the teacher refers to it, their friends joke about it. Feelings of shame, and at times of pride too, were frequently referred to in the course of the study. Nor were the parents immune, as the foregoing pages have shown. All of this combines to create an awareness of the family as a group and as a distinct and unique aspect of one's experience. Needless to say, such feelings of family awareness are lacking in the small family.

5. Group existence and awareness make for group functioning, and this in turn calls for organization and leadership. A large number of persons, of differing ages and sexes, living within a limited space, on a limited income, and with limited living facilities of various kinds, make organization, administration, authoritarian control, and executive direction inevitable to some degree, and our judgment is that the larger the family group becomes the more such developments will appear. This naturally makes for a dominant role of the father, the mother, and/or the elder siblings.

Many of the problems and values that characterize large families are those involved in group leadership and group functioning. The data of the present study make it abundantly clear that the good father is the wise executive director, the effective mother is the able household manager, and the older brother or sister most respected is the good leader. Conversely, the bad father is the too autocratic one, who tries to handle all problems by the ordering-and-forbidding technique, and the mother most criticized by the siblings is the ineffective one. Favoritism is a frequent cause of trouble. These are all aspects of faulty administration.

6. With large family living go emphases on qualities of behavior which are group essentials. Conformity is valued above self-expression. Listening is the rule rather than talking: at least one learns to give and take turns in conversation. Earlier forms of heating houses, with their open hearth around which the family gathered to keep warm, aided and abetted this tendency. Modern methods of heating, which make all rooms of even temperature, permit a cell-like type of existence, with a radio in every cell. All this suggests, and there is nothing facetious in this comment, that the current cocktail-party pattern of everyone talking and no one listening may be the result of family conditioning rather than a psychopathic group emergent.

Another necessary group virtue is coöperation. What siblings most complain about each other is not doing one's share, failure to do team work, "getting out of line." The family must function as a group to do its group chores, and that calls for coöperation. The material of this study contains little mention of the child that excels at large, as is so common with small family children; there is little comparison with the neighbor's children; the emphasis is upon duty, not spectacular achievement.

7. Whenever any considerable number of people function together, rules of conduct and procedure become necessary,

and, as a rule, the greater the number of persons in the group the more numerous and stringent the rules. Applied to the present study, this means that discipline is stressed in the large family. The relatively rigid pattern of family diets, referred to in Chapter 7, is an illustration in kind, but the point has general application.

Discipline is not only the inevitable accompaniment of large family living, but its proper exercise is much stressed. Much of it is exercised in the name of the paternal constitutional monarch, but its execution often is left to the siblings. Children in a large family discipline each other, adjustments must be made to peers, not primarily to adults. And discipline of children by children has its own distinctive features. First of all, it is realistic, not ideological; it is practical, not theoretical. Children understand each other, and their minds are not yet cluttered with theories of child rearing. They "see through" each other, they realize the implications of each other's behavior better than adults do. And, what is more, they know how to deal with each other. It is often said that children are diabolically cruel to each other, and this is true: first, because they know what is important—to children; and second, they know what to do about it. Significantly, then, the disciplinary measures they use are often more subtle than overt. For the nonconforming member, there are obvious indications of impatience; for the odd one, there is ridicule; for the vexing transgressor, there is disdain.

The complement to this sibling-rearing-by-sibling is a pattern of parental behavior quite different from that which obtains in the contemporary small family. The oversolicitous mother is strangely out of place in a family of twelve. The nagging parent, the type who says, "Mary, go out and see what Johnny is doing and tell him to stop," is too much occupied in a large family to "ride" any one child. Both parent and child in a large family are apt to be less demanding and less possessive in their attitudes toward each other. The stark realities of large family living laugh to scorn the neurotic sins of the small family. In short, our hypothesis here tends to agree with George Bernard Shaw's comments years ago: "The old observation," he writes, "that members of large families get on in the world holds good because in large families it is impossible for each child to receive what schoolmasters call 'individual attention.' The children may receive a good deal of individual attention from one another in the shape of outspoken reproach, ruthless ridicule, and violent resistance to their attempts at aggression; but the parental despots are compelled by the multitude of their subjects to resort to political rather than to personal rule, and to spread their attempts at moral monster-making over so many children, that each child has enough freedom, and enough sport in the prophylactic process of laughing at its elders behind their backs, to escape with much less damage than the single child." [6]

8. Ten children born in the same family are not going to behave alike any more than they are going to look alike. Differences of behavior manifest themselves early in life, on the basis of age, sex, abilities, interests, duties assigned, and conceptions of role developed by both individual and group alike. Particularly important is the specialization in the tasks assigned customarily to different members. On the basis of these assignments, and the siblings' adjustment to them, emerges the unity of larger patterns of behavior which constitute the core of personality.

Specialization of role and function among the children is another characteristic of the large family system. Obviously, this takes many forms. Earlier, it was quite customary in large families to direct the children, particularly the sons, into different occupations. Thus, one son might be given to the church, another to the army, another to the law. If today there is less practice of routine occupational assignment, the

[6] George Bernard Shaw, *Misalliance* (New York: Brentano's, 1914), pp. xix, xx.

distinction between personality patterns is no less pronounced, as the analysis in Chapter 10 clearly showed.

This specialization of role among the siblings is particularly important in the large family. First, there is the principle that the degree of specialization correlates with increases in the size of the group. Emile Durkheim, the French sociologist, first developed this in his analysis of the division of labor, pointing out that the larger the number of people living together the greater the division of labor and specialization of function there are apt to be.[7]

A second important fact in this connection is that the number of siblings limits the range of choice of those lower in the order of birth. Only the oldest child has a relatively unlimited choice. Since no one wants to duplicate the role of another sibling, each succeeding child's choice is limited by the choices of his predecessors in the order of birth. Specialized roles are pre-empted by the older siblings: they come to be firmly held with the progress of time. Thus the younger children in a large family may have greater difficulty in finding satisfactory roles within the family group. Also, they may be under greater temptation to develop patterns of rebellion. At any rate, our hypothesis is that such specialization of role, and the individual response to it, come early in life for members of large families; that such experience is of importance in shaping the patterned form of adjustment to life; and that both the early acceptance of assigned role in the group, or rebellion to it, are important determinants in shaping the personality. Often, the subsequent effort to escape an early assigned role and transfer to another becomes one of life's basic drives.

9. Durkheim points out still another principle of value in the study of the large family system. The greater the degree of specialization, he says, the greater the degree of inter-

[7] George Simpson, *Emile Durkheim on the Division of Labor in Society* (New York: The Macmillan Co., 1933), Book II.

dependence that comes about. This in turn demands *consensus*, a term and idea which Durkheim has contributed to sociology. It is this *consensus* which gives unity to the group, binds the members together, and "the greater the diversity of relations . . . , the more it creates links which attach the individual to the group." [8] It is our hypothesis that the larger the family group, that is, the more persons that are living together in a family, the more family consensus tends to develop, the stronger its hold upon individual members becomes, and the stronger the position of the father as its directive symbol becomes.

10. Other things being equal, the large family system makes for a certain balance and sanity in child rearing. Our material tends to show that having many children makes for an extended accumulation of parental experience, which in turn results in a certain detached and objective attitude toward child problems. The large family parent, instead of rushing to the doctor or psychologist or psychiatrist about Mary's present annoying behavior, has seen the same symptoms with Mary's three older sisters, and knows that nothing is so helpful as a liberal dose of judicious neglect. Parents of small families often act neurotically about these phases and tend to communicate their neurotic concern to the child; parents of large families, viewing similar problems from the vantage point of historical perspective, learn to take them in patient stride. One wonders, too, of the effect of this upon the older children. They, too, see the younger children go through the same stages that they did, and they likewise come naturally by an objectivity toward human behavior which cannot be expected of the small family child.

It is at this point that one becomes aware of the need of long-range studies of the large family. Only recently has the importance of historical studies of individual families come to be appreciated. Such observations as have been made

[8] Simpson, *op. cit.*, p. 109.

have revealed the existence of a family cycle, with distinct stages, each with its own crises, preoccupations, and problems. Parenthood is one of these stages, with child bearing, child rearing, and child launching as clearly defined substages. This concept of the family cycle has proven to be very helpful in the analysis of family life and child development.

Unfortunately, these studies and the concept of the family cycle as thus far developed have been based almost wholly on the small family system, in which each stage of the cycle tends to be distinct, and where the various stages follow each other in a rather clear-cut sequence. This is far from the case in the typical large family, where the last children may be born or be in the pre-school period at the same time that the first born are leaving home and embarking on their adult careers. Thus one finds in such families, not a succession, but an accumulation, of stages.

What is the significance of this for the older children? Our case material suggests that the fundamental problem of the older children in large families lies in the fact that by the time they reach the need-to-be-launched stage, their parents are still occupied with the tasks of the child-rearing and child-bearing stages. There are, to be sure, those few remarkable parents, so energized or financed, that they can bear, rear, and launch a dozen children with noticeable effectiveness, but they are nonexistent thus far in our study. Mostly, the older children in large families launch themselves, if indeed they are launched at all, or, in recent years, they are launched in and by the armed forces of their country.

Similarly, one wonders what are the special problems of the younger children in those cases where all of the substages of parenthood are present at the same time in the family history. Is there a jaded parent, surfeited with an undue prolongation of the joys of parenthood? Is there a foolish parent, bent on prolonging parenthood with the last born?

The Large Family System

Is there a tired parent, worn out with the tribulations of the years? A preliminary study of children of overage parents suggests a wide variety of complications for the child of such parents.[9]

11. *To grow up in a large family is to come to terms with life.* This seems the best way to designate the almost inevitable socializing process of large family living. There are many aspects of this process—learning to live with people, learning to play with them, to work with them, to share with them, to endure and enjoy with them. To grow up in a large family means that one must accept people, not as a pleasant interlude from which one can withdraw as fancy dictates, but as a constant bill of fare. It is this fact of constancy which seems basically important. From infancy, the large family child (except the first one for a limited time) is surrounded by other children, always. One wakens with one or several in the same room, perhaps in the same bed. One lives with them before breakfast and in the disarmed moments at bedtime. One shares with others constantly, and thus one just comes to accept the presence of other persons. It is on this basis, of the acceptance of the constant presence of other persons, that the patterns of adjustment are formed.

This suggests a problem of great import. Is there any relation between the size of the family group in which a person is reared and the size of the working group in which he or she makes his best occupational adjustment?

Tentative data gathered by the authors over a period of several years seem overwhelmingly positive in the answer they indicate. Persons reared as only children or in small families are happiest in jobs where they work alone or with one other person. Similarly, it seems that persons reared in large families make better occupational adjustments when working in larger groups. It is hoped that a more pretentious research study will be made to answer the question, for its

[9] Bossard, *Parent and Child: Studies in Family Behavior*, chap. X.

answer would be of great help in placement and personnel work.

12. As a system, the large family seems not to perpetuate itself. Rates of marriage and of reproduction are relatively low, as compared with the population as a whole. Many reasons for this appeared in the course of the study. Economic pressure resulting from the mere fact of numbers; the crises, often major ones, that appeared in so many families; the problems that arose from incompetent or unwise parenthood; the stresses and strains of limited space—all of these and others overshadowed often the other compensations of the large family. In only 30 per cent of the families were parents and informants agreed that it was wholly good. Most often, the overall attitude of siblings could be expressed in the words of one informant: "It was nice, it was fun, but—" It is the "but" which is the key word in interpreting the failure of the large family system to perpetuate itself.

Perhaps what the data from the study on this point seek to tell is something like this—there are advantages to having a number of children, but there are rational limitations that should be considered. The number should not lose sight of the economic circumstances of the parents, but should be adjusted to some considerable extent to the available economic resources. Similarly, the number should bear some relationship to the capacities for parenthood in the particular family. What this means is that, while some persons should limit the size of their families, others should increase them, both in the interests of better family life. Mathematically, this may mean that it is not the small family system with its one or two children, nor the large one which this study has considered, but a medium-sized one, with from four to five children.

EPILOGUE

Now that the study is completed, this is the message that comes clear.

Good family life is never an accident but always an achievement by those who share it.

Growing up is life's most unique experience; being a parent is life's most important responsibility.

If every person has a soul, as most people believe, then to bring a child into the world is to usher into being a spark of the Divine.

If a child's life can be molded and directed, as human experience shows, then man has the ability, to some extent, to create others in the social image that he desires.

To the extent, then, that man can create and control life, he owes it to himself to learn how and to what extent these can best be done. To contribute to this end has been the purpose of the present study.

Subject Index

Adjustment of siblings, 252–61; by birth order and sex, 255–56; main findings about, 253–61; poor, 257–60

Attitudes, alternating, toward family size, 282–84; concluding comments on, 70–74; conflict in, 59; of parents toward large families, 53–59; of racial and religious groups, 60; of shame, 103; of siblings, 59; selected types of, 64–70; toward economic security, 231; toward emotional security, 224; toward possessiveness, 244

Birth, time interval between, 186
Birth order, sibling attitudes toward, 205; and adjustment of siblings, 255
Birth, time interval and sex sequence of, 48
By-products, of large family living, 222 ff.

Child, first born, 207–08; inbetween, 207, 209; youngest, 207, 209
Child management, *see* Child rearing
Child rearing, as a process, 126; by siblings, 148–66; by whom, 131; coöperation between parents in, 139; crises in, 142; differentials in, 127–31; in the large family, 126–47; interference in, by relatives, 133; methods of, 134; other than physical methods, 137; physical punishment in, 135–37; role of size of group in, 141; sex distribution and, 144
Children, age distribution by size of families, 41; born to large family siblings, 267; by sex and number, 39; differentials in, 272–80; discipline of, 131; in a hundred large families, 39–52; oldest, as types, 162–65; reactions of, to sibling discipline, 151
Combines, intrasibling, 189

Death, of large family parents, 109–11
Depression, impact of, 118–19
Dietary habits, 141
Discipline, *see* Child rearing
Drunkenness, of large family fathers, 108

Economic pressure, in large families, 116
Extramarital relations, of large family parents, 107

Families, large, adjustment problems in, 111; and the depression, 118; and the socialization process, 194–200; and the war, 119; as a family system, 305–20; attitudes toward, 53–75; by age of parents, 21; by father's occupation, 19; by nativity and race, 19; by religious preference, 19; by state of residence, 21; by type of community, 20; children in, 39–52; dietary habits in, 141; divorce in, 107; economic pressure in, 116; happiness in, 81; medium happiness in, 94–104; sticking together in, 122; unhappiness in, 83, 91; vulnerability of, 106–25
Family culture pattern, 15
Family formation, in the next generation, 262–81
Family interaction, in large families, 76; laws of, 77–78; peculiar nature of, 79–80

Subject Index

Family life patterns, in different countries, 17
Family of interaction, 45–48
Family size, as determinant factor, 16
Family system, large, 305; characteristics of, 309–20; number of, 14; purpose of study, 13–22
Family system, small, 306–09

Happiness, lack of, in families, 83, 91; marital, of persons reared in large families, 285–304; medium, in large families, 94–104; of large families, 81; ratings of large families for, by siblings, 84; selected aspects of, 85–91

Informants, age of, 31; marital status of, 32; order of birth, 31; sex of, 31
Information, on large families, sources of, 30–34, 53
Insecurity in the large family, 233; by birth order, 235; by family size, 235; by father's occupation, 238; by living area, 237; by religion, 237; by sex, 234
Interaction, among the siblings, 148–200; family, 45–48; within the large family, 76
Isolates, family, 216

Laws of family interaction, 77–78
Life-history documents, 24–26

Method, of securing information, 29; of studying large families, 24
Methodology, footnote on, 34–37

New York Times, The, 18

Parenthood, requisites for success in, 145–46
Patterns, of personality, among siblings, 201–21
Possession, sense of, 240–51; and personality types, 247; as part of personality structure, 240; related to selected factors, 250–51

Questionnaire, use of, 35

Remarriage, of large family parents, 113–15
Role, and personality patterns, 202; as seen by informants, 211–21; sex differentiation in, 210; specialization of, 201

Security, differentials in feelings of, 234–38; economic, 231; emotional, 224; feelings of, 210
Sex differentials in roles, 210
Sex distribution, and child rearing, 144, 191
Sex order, in birth of siblings, 132
Siblings, adjustment of, 252–61; age and sex of, 185; as surrogates, 156; attitudes of, toward birth order, 205; attitudes of, toward large families, 59, 61; child rearing by, 148; children born to, 267; combines among, 189; factors in relations of, 190–94; interaction among, 148–200; learning to live together, 173–77; light on, 62; marital status of, 262–65; marriage of older, 266; personality patterns among, 201; playing together, 167–70; relations in later life, 183–85; rivalry and conflict, 177–83; sacrifice of, 120, 158; sex order in birth of, 132
Socialization, in the large family, 194–200
Step-parents, 111–13
Sticking together, 122
Surrogates, siblings as, 156

Time interval, between birth of siblings, 186; sex sequence of, 48

Vital Statistics, National Office of, 14

Index of Authors

Baldwin, A. L., 145
Bales, Robert F., 77, 307
Barclay, Mrs. Dorothy, 18
Barker, Roger G., 24, 25
Benedict, Ruth, 241
Berent, Jerzy, 276, 278
Boll, Eleanor S., 36, 86, 87, 222, 308
Bosanquet, Helen, 79
Bossard, James H. S., 18, 36, 43, 46, 76, 86, 87, 100, 120, 205, 210, 226, 281, 306, 307, 308, 319
Breese, F. H., 145
Burgess, Ernest W., 81, 82, 286, 287, 289, 290, 294, 301

Cottrell, Leonard S., Jr., 81, 82, 286, 287, 294, 301
Cutts, Norma E., 290

Damrin, Dora E., 205
Durkheim, Emile, 172, 173, 202, 203, 316, 317

Freeman, Douglas Southall, 157
Fromm, Erich, 242

Goldhamer, Herbert, 77
Greco, Marshall C., 72

Hare, Alexander Paul, 77, 307
Hill, Reuben, 170, 171
Hobbs, A. H., 222
Homans, George, 77
Huestis, R. R., 276

James, John, 307

Kalhorn, J., 145
Kephart, William M., 77, 78, 307
Kinsey, Alfred C., 299

Landis, Judson T., 82
Lang, R. O., 82, 286, 294
Larson, Carol M., 77

Lee, Alice, 276
Lees, J. P., 162, 163
Lincoln, Abraham, 93

Maxwell, A., 276
Mead, Margaret, 308
Meyer, Eugene, 254
Moseley, Nicholas, 290
Murchison, Carl, 77

Opler, Morris E., 306

Pearson, Karl, 276
Plant, James S., 226, 229
Popenoe, Paul, 82, 290

Reed, Robert B., 82
Reyher, Rebecca, 37
Rose, Don, 73, 116, 119, 120

Sanger, Winogene Pratt, 18
Sears, Robert R., 205
Shaw, George Bernard, 315
Simmel, Georg, 77
Simpson, George, 173, 202, 316, 317
Somervell, D. C., 223
Strecker, Edward A., 254

Terman, Lewis M., 82, 287, 294
Thelen, Herbert A., 77
Thomas, Dorothy S., 35
Thomas, W. I., 35
Thrasher, Frederic M., 201
Toynbee, Arnold J., 223, 224, 230

Volkart, Edmund H., 35

Wallin, Paul, 289, 290
Washington, George, 157
Waters, Ethel, 127
Wolf, Kurt H., 77
Wright, Herbert F., 24, 25
Wright, Richard, 127